Global Power Shift

Series Editor

Xuewu Gu, Center for Global Studies, University of Bonn, Bonn, Germany

Managing Editor

Hendrik W. Ohnesorge, Center for Global Studies, University of Bonn, Bonn, Germany

Advisory Editors

G. John Ikenberry, Princeton University, Princeton, NJ, USA

Canrong Jin, Renmin University of Beijing, Beijing, China

Srikanth Kondapalli, Jawaharlal Nehru University, New Delhi, India

Beate Neuss, Chemnitz University of Technology, Chemnitz, Germany

Carla Norrlof, University of Toronto, Toronto, Canada

Dingli Shen, Fudan University, Shanghai, China

Kazuhiko Togo, Kyoto Sanyo University, Tokyo, Japan

Roberto Zoboli, Catholic University of Milan, Milano, Italy

Ample empirical evidence points to recent power shifts in multiple areas of international relations taking place between industrialized countries and emerging powers, as well as between states and non-state actors. However, there is a dearth of theoretical interpretation and synthesis of these findings, and a growing need for coherent approaches to understand and measure the transformation. The central issues to be addressed include theoretical questions and empirical puzzles: How can studies of global power shift and the rise of 'emerging powers' benefit from existing theories, and which alternative aspects and theoretical approaches might be suitable? How can the meanings, perceptions, dynamics, and consequences of global power shift be determined and assessed? This edited series will include highly innovative research on these topics. It aims to bring together scholars from all major world regions as well as different disciplines, including political science, economics and human geography. The overall aim is to discuss and possibly blend their different approaches and provide new frameworks for understanding global affairs and the governance of global power shifts.

Selected volumes published in this series are indexed by the Web of Science.

More information about this series at http://www.springer.com/series/10201

Jan Eichler

NATO's Expansion After the Cold War

Geopolitics and Impacts for International Security

 Springer

Jan Eichler
Institute of International Relations
Prague, Czech Republic

ISSN 2198-7343 ISSN 2198-7351 (electronic)
Global Power Shift
ISBN 978-3-030-66643-9 ISBN 978-3-030-66641-5 (eBook)
https://doi.org/10.1007/978-3-030-66641-5

© The Editor(s) (if applicable) and The Author(s), under exclusive license to Springer Nature Switzerland AG 2021
This work is subject to copyright. All rights are solely and exclusively licensed by the Publisher, whether the whole or part of the material is concerned, specifically the rights of translation, reprinting, reuse of illustrations, recitation, broadcasting, reproduction on microfilms or in any other physical way, and transmission or information storage and retrieval, electronic adaptation, computer software, or by similar or dissimilar methodology now known or hereafter developed.
The use of general descriptive names, registered names, trademarks, service marks, etc. in this publication does not imply, even in the absence of a specific statement, that such names are exempt from the relevant protective laws and regulations and therefore free for general use.
The publisher, the authors and the editors are safe to assume that the advice and information in this book are believed to be true and accurate at the date of publication. Neither the publisher nor the authors or the editors give a warranty, expressed or implied, with respect to the material contained herein or for any errors or omissions that may have been made. The publisher remains neutral with regard to jurisdictional claims in published maps and institutional affiliations.

This Springer imprint is published by the registered company Springer Nature Switzerland AG
The registered company address is: Gewerbestrasse 11, 6330 Cham, Switzerland

*To the memory of my excellent wife Anna
(1952–2019)*

Acknowledgement

This book has been written thanks to a Technological Agency of the Czech Republic research project, Migration from the Middle East, sub-Saharan Africa and Asia: geopolitical and security context, consequences and recommendations for the Czech Republic.

Number: TL01000432.

Contents

1 **Introduction: A New Bipolarisation in Europe** 1
   Sources 7
2 **The NATO Post-Cold War Enlargement: Realist and Neorealist Approaches** 9
   2.1 Realism and Neorealism as the Basic Theoretical Inspiration 9
   2.2 Three Great Neorealists 11
       2.2.1 Kenneth Waltz 12
       2.2.2 Stephen Walt 12
       2.2.3 John Mearsheimer 15
   2.3 The NATO Post-Cold War Enlargement as an Expansion Sui Generis 17
       2.3.1 Expansion as the Central Concept of This Book 17
       2.3.2 Target as a Key Concept of the Neorealist Approach to the Process of Expansion 18
       2.3.3 NATO Expansion as a Security Dilemma 19
       2.3.4 NATO Expansion as a Greedy Behaviour? 19
       2.3.5 Three Stages of NATO Expansion 20
       2.3.6 An "Expansion by Invitation" 22
       2.3.7 Balancing Theory and Its Importance for the Study of NATO Expansion 23
   2.4 Positive and Negative Peace 25
   2.5 Research Questions 28
   2.6 Methodology 29
   Sources 30
3 **From Hamburg and Munich to Tallinn and Burgas** 33
   3.1 The First Reflexions About the Expansion of NATO Under the Presidency of G. Bush Senior 33
       3.1.1 The Most Important Open Declarations 33
       3.1.2 The Most Important Secret Negotiations 35
       3.1.3 Key Common Denominators of the Proponents of the TLDA Strategy 35

		3.1.4	Between Consistency and Hypocrisy	37
	3.2	The End of the USSR and Its Consequences		38
	3.3	Bill Clinton as a Political Guarantor of the Second Wave of NATO Expansion		38
		3.3.1	Supporters of NATO Expansion	39
		3.3.2	Sceptical and Critical Authors	41
	3.4	The PfP as the First Step of NATO Expansion		45
		3.4.1	Key Important Milestones	45
		3.4.2	The First Round of NATO Expansion in the Light of Kenneth Waltz	47
	3.5	George W. Bush as a Political Guarantor of the Second Wave of NATO Expansion		48
		3.5.1	The Zero-Sum Game	48
		3.5.2	The Baltic States as a New North-Eastern Frontier of NATO	49
		3.5.3	The Black Sea Area as a New South-Eastern Border of NATO	50
	3.6	Russian Internal Balancing and Its Consequences		51
		3.6.1	Historical Aspects	52
		3.6.2	Russian Balancing Face to Face with the First Two Rounds of NATO Expansion	52
		3.6.3	The Russian A2/AD Systems	53
		3.6.4	Russian A2/AD Systems in the Light of Neorealism	54
		3.6.5	A Security Controversy Between NATO and the RF	55
		3.6.6	A Clash of Perceptions and New Spirals of Security Dilemmas	56
	3.7	Conclusion		56
	Sources			58
4	**From the War Against Georgia to the Annexation of the Crimea and the Following Increase of Military Tension**			**65**
	4.1	From Munich 2007 to Georgia 2008		66
		4.1.1	The First Negativist Speech by Putin	66
		4.1.2	The Five Days War Between the RF and Georgia and Its Consequences	67
		4.1.3	Doctrinal Reactions of the Russian Operational Realists	70
	4.2	Basic Differences Between NATO and the RF After the Second Wave of the NATO Expansion		71
		4.2.1	External vs. Internal Balancing	73
		4.2.2	Virulent Reproaches of Two Presidents	73
		4.2.3	The Annexation of the Crimean Peninsula and Its Consequences	75
		4.2.4	Russian Doctrinal Documents Approved After the Annexation of Crimea	83

	4.3	The Academic Debate After the Annexation of the Crimea	84
		4.3.1 The Strongly Critical Authors	84
		4.3.2 The Non-Critical Authors	86
		4.3.3 Authors with Impartial Attitudes	89
	4.4	The Conclusion of the Chapter	90
	Sources		91
5	**The Growing Militarisation of the Baltic and Black Sea Areas After the End of the Cold War**		**99**
	5.1	The Smoothly Growing Militarisation After the End of the Cold War	99
		5.1.1 The U.S. NGSPP as a Forerunner of a Future Expansion	99
		5.1.2 The Baltic Military After the End of the Cold War	100
		5.1.3 The Black Sea Military After the End of the Cold War	101
	5.2	The Doctrinal Development of NATO Before the Annexation of Crimea	101
		5.2.1 Lisbon 2010	102
	5.3	The New Eastern Frontier of NATO	103
		5.3.1 NATO in the Black Sea Area	103
		5.3.2 NATO in Romania	105
	5.4	Military Consequences of the Russian Annexation of Crimea	108
		5.4.1 The European Reassurance/Deterrence Initiative	108
		5.4.2 Reactions of NATO	113
		5.4.3 Reactions of the New Member States of NATO	114
		5.4.4 Military Exercises After 2014	117
		5.4.5 The Russian Exercise Zapad 2017	121
		5.4.6 Military Incidents Between the RF and Western Countries	123
	5.5	And What's Next	124
		5.5.1 Stoltenberg's Doctrinal Speeches	125
		5.5.2 NATO's New Strategy of "Stability Generation"	127
		5.5.3 Rand 2019	128
	5.6	Conclusion of the Chapter	129
	Sources		130
6	**American Military Doctrines of the New Generation**		**137**
	6.1	Key Concepts	137
		6.1.1 The Basic Concepts of This Book	138
		6.1.2 The International and Military Context of the US Doctrinal Documents Approved Between 2012 and 2015	139
	6.2	From the NSS 2010 to the JCRA	142
		6.2.1 The Grand Strategy and Security Culture of Barack Obama	142
		6.2.2 NSS 2010	144

		6.2.3	Sustaining U.S. Global Leadership: Priorities for Twenty-First Century Defense	145
		6.2.4	The Joint Operational Access Concept (JOAC) of January 2012	148
		6.2.5	Air-Sea Battle, May 2013	150
		6.2.6	The Joint Concept for Entry Operations (JCEO) of April 2014	154
		6.2.7	The Joint Concept for Rapid Aggregation (JCRA) of May 2015	156
	6.3	The Conclusion of the Chapter		157
		6.3.1	The Primordial Importance of the Bay of Finland	159
		6.3.2	Military Exercises and Growing Tension	159
	Sources			160
7	**Conclusion: Waiting for a New Gorbachev and for a New Reagan**			165
	7.1	NATO Expansion in the Light of the Key Pillars of Realism		168
	7.2	NATO Expansion in the Light of the Key Pillars of Neorealism		168
	7.3	Likudisation as an Inspiration for the NATO Expansion?		170
	7.4	A Clash of Two Contradictory Narratives		171
	Sources			173

Abbreviations

ABCT	Armored Brigade Combat Team
ABM	Antiballistic Missile
AD	Air Defence
ADR	Annual Defence Review
AFCENT	Allied Forces, Europe
APS	Army Prepositioned Stock
ATV	All-Terrain Vehicle
AWACS	Airborne Warning and Control System
BCT	Brigade Combat Team
BS-AST	Black Sea Area Support Team
C3I	Command, Control, Communications and Intelligence
CFE	Conventional Forces in Europe
CFSP	Common Foreign and Security Policy
CIA	Central Intelligence Agency
CIMIC	Civil—Military Cooperation
CJET	Combined Joint Enhanced Training Initiative
CJTF	Combined Joint Task Forces
CSAR	Combat Search and Rescue
CSBM	Confidence and Security—Building Measures
CSCE	Conference on Security and Cooperation in Europe
DCA	Defense Cooperation Agreement
DCI	Defence Capabilities Initiative
DD	Defence Department
DPC	Defence Planning Committee
DPKO	Department of Peacekeeping Operations ECAP—European Capabilities Action Plan
DPRK	Democratic People's Republic of Korea
DRV	Democratic Republic of Vietnam
EDA	European Defence Agency
EDI	European Deterrence Initiative
EETAF	Eastern European Task Force
EFP	NATO Enhanced Forward Presence

ERI	European Reassurance Initiative
ESDP	European Security and Defence Policy
EU	European Union
EUFOR	European Force
EUROFOR	European (Rapid Deployment) Force
FMF	Foreign Military Financing
FMF/DCC	Foreign Military Financing of Direct Commercial Contracts
FMS	Foreign Military Sales
FY	Financial Year
FYROM	Former Yugoslav Republic of Macedonia
GDP	Gross Domestic Product
GPS	Global Positioning System
GWOT	Global War on Terror
HUMINT	Human Intelligence
IAMD	Integrated Air and Missile Defense
ICBM	Inter Continental Ballistic Missile
IFOR	Implementation Force
IGC	Intergovernmental Conference
IMET	International Military Education and Training
INF	Intermediate-Range Nuclear Forces
ISAF	International Security Assistance Forces
ISR	International Security Relations
ISTAR	Intelligence, Surveillance, Target Acquisition and Reconnaissance
JDAM	Joint Direct Attack Munition
JTF-E	Joint Task Force-East
KFOR	Kosovo Force
LGM	Little Green Men
MIRV	Multiple Independently Targetable Re-entry Vehicle
MKAF	Mihail Kogălniceanu Airfield
MNDSE	Multinational Division Southeast
NAC	North Atlantic Council
NATO	North Atlantic Treaty Organisation
NATO BAPM	Baltic Air Policing Mission
NATO CCDCE	Cooperative Cyber Defense Center of Excellence
NATO MC	NATO Military Committee
NBC	Nuclear, Biological and Chemical
NDS	National Defence Strategy
NGSPP	National Guard State Partnership Program
NPT	Non-Proliferation Treaty
NRF	NATO Response Force
NSIP	NATO Security Investment Program
NSPA	NATO Support and Procurement Agency
NSS	National Security Strategy
NSTA	Novo Selo Training Area
NVC	Network Centred War

Abbreviations

NW	Nuclear Weapons
NWFW	Nuclear Weapons Free World
OAR	Operation Atlantic Resolve
ODS	Operation Desert Storm
OEF	Operation Enduring Freedom
OIF	Operation Iraqi Freedom
OOA	Out of Area
OSCE	Organisation for Security and Cooperation in Europe
PFOS	Permanent Forward Operating Site
PfP	Partnership for Peace
PGM	Precision—Guided Munition
PRC	People's Republic of China
RAP	Readiness Action Plane
RC	Regional Conflict
RMA	Revolution in Military Affairs
RV	Republic of Vietnam
SACEUR	Supreme Allied Commander Europe
SACLANT	Supreme Allied Commander Atlantic
SALT	Strategic Arms Limitation Talks
SFOR	Stabilisation Force
SHAPE	Supreme Headquarter Allied Powers Europe
SITCEN	Situation Centre
SLBM	Sub-Marine Launched Missiles
SOF	Special Operations Forces
SOFAs	Status of Forces Agreements
SPG	Strategic Planning Guidance
START	Strategic Arms Reduction Treaty
TD	Total Defense
TSCP	Theater Security Cooperation Program
UAV	Unmanned Aerial Vehicle
UN	United Nations
UNCS	United Nations Security Council
USAREUR	United States Army Europe
UW	Unconventional Warfare
WMD	Weapons of Mass Destruction

Chapter 1
Introduction: A New Bipolarisation in Europe

This book will analyse two mutually intertwined topics. The first of them is the geopolitical and geostrategic context of the post-Cold War process of NATO expansion into the former sphere of influence of the USSR. The second topic is represented by the long-term consequences of this process and of its dynamics. In analysing and evaluating these two topics, the text will draw on the related documents (doctrines, declarations, programs and speeches of the most influential decision-makers), monographs, articles and other analyses. The aim of this book is to present a synoptic evaluation of the process of NATO expansion after the end of the Cold War and its consequences for the international security relations (ISR) in Europe.

The process of NATO expansion is a major subject of long debates in two important spheres. First, in the political sphere, particularly in all the new member states, it is perceived as the most important event after the end of the Cold War. With the exception of the communist parties (which are increasingly marginalised) and nationalist political parties (which are, unfortunately, increasingly influential), this process is appreciated and viewed highly positively by the political parties in these countries. It is interpreted as an important milestone which opened a new future for the former satellites of the USSR.

Second, the same approach is typical for the academic sphere. Its strong majority unequivocally shares the conviction that the post-Cold War opening of NATO to the former member states of the Pact of Warsaw (POW) was an excellent decision not only for these states, but also in terms of the international security relations (ISR) in all of Europe. The academic mainstream, which is enormously strong and influential, unreservedly shares the conviction that NATO is the most important and successful alliance in the entire history of humankind (Göncz 2009) and a guarantor of peace, prosperity, democracy and liberty (books.google.cz). This mainstream view categorically refuses to discuss the possible counterproductive and disturbing consequences of this process. Openly articulated doubts or critical points of view regarding this matter are a taboo in the best case, and in the worst case, they are followed by personal attacks, and the individuals expressing such views are often labelled as agents of Putin (Dobrovský 2016).

© The Author(s), under exclusive license to Springer Nature Switzerland AG 2021
J. Eichler, *NATO's Expansion After the Cold War*, Global Power Shift,
https://doi.org/10.1007/978-3-030-66641-5_1

This book has been written with two basic motivations. In the negative sense, its mission is neither to defend the positions and the security interests of the Russian Federation, nor to advocate Putin´s decisions and his long-term security strategy based on an active (and, in the case of the Crimea, even aggressive) resistance to NATO and its enlargement in the post-Soviet space. And in the positive sense, the central aim is to shed a new light on the geopolitical and geostrategic context and circumstances of the five waves of the expansion of NATO, and to present an assessment of their impact on the international security relations in Europe and their long-term consequences. The preceding paragraph indicates that this book offers, in comparison with the mainstream academic literature in the new NATO member states, an alternative view which is based on two pillars. First, this book doesn't use the generally shared and often repeated expression "NATO enlargement." Instead it prefers and consistently uses the phrase "NATO expansion." The reasons for this approach are explained in detail in Chapter 2, which is consecrated to the theoretical anchoring and the definitions of key concepts. This author's preference is based on the terminology of mathematics, natural sciences, and geopolitics. It is also necessary to underline that the word expansion is not used here in a pejorative sense; it is simply used with the aim to call things by their proper names.

Second, this book does not question the substance of the process of NATO expansion and it is very far from condemning it. The book simply warns that this process has not only positive results, but also some controversial consequences which are symbolised particularly by the growing militarisation of the entire post-Soviet space, the doctrinal accents on offensive operations, and the growing numbers of military exercises in the Baltic Sea and Black Sea areas, which are accompanied by serious military incidents with a highly explosive potential. After a detailed analysis of these dangerous events, the book concludes that the entry of NATO into the post-Soviet space resulted in a high political and military tension. The book states that these controversial consequences should not be underestimated and that the actors of this new bipolarity should make a big effort to reverse this growing tension and advance on the way from the contemporary negative peace towards a positive peace.

The key argument of this book is articulated in the following manner: from its beginning until today, the process of NATO expansion has been enormously controversial because it was conceived as a zero-sum game between the winner of the Cold War on one hand and its loser on the other. This process had two important consequences. First, it profoundly redrew the geopolitical map of the so-called Old Continent and resulted in its new bipolarisation, a form of the international order which had been so typical for the four decades of the Cold war. And second, it has been accompanied by a growing international tension and a long series of increasingly dangerous military incidents at the new Eastern frontier of NATO.

The role of the loser of the process of NATO expansion has been assumed by only one actor: the USSR. From its creation until the end of the 1930s, this state pretended to the role of a messianic state and a challenger of global capitalism. Its geopolitical ambitions were significantly strengthened after the end of WW II, when it obtained an immense and enormously deep sphere of influence of strategic and historic importance. And in 1957 (in the context of the Sputnik crisis), it succeeded in acquiring the status of the second nuclear superpower of the bipolar divided world. During all of its existence, its ruling elites preferred the Russian nationality, and they imposed the Russian language and culture on other nations to the detriment of these nations and their languages and cultures.

And during the four-decades-long period of the Cold War, this state imposed its brutal mode of reigning on all states of its sphere of influence, transforming them into subordinated and underestimated satellites. Despite this, these states were incorporated into the USSR or into its exclusive sphere of influence,[1] an artificial block based on a distorted social engineering. Moreover, the ruling elites of the USSR did not hesitate to resort to military interventions and following long-term occupations in two satellite countries which had previously manifested their refusal of the so-called Pax Sovietica and their determination to independently choose their own paths.[2] All the Soviet bloc countries were thus condemned to wait for the arrival of the last General Secretary of the Communist Party of the USSR, who was later the president of this colossal state, with his emphasis on the so-called new political thinking (Holloway 1988), on the profound changes in the USSR's internal as well as foreign policy (Gorbatchev 1988), and, especially, on the so-called Sinatra doctrine (Tatu 1987).

In the light of the above mentioned historical factors, it is no surprise that the camp of winners of the Cold War has been much more numerous and representative. Besides the USA as the key winner, it contains its allies from the four-decades-long period of bipolar confrontation. But at the same time, this camp contains all the former Soviet satellites and even all the former member states of the ruined USSR. In these states, with the exception of the Russian Federation, the successor state of the former USSR, the end of the Cold War was appreciated as the end of their submissive position in an alliance by coercion and as the beginning of a new era, an era of their emancipation.

All the above-mentioned facts had an enormously important role to play in the historically as well as strategically important process of the NATO expansion. In the light of these facts, this process will be analysed and explained as an expansion started after a long series of intensive solicitations of leaders of the former Central European states of the Pact of Warsaw.[3] As a result, the process of the NATO enlargement after the end of the Cold War will be called an "expansion by invitation." The qualifying phrase "by invitation" will be systematically used as an opposite to the "by coercion"

---

[1] This zone became the victim of a brutal Sovietisation which resulted in the abolition of the market economies in these countries, the establishment of one-party systems in them and their complete dependence on Russia in foreign and security policy matters.
[2] This was the case with Hungary in 1956, and Czechoslovakia in 1968. In the first case, the intervention was followed by political trials and even by a lot of executions. It both cases, the Soviet intervention provoked massive waves of emigration of the countries' élites.
[3] This pact existed from 14 May 1955 until 1 July 1991.

quality of the former Warsaw Pact, which was based on the coercion applied by the USSR against its satellite states.[4]

It is necessary to mention that the strategy of the NATO expansion has been openly articulated for the first time on the pages of the 1995 Study on NATO Enlargement. Twenty-five years later, we have a new Alliance, an alliance which has been enlarged in five waves and which controls the territory from the Baltic Sea to the Black Sea in the North-South direction, and the territory from Split and Tirana to Burgas and Constanza in the West-East direction. This space includes fourteen new member states which create an important strategic depth.[5]

All fourteen of the new member states received two big benefits. In the negative sense, they have the certitude that they are no longer exposed to the threat of economic, political, and diplomatic pressures, if not direct military interventions from Moscow. And in the positive sense, they entered a new security community based on shared values, security guaranties and respect for every member state and its dignity and interests. They became members of an alliance in which they are no longer satellite states, but respected client states.

Nevertheless, there is no rose without thorns. On the other hand, we are witnessing a disturbing return of the situation of the period between 1979 and 1985. This is especially the case with the growing militarisation of the ISR, the build-up of new big military units (especially the Western Military District in St. Petersburg), various very dangerous military incidents (especially those in the Baltic and Black Sea areas) and even the return of the temptations to use nuclear weapons in case of an unfavourable development of a conventional conflict. Forty years ago, these temptations were typical for NATO, while today they are typical for the doctrinal thinking of some strategists of the RF.[6] In both cases, these temptations resulted from disturbing feelings of conventional inferiority. Despite the above-mentioned differences, these doctrinal temptations are enormously dangerous (Russia's Nuclear Weapons 2020).

In developing the above-mentioned argument, this text will focus on the four following important decision-making milestones and their consequences for the contemporary ISR:

(1) The first wave of the NATO expansion, which included "only" three countries of Central Europe. Even if those countries had no direct frontier with the RF (with the exception of Kaliningrad), this act opened a new Pandora's box of the post-Cold War Europe.
(2) The second wave of the NATO expansion, which was, strategically speaking, much more important because it included three post-Soviet countries of the Baltic region and two countries of the Black Sea region, with Slovakia and

---

[4]The inspiration for this idea has been taken from: Empire by Invitation? The United States and Western Europe, 1945–1952 Author(s): Geir Lundestad. *Journal of Peace Research, 23*(3) (September 1986), 263–277, published by: Sage.

[5]Hungary, Poland, and the Czech Republic (which joined NATO in 1999), Bulgaria, Estonia, Latvia, Lithuania, Romania, Slovakia, and Slovenia (2004), Croatia and Albania (2009), Montenegro (2017) and North Macedonia (2020).

[6]These highly disturbing temptation will be analysed in detail in Chapter 4.

Slovenia being much less important. By expanding to these countries, NATO obtained almost one million km^2 of new territory, and this importantly, if not dramatically, shortened the distance between its Eastern frontier and the Western part of the RF. Strategically speaking, this means that the St. Petersburg and Moscow regions are within the range of the expanded NATO.

(3) The opening of the debate about the invitation for Ukraine to become a new member state of NATO with all the usual security guaranties. This debate provoked a strong irritation on the part of the Russian political and military operational realists (especially the latter), which resulted in the annexation of the Crimea and the outbreak of a protracted civil war in Eastern Ukraine. This will be profoundly analysed in Chapter 4.

(4) Since the second wave of NATO expansion, we are witnessing a new form of the vicious circle of measures and countermeasures which had been so typical for the Cold War. At the same time, we are witnessing a high level of international tension, political as well military, which covers even the doctrinal level. This development results in a continuing worsening of the contemporary ISR.

This book has two basic definitions: the first is a negative one, and the second is positive. The negative definition is as follows. This book will not analyse the wars waged by NATO after 1990 or its active participation in such wars. The book will pay hardly any attention to the controversial Operation Allied Force, the first "out of area" operation which was waged without a mandate of the UNSC. At the same time, this book will describe neither the missions ISAF and Resolute Support in Afghanistan nor the missions in Iraq waged within the framework of the long term GWOT, even if these operations gave a lot of new experiences to the soldiers of NATO as well as to the local militaries. Even Operation Ocean Shield as well as Operation United Protector, which was carried out in Libya in 2011 with the active participation of all leading powers of NATO, will remain outside of the interest of this book. All these operations are only mentioned in the book, but not analysed. Lastly, the book does not analyse the Mediterranean Dialogue or the ICI either, even if they represent two very important activities of NATO.

The above-mentioned negative definition does not mean any disrespect toward the fact that NATO's military activities (especially its out of area operations) after 1999 represent an extremely important and interesting subject for the analysis of the contemporary international security relations (ISR); these activities will be only briefly remembered in this book. The absence of the above-mentioned activities on the pages of this book simply means that all the attention of the following chapters will be aimed at the subject of NATO expansion and its consequences for the ISR in Europe.

The text is divided into four chapters. Chapter 2 defines the theoretical and methodological profile of the analysis. It explains why neorealism has been chosen as the theoretical framework and which authors will be the most often cited. At the same time, this chapter explains why, in the present book, neorealist postulates are combined with the theory of greedy states vs. security seeking states articulated by Charles Glaser. This combination may appear as surprising; nevertheless it offers an original framework for the study of the process of NATO expansion after the end of the Cold War. The chapter continues with an explication of the ontological and epistemological preferences. Last but least, this chapter presents four research questions which create the basic framework of this entire book.

The third chapter covers the first decade after the end of the Cold War and explains the development from the first reflexions about the expansion of NATO under the presidency of G. Bush Senior until the first round of the expansion realised under President B. Clinton. It presents this period as a time of movement between consistency and hypocrisy on the part of western, especially American, politicians. The second part of this chapter is consecrated to the implosion of the USSR and its international consequences. The following part analyses the role of G. W. Bush as a political guarantor of the second wave of NATO expansion. It also compares the arguments of various supporters of this historically important process.

At the same time, it analyses the arguments of authors sceptical of it, particularly George Kennan, who opposed this process and warned of its counterproductive consequences. The chapter continues with an analysis of the first two waves in the light of the theories of Stephen Walt (the theory of the balance of threats) and Charles Glaser (the theory of security seeking states vs. greedy states). And the last part of the chapter states that in the light of the theoretical framework of the book, the first two waves of NATO expansion resulted in a dangerous move from a promising and hopeful security cooperation (which was so typical for the first half of the 1990s) to the military incidents at the RF's western flank and the threat of a direct confrontation (which was typical for the second half of the 2010s).

Chapter 4 begins with a set of tables which present the key ideas and arguments which will be analysed in the following pages. In this chapter much attention will be paid to the growing controversy between the enlarged NATO and the RF, whose security strategy and behaviour were increasingly predetermined, once again, by the resurgence of its deeply rooted growing security fears of being like an encircled fortress. The chapter offers an impartial comparison of the measures of the American and Russian operative realists and their consequences. This comparison is aimed particularly at the changes in the field of military doctrines, new arms systems, and the formation of new military units and commandments. The following part of this chapter will analyse the Russian hybrid/asymmetric warfare, particularly the annexation of Crimea and its international consequences. As in the case of the preceding chapter, much attention is paid to the related academic discussion, namely to the arguments of the critics of the annexation on the one hand, and the counterarguments of the authors who do not agree with these critical arguments and do not even hesitate to articulate an understanding for this controversial measure of the Russian operational realists led by V. Putin, on the other.

Chapter 5 analyses the growing militarisation and presents it as a direct result of the two decades long process of the NATO expansion. It starts by the analysis of the modernisation of the armed forces of the new member states and of their cooperation with the USA. A big attention is payed to the Lisbon summit of NATO (2010) which send the call for the Eastward relocation of the Russian Western military district units and which announced the decision to offer the strategic partnership to Ukraine and

Georgia, two other post—Soviet states. The chapter continues by the analysis of a massive US program European Deterrence Initiative (EDI), namely of the installation of the Army Prepositioned Stocks) and by the NATO´s initiatives Enhanced Forward Presence (Poland, Latvia, Estonia, and Lithuania) and Tailored Forward Presence (Bulgaria and Romania). All these programs are presented as the Western answer to the annexation of the Crimea (2014). Lastly, the chapter analyses the growing numbers and intensity of military exercises of NATO and Russia and of military incidents between these two rivals.

The last chapter is consecrated to a detailed analysis of the American doctrinal documents approved after 2011 which defined the new US security priorities and military ambitions. All those documents are oriented towards the A2/AD systems which are in the possession of the so-called challengers, and fix concrete tasks for the US armed forces. The most important of these challengers is Russia with its armed forces, especially the Western Military District in St. Petersburg. Much attention is paid to analysing military doctrines and military exercises which led to a long range of dangerous military incidents. This chapter leads to a worrying conclusion: the area which includes the new eastern frontier of NATO and the western frontier of the RF represents a dangerous zone of a growing military tension with a growing number of military incidents which could escape political control and menace the peace in this important part of the so-called Old Continent.

Sources

books.google.cz. In the Stream of History: Shaping Foreign Policy for a New Era.
Dobrovský, L. (2016). Polemika s neorealistickými teoriemi mezinárodních vztahů, o něž se opírá článek Jana Eichlera Černomořská dimenze války na Ukrajině ve VR 2016/1. *Vojenské rozhledy*, 25(57, 2), 144–147.
Göncz, K. (2009). The Most Successful Alliance: Sixty Years of Collective Defense. *American Foreign Policy Interests*, 31(2), 90–99.
Gorbatchev, M. (1988). *Perestroïka et la nouvelle pensée pour notre pays et pour tout le monde.*
Holloway, D. (1988). Gorbachev's New Thinking. *Foreign Affairs*, 68(1).
ISAF's Mission in Afghanistan (2001–2014) (Archived)—NATO. (2015, September 1). Available: https://www.nato.int/cps/en/natohq/topics_69366.htm.
Lundestad, G. (1986). Empire by Invitation? The United States and Western Europe, 1945–1952. *Journal of Peace Research*, 23(3), 263–277.
NATO and Libya: Operation Unified Protector—NATO. (2011, February–October). Available: www.nato.int/cps/natolive.
Russia's Nuclear Weapons. Doctrine, Forces, and Modernization. (2020, January 2). Congressional Research Available: Service https://crsreports.congress.govR45861.
Resolute Support Mission (RSM)—SHAPE—NATO. Available: shape.nato.int/ongoingoperations.
Study on NATO Enlargement. Official text, 3 September 1995. Available: http://www.nato.int/cps/en/natohq/official_texts_24733.htm.
Tatu, M. (1987). *Gorbatchev: l'URSS va-t-elle changer?* Paris: le Centurion.
Topic: NATO Mission Iraq—NATO. (2010, February 17). Available: https://www.nato.int/cps/en/natohq/topics_166936.htm.
Topic: Mediterranean Dialogue—NATO. (2019, February 22). Available: http://www.nato.int/cps/en/natohq/topics_52927.htm.

Chapter 2
The NATO Post-Cold War Enlargement: Realist and Neorealist Approaches

The aim of this chapter is to define the theoretical and methodological positions of the entire book. It will pay the same amount of attention to both the factors of the so-called hard power and the factors of soft power, and view them as equally important (Nye 2011). As all of this book is based on the theoretical approaches of academic neorealism, this chapter starts with a presentation of the key pillars of the realist and, particularly, neorealist schools of thought. The US political and military engagement in the post-Soviet space will be analysed and presented as a clear signalisation of two important phenomena. The first of them is the American military primacy and superiority, and the second is the US determination to use this primacy to satisfy the solicitations of the political and military élites of the former member states of the Pact of Warsaw (PoW) and of the USSR (the three Baltic States) which identify their future with the US security guarantees.

2.1 Realism and Neorealism as the Basic Theoretical Inspiration

First of all, it is necessary to remember that the realists are divided into two basic groups: the academic realists and the operational realists (Hill and Gaddy 2015). The first group includes the most known and often cited realist authors who publish their conclusions on the pages of their monographs or journals with a high IF. The second group is represented by the so-called decision sphere: presidents, ministers, and generals. These politicians take important decisions and implement them, and the soldiers prepare military doctrines and direct the build-up of the armed forces and their military training. And if necessary they wage wars.

In the light of the above-mentioned facts, this book has two basic characteristics. On the positive level, it will be dominantly based on a profound analysis of so-called primary sources. This means that the important doctrinal documents will be profoundly analysed and very often cited. At the same time, the approaches and

Table 2.1 Key pillars of realism

Groupism	Security via coalitions or alliances
Egoism	A priority of the national interests
Power-centrism	States are power maximisers and security maximisers

Source Compiled by the author

conclusions of the academic realists will be studied and cited. Besides this, much attention will be paid to the analysis of the attitudes and conclusions of the operative realists. The assessment of these types of sources will by the primary ambition of this method.

And on the negative level, this book will present no judgements of the behaviour of key actors of the process of NATO Expansion. At the same time, it will offer no particular recommendations for the decision-makers. In other words, this book has no normative ambition (Table 2.1).

This book is not about an ideal world, but about the existing world, which is characterised specifically by groupism, egoism a power-centrism (Wohlforth 2010). Groupism means that politics takes place within groups and between them. This expression reflects the fact that life at the interpersonal, national, and international levels is impossible without cohesion and group solidarity. Groupism has two basic connotations. The negative one results from the fact that group solidarity can generate conflicts with other groups. The positive meaning becomes visible in periods when different groups of states share a mutual respect for their security interests and have a basic confidence which enables them to avoid a direct confrontation and develop a reliable security cooperation.

Egoism as the second basic concept results from the fact that on the field of the ISR, any state can fully rely on the help of other states (Huntington 1958, pp. 41–86). Egoism is generally defined as the imposition of security interests of certain states regardless of the interests and attitudes of other states, and it very often generates potential for clashes of interests and for direct confrontation. This security behaviour is typical for assertive rising states, for aggressive revisionist powers, for the hegemons who push important international power transitions (Tammen et al. 2000), and, lastly, for greedy states.

Lastly, power centrism very often provokes great inequalities of power distribution and following destabilisations, clashes of interests, and, in extremis, wars. Struggles for power are mutually intertwined with hegemony ambitions, which are motivated by the desire to control new territories with their resources, govern a new international system, and impose new sets of rules (Gilpin 1981).

All three of the above-mentioned pillars of realism are very important because they offer three important ways to systematically study the NATO expansion. In the light of groupism, the expansion can be analysed as the enlargement of the group of states which are covered by the security guarantees of the central and the most powerful state of NATO. From the egoism point of view, this process is mainly about the satisfaction of the ambitions of political and military élites of the new member countries. And power centrism leads us to an attentive examination of the redistribution of power (hard power as well as soft power) after the end of the Cold War.

All classical realists pay much attention to the concept of the balance of power (Paul et al. 2004). The balance of power (BoP) theory in international relations is based on the statement that security and survival represent the most important value and aim of all states (Kegley and Wittkopf 2006). The threats to the security of states may be mitigated, prevented, or eliminated by modernizations of military forces or by diplomatic means—namely by adhesion to alliances. According to Kenneth Waltz, "balance-of-power politics prevail wherever two, and only two requirements are met: that the order be anarchic and that it be populated by units wishing to survive" (Waltz 1979, pp. 118–121).

At the same time, all realists are convinced that, from the international point of view, balance-of-power is the best solution because it opens the way towards international stability. When states are confronted with a security threat, they may apply the strategy of balancing in the cooperation with their allies (Walt 1987, pp. 5, 1–29). And during the last years of the Cold War, this theory (BoP) was enriched by Stephen M. Walt (1987), who came with the balance of threat (BoT) theory.[1] This theory is mainly based on three key variables: aggregate capabilities, geography and perception of aggressive intentions (Wohlforth 2010, pp. 15), and it represents one of the pillars of a relatively new (1980s) school of thought which has the name neorealism.

2.2 Three Great Neorealists

The neorealist school of thought came on the scene just before the end of the Cold War and has represented an important inspiration for the study of ISR until today. The reason why this theory has been chosen as the key inspiration for this book is that all authors of this school underline the importance of structures of international security relations (Keohane 1988, pp. 169–76). Their contribution results from the fact that they analyse security threats as social phenomena which result from the power of states, the distance between states and, especially, the distance between their armed forces, and their respective attack capabilities and security intentions (Keohane 1986, pp. 378). If a state is weak, it can become a "target" of its strong neighbour; it can even become an object, if not a victim, of its expansion.

---

[1] First mentioned in "Alliance Formation and the Balance of World Power", an article published in the journal *International Security* in 1985 and later further elaborated in his internationally known book *The Origins of Alliances* (Walt 1987).

Table 2.2 Key pillars of the theory of K. Waltz

International level	State-level
Every state operates in an anarchic environment	As a result, the security strategy of states is state-centric and state-based
In international politics, there is no overarching global authority	As a result, every state is a security maximiser
In the field of security, self-help is a key principle of the security and strategic culture of every state	As a result, every state prefers a balancing which has two basic forms: Internal balancing; External balancing, namely with coalitions (Wohlforth 2010, p. 15)

Source Compiled by the author

2.2.1 Kenneth Waltz

In the field of neorealism, Kenneth Waltz, its generally respected founding author, gives us an invaluable inspiration thanks to his definition of three levels of analysis: the individual, state, and international levels (Waltz 1959). The last of these levels will be dominant in this book. This thinker enriched the theory of ISR with the following important canons. First, every state operates in an anarchic environment, which means that on the field of international politics, there is no overarching global authority on which states could rely to assure their security interests. John Mearsheimer explains it in the following way: there is no night-watchman who would rescue states when they are threatened, and when a state calls the emergency services for help, there is nobody in the international system to answer the call (Mearsheimer 2007, pp. 74).

And second, on the field of ISR, self-help is a key principle of the security and strategic culture of every state. This means that all states promote their own security interests and rely on their own resources and forces. Nevertheless, at the same time, they try to create alliances with states that face the same security threats and have the same interests in and expectations of the shared peace (Table 2.2).

2.2.2 Stephen Walt

The second prominent author of the neorealist school of thought is Stephen Walt (1987), who enriched this school with the definition of five dimensions of security threats. The first of them is the geographic distance between states, which can be exactly measured in kilometres, but also the strategic depth of the compared actors who are in the role of competitors. The second is the offensive strength of their armed forces, which can be measured on the basis of clear quantitative parameters like the absolute volumes of military expenditures, the numbers of modern arms systems (conventional as well as nuclear), and the total numbers of soldiers. The third is the perception of the imminence of the security threats, which is hardly measurable and

2.2 Three Great Neorealists

Table 2.3 Five dimensions of security threats

Distance between states	It is measurable in kilometres
Offensive strength of armed forces	It is measurable if we take into consideration military expenditures and numbers of soldiers and the quality as well as quantity of their arms systems
Perception of the imminence of security threats	It is dominantly a subjective factor; nevertheless, it can be articulated by military arguments
Balance of security threats	It is measurable on the basis of the quantitative parameters
Ideology as a secondary factor	An unmeasurable, but enormously important factor

Source Compiled by the author

requires a necessary degree of empathy. The fourth dimension, balance of security threats, which is Walt's basic contribution to the theory of ISR, must also be taken into consideration. Lastly, ideology as a secondary factor plays a non-negligible role as an instrument of the rationalisation of the expansion, and as a basis of the production of necessary arguments (Table 2.3).

All the above-mentioned dimensions of security threats offer an excellent instrument for the analysis of the results and consequences of the process of NATO expansion after the end of the Cold War. Some of them can be easily measurable or evaluable (namely the distances, military budgets, and numbers of arms systems) while the others are subjective, and hardly measurable if not totally unmeasurable (like, for example, perceptions or ideologies). Nevertheless, all of them play an important role in the field of ISR. Despite their big differences in the field of measurability, all these dimensions have a common denominator: during discussions about them it is necessary for the parties to have a sufficient degree of willingness to listen each other, try to understand why the other is so disturbed and look for bilaterally acceptable compromises.

All the above-mentioned ideas are not a purely idealist theory; they reflect something that can happen even within the framework of ISR between rivals who do not share the same values and expectations. As a generally known and still relevant example, we can remember the behaviour of Ronald Reagan after the crisis provoked by the big exercise Able Archer in 1983, when he understood that the NATO military planes approaching the Soviet air defence systems provoked panic and fears in the USSR and had, as a result, the potential to culminate in a direct confrontation, which, in reality, nobody wanted (Barras 2016, pp. 7–30).

The following chapters will examine the situation after the second wave of NATO enlargement in the light of the neorealist canon of Stephen Walt which states that in terms of geography, there is a big difference between sea powers (specifically the USA) and continental powers (specifically the RF). They will also look at the advantages of the former (it is very far from the possible line of confrontation),

Table 2.4 The theoretical heritage of Stephen Walt

Two basic forms of balancing
Internal balancing as the exploitation of internal resources of states, which has two main forms: • *arming* • *imitation*: (**a**) quantitative: build-up of new military forces and modernisation of their equipment; (**b**) qualitative: new military doctrines and the modernisation of military training
External balancing as the exploitation of resources of other states

Source Compiled by the author

as well as the disadvantages of the latter (it has units of its competitor just on its frontier) (Little 2007, pp. 238–239). The latter is situated near its new competitors, and can, as a result, be involved, even despite their intentions, in a direct military confrontation with unpredictable outcomes (Blagden et al. 2011, pp. 190–202) while the sea powers can profit from their geopolitical position far away from the possible line of confrontation.

Table 2.4 indicates that the following two chapters will largely use not only the classification of security threats articulated by Stephen Walt, but also his theory of balancing. This instrument will be used for the analysis of the big differences between states which could make use of external balancing (like the USA thanks to its new allies after the two main waves of the NATO expansion) and states which can rely only on the resources of internal balancing (like the RF after the end of the Cold War).

Specifically speaking, the following chapters will analyse the opportunities which result from the external balancing of the USA in the space of the former POW. The following chapters will pay attention to the study of important directions in which the operative realists of the new member countries have proven helpful to NATO from the beginning of their memberships until today. First, Chapter 3 will analyse the political value of the invitation from the presidents of Poland and of the Czech Republic just a few years after the end of the Cold War in the beginning of the 1990's, which had the form of an urgent solicitation for the security guarantees of the USA. In other words, it was a direct invitation for the security engagement of the USA in this important part of the post-Cold War world. And this invitation became a great inspiration for the following waves of the NATO expansion.

Secondly, the second direction is symbolised by the offer for the USA to use the military bases of the new member states, which provide the possibility of an eastward projection of military forces towards the territory of its competitor. Thirdly, the armed forces of member states can be used during exercises, and, if necessary, during a possible direct military confrontation. Last but not least, significant attention will be paid to the political reliability of the new member states and to their ideological

Table 2.5 The theoretical heritage of John Mearsheimer

Two types of realism	Two basic groups of states
Offensive realism	Status quo states
Defensive realism	Revisionist states

Source Compiled by the author

kinship because they represent a very important source for the production of arguments for the justification of the expansion of an actor who expands and uses all the advantages of external balancing.

2.2.3 John Mearsheimer

John Mearsheimer (2001), as the third leading neorealist, represents a big inspiration for the present study thanks to his definition of the difference between offensive and defensive realism. Generally speaking, offensive realism puts a decisive emphasis on hegemony, which is perceived as the best way to guarantee the survival of states and as a guarantee of stability and peace (Mearsheimer 2007, p. 75). Offensive realists recommend that states use every opportunity to gain as much of power as possible. In connection with this, he pays much attention to the expansion of large states as well as to the significance of offensive armament and the respective national strategies.

In contrast, defensive realists focus on the relevance of defensive national strategies and especially on the significance of arms control (Nau 2012, p. 70). They believe that to be obsessed with hegemony is a foolish strategy. They recommend that states forget the temptations to maximise their power and instead prefer an "appropriate amount of power" (Waltz 1979, p. 40). In addition, Mearsheimer's emphasis on the status quo allows us to conclude whether any given state is a status quo or a revisionist power. Besides John Mearsheimer, it is necessary to mention other defensive realists, namely Barry Posen (1984), Jack Snyder (1991) and Stephen Van Evera (1999). And defensive realism is not only a grey theory, but it can be applied to a lot of examples in modern history. One of them is the security culture of Otto von Bismarck[2]: after two stunning victories in the Austro-Prussian (1866) and Franco-Prussian wars (1870), he understood that too much power could be counterproductive for his country, and his neighbours could start ta balance against him. As a result, he stopped the strategy of the German expansion (Table 2.5).

Specifically speaking, the approach of John Mearsheimer offers the inspiration for basic angles from which we could see and analyse the interactions between Russia and the expanding NATO (Mearsheimer 2007, p. 75). Mearsheimer indicates that in the light of the key premises of offensive realism, Russian operative realists are determined to restore their hegemony in Eastern Europe and in doing so, they will act like their predecessors in the 1950s and in 1970s, and even use military instruments.

---

[2] The German Chancellor between March 1871 and March 1890.

Table 2.6 The three great neorealists and their ideas which inspired the present book

Kenneth Waltz	Three levels of analysis
	States are security maximisers
Stephen Walt	From the balance of power to the balance of threats
	Five dimensions of security threats[a]
	Internal and external balancing
John Mearsheimer	Offensive vs. defensive realism
	Status quo vs. revisionist powers

Source Compiled by the author
[a]These are the following: aggregate power, geographic proximity between states and between their armed forces, the imminence of the threat, offensive power of key actors, and their respective aggressive intentions

This means that the US must be present in this area and use all its possibilities and instruments to prevent the Russian leaders from being tempted by revisionism and revanchism. A security cooperation with them is impossible. According to this approach, the NATO expansion into the post-Soviet space based on the external balancing is not only a possibility, but even an obligation for the USA.

Under the light of the key premises of defensive realism, which offers a more optimistic approach and story (Mearsheimer 2007, pp. 83–85), it is hard to imagine that Russia would conquer its neighbours which entered NATO during the first and the second wave of NATO expansion. On the contrary, Russia can peacefully coexist with them. Moreover, this weakened state could be able to understand that the benefits of an aggressive posture towards its Eastern neighbours will be outweighed by its costs. As a result, it is possible to hope that if they do not want a new wave of NATO expansion in the post-Soviet space, the Russian operative realists will act like Bismarck, and not like Wilhelm II or Adolf Hitler; or like Khrushchev[3] and Gorbachev,[4] and not like Stalin[5] or Brezhnev.[6]

All this means that the window of opportunities for a security cooperation is not definitively closed. We can conclude this section with the statement that the contemporary defensive realism is a continuation of the approach defined by John Kennan at the beginning of the Cold War, when he was convinced that the USSR (a much more influential and self-confident actor than the contemporary RF) was unlikely to start a war and preferred political to military methods (Harper 2012, pp. 157–166) (Table 2.6).

Last, but not least, all neorealist thinkers agree with Samuel Huntington (a classical realist) that in the field of security, states cannot rely on other actors (Huntington 1958, pp. 41–86). Within this self-help system, the security of states is very expensive

---

[3]This controversial politician merits a positive evaluation particularly for his sincere efforts to reduce the military expenditures and numbers of soldiers and military units.

[4]He entered modern history as a major figure thanks to his emphasis on arms control, détente, and the so-called new thinking, which resulted in the peaceful end of the Cold War.

[5]In the sense of his brutal expansion into Central Europe.

[6]In the sense of his military intervention in Czechoslovakia in 1968.

(Waltz 1979, p. 33) and an underestimation of this issue can have fatal consequences. Moreover, neorealist thinkers underline the priority of structural factors, which means that small and declining states and their leading politicians must accommodate them (Parent and Rosato 2015, pp. 51–86).

2.3 The NATO Post-Cold War Enlargement as an Expansion Sui Generis

The central concept of this book is a word which is composed of 9 letters: "expansion." This word will be used strictly without any political or ideological connotations. It will be used here in all its variants regardless of the state which expands and also regardless of the direction of its expansion and the arguments used for its justification. This approach is deduced from the natural sciences. First, mathematics, the "Queen of all sciences," has the following definition: $(a + b)^2$ is the basic formula, while $a^2 + 2ab + b^2$ is the expanded formula. Second, in physics, the word "expansion" is used to describe an increase in the volume of working fluid. Lastly, in geography, expansion means that a country enlarges its frontiers or its dominant influence in the world.[7] In other words, the term "expansion" will be used without any pejorative or normative context or meaning.

2.3.1 Expansion as the Central Concept of This Book

The expansion of NATO as a specific and particular form of expansion will be studied on three levels. On the geopolitical level, the key attention will be paid to the seizure of a new territory and its resources, which results in changes of distances between states which play an important role in the field of ISR. On the military level, the main attention will be aimed at an analysis of particular measures. The first of them is the sending of expeditionary forces abroad and it is defined by M. Mandelbaum (1995, pp. 9–13). And the following measures have been defined by great neorealist authors: the changes of distances between armed forces (Yale Journal of International Affairs 2010), and the changes of the threat balances and of security threats. And on the ideological level, the imposition of new norms, a new ideology (Aron 1954) and a new doctrinal thinking is the most typical symptom of every expansion. All these measures are symbols of the process of the expansion of NATO and they will be attentively analysed on the following pages.

Table 2.7 presents the most important relevant authors and their approaches to the concept of expansion. At the same time, it mentions some possible consequences of expansions. Under these lenses, the process of NATO enlargement will be studied as an expansion sui generis.

---

[7] www.larousse.fr/dictionnaires/francais/expansion/322147.

Table 2.7 Forms of expansion

Levels	Key features	The authors of the definitions
Geopolitical level	Expansion of influence	Larousse
	Seizure of new territory and its resources	Raymond Aron (1962)
	Changes in distances between states	Stephen Walt
Military level	Sending of expeditionary forces abroad	Michael Mandelbaum
	Changes in distances between armed forces	Stephen Walt
	Breaks/violations of the threat balances	
	Changes in perceptions of security threats	
Ideological level	Control of new territories	Michael Mandelbaum
	The imposition of new norms	Stephen Walt
	Expansion of ideological solidarity	Raymond Aron
	The imposition of a new ideology	Larousse
	Doctrinal expansion	

Source Compiled by the author

2.3.2 Target as a Key Concept of the Neorealist Approach to the Process of Expansion

The word "target" is used to refer to the territory which is at stake in the process of expansion. In the case of this book, it is the territory of the new member states of NATO which entered this organisation of collective defence after the end of the Cold War, namely the former member countries of the Pact of Warsaw (POW) and/or the USSR. Table 2.8 presents a framework for the classification of the actors of the expansion and of its possible consequences, political as well as military. The process of NATO expansion will be analysed in the light of the difference between two groups of actors: active and passive ones.

Table 2.8 Expansion in the light of key actors and possible consequences

Actors of expansion	Active actors Only strong states can expand (Mandelbaum 1988, pp. 143–155)	Passive actors Weak states in decline are looking for ways to face the expansion of strong states (Mandelbaum) Those weak states or the areas surrounding them are in the role of "targets" (Keohane 1986, p. 378)
Possible consequences	Growing international tension (Jervis)	Military consequences Growing military tension Military incidents Direct military confrontation

Source Compiled by the author

2.3 The NATO Post-Cold War Enlargement as an Expansion Sui Generis 19

2.3.3 *NATO Expansion as a Security Dilemma*

As the process of NATO expansion became the most important point of contention in the security relations between the US and the RF, *Robert Jervis* (1978, pp. 167–214) serves as another basic theoretical inspiration of this book. Namely, his model of the security dilemma process will be applied to the study because ever since the first wave of NATO expansion we are witnessing a long and endless vicious circle, a dangerous process of measures, countermeasures, counter-countermeasures, etc.

The Russian leaders condemn the process of the NATO enlargement as a malign and even aggressive strategy. They identify it with the alleged malign (offensive) intents of NATO, namely of the USA as its hegemon. Similarly, the annexation of the Crimea will be studied and explained as a result of Moscow's long-term obsession with worst-case assumptions and worst-case scenarios (Tang 2008) in their analyses and interpretations of the process of NATO enlargement and its consequences for the security of the RF.

2.3.4 *NATO Expansion as a Greedy Behaviour?*

Jervis's concept of the security dilemma has been revisited, refined, and enriched by *Charles Glaser* thanks to his distinction between security-seeking states and greedy states (Glaser 1997, pp. 179–180). This concept opens a way to the study of the process of NATO expansion in a new light, in the light of its possible counterproductive results and consequences. Glaser argues that expansion is propelled by the greedy intentions of some states and warns that it can have two negative consequences. First, a greedy state can provoke the state in the role of the target of its expansion and this targeted state can react with a substantial increase of its military expenditures, purchases of new arms systems and even important changes in its doctrines. This spiral of measures and countermeasures was typical for all four decades of the Cold War.

And secondly, the provoked state can react with a counter-expansion. A typical behaviour of this sort occurred in 1967, when Egypt blockaded the Straits of Tiran, mobilised its forces on the frontier with Israel, and asked the UN peacekeeping forces to evacuate the Sinai (Ripsman et al. 2016). Faced with Egypt's expansionist behaviour, the Israeli leaders reacted with a pre-emptive strike (Bass 2002) which was crowned by an enormous success and which resulted in a new international order in the Middle East (Oren 2002).

In the light of this inspiration, Chapter 3 of this book will show that this mechanism has been applied by the RF in two cases. The first of them was the first instrumentalization of separatism against the process of NATO enlargement, which happened in 2008 in Georgia. The second, even more important and disturbing one came in 2014 when Russia carried out its second instrumentalization of separatism against

Table 2.9 Key differences between security-seeking states and greedy states

Security-seeking states	Greedy states
They do not try to actively influence their neighbourhood	They actively and assertively influence their neighbourhood and/or the world
They do not spread their ideology and/or their religion	They actively and assertively spread their ideology and/or their religion
They are satisfied with the levels of their armed forces	They are obsessed with military supremacy and modernisation
Their military doctrines emphasise the defence of their territory	Their military doctrines emphasise the projections of military forces
The build-up of their armed forces strictly respects the principles of strategic sufficiency	The build-up of their armed forces largely exceeds the level of the defence of their territory
They prefer security cooperation; they do not apply methods of political pressure	They do not rule out political pressure, security competition or even confrontation
They refuse any forms of expansion	Expansion is an integral and important part of their strategy

Source Compiled by the author

the process of NATO enlargement, which was crowned by the annexation of the Crimean Peninsula, a part of Ukraine (Table 2.9).

It is generally known that Charles Glaser supported the process of NATO expansion since its beginning (Glaser 1993). Nevertheless, his theoretical heritage is so strong and inspirational that it can be applied to a critical, maybe partly heretical, reassessment of the process of the NATO expansion after the end of the Cold War. This means that in this book, the movement of the Alliance towards the western frontiers of the RF will be studied and interpreted as a specific form of greedy security behaviour.

But this book will not cover all the history of NATO expansion; it will avoid the four decades long period of the Cold War, which saw three waves of NATO expansion. The first of them came in 1952 with the adhesion of Greece and Turkey, when, as a result, NATO entered the new, strategically important space of the Aegean Sea and the Black Sea. The second wave happened in 1955 with the adhesion of West Germany. And the last wave brought into the Alliance an important Mediterranean country—Spain. Nevertheless, these waves will not be analysed in this book, even if they had important and sometimes dramatic consequences for ISR in Europe.

2.3.5 *Three Stages of NATO Expansion*

The main attention will be paid to the NATO expansion after the end of the Cold War and its consequences for the international security relations. Chapters 3 and 4 will analyse and explain this process by dividing it into three stages. During the *first stage*, two former states of the Warsaw Pact, namely Poland and the Czech Republic, acted as security-seeking states and just some years after the end of the Cold War, they invited the USA to give them its security guarantees. Their solicitation will be studied as a demonstration of similar activity as that of the Western Europe states in spring 1949, after the first Berlin crisis, when they solicited the USA to create the security community which entered modern history under the name NATO (Schmidt 2001). This newly created alliance declared that its mission was to face the behaviour of the USSR under the reign of the unscrupulous dictator J.V. Stalin, which had been perceived as an imminent security threat for all of the free world.

Chapters 3 and 4 will show that the *second stage* of the post-Cold War NATO expansion had the same basic feature as the first one: a solicitation sent to the USA by states seeking its security guarantees. In a profoundly changed geopolitical situation, there was the same addressee, the same solicited state: the USA. But this time, the same solicitation was sent by new transmitters: the former member states of the Warsaw Treaty Organisation (WTO), which were also former Soviet satellites. Despite the new historical and geopolitical framework, the solicitations of these states were based on the same rationale as the previous solicitation: they had security fears related to the same country that the solicitors in 1949 feared. Of course, this time, it was not the USSR, but only the Russian Federation as the largest and strongest of its successor states. And, like in 1949, the USA complied with these solicitations and it did so in two main waves (in 1999 and 2004).

Finally, the *third stage* started in 2008 with the war between Georgia and Russia and culminated in 2014 with the Russian annexation of Crimea. These two military measures resulted from the enormously strong security fears of the "operative realists" in Moscow, who reacted in this way to the preceding two waves of the process of NATO expansion, namely its expansion to the Black Sea area (these operative realists were President B. Yeltsin in the case of the first wave and V. Putin in the case of the second wave, plus their ministers and generals). The decision to support the Russian separatists in Eastern Ukraine and, especially, the annexation of Crimea will be analysed as a specific form of the greedy behaviour of the RF which was motivated by the aim to stop the process of NATO expansion and gain a strategic depth for itself as well as an instrument for its politics of blackmail.

Moreover, the above-mentioned waves were followed by other adhesions, which happened during the third stage, and started with the entry of two other states of Eastern Europe into NATO. This process started in April 2009, sixty years after the creation of NATO, with the adhesion of Croatia (56,594 km^2 with 4 million of inhabitants) and Albania (28,748 km^2 with 2,8 million inhabitants). And the expansion continued with the entry of Montenegro (13,812 km^2 with 4 million inhabitants) in June 2017 and was crowned in March 2020 by the entry of North Macedonia (25,713 km^2 with 2 million of inhabitants). In total, the territory that was added to NATO consisted of 125,000 km^2 with 13 million inhabitants. From the quantitative point of view, however, neither the size of the area, nor the number of inhabitants plays any extraordinary role.

But from the geopolitical and geostrategic point of view, between 2004 and 2020, NATO entered the area of the Adriatic Sea, which is very important. Thanks to this wave of expansion, NATO gained the possibility of a direct control of the following areas of a high strategic importance:

- In the North, it is the Baltic Sea, including the Bay of Finland, which opens a direct access route to the area of St. Petersburg, the second largest city of the entire Russian Federation;
- And in the South, it is the Adriatic Sea, which includes an important part of the post-Yugoslav space;
- Thanks to its gaining the Southern part of the former Yugoslavia, NATO gained an important continuous and unbroken strip between two European seas: the Black Sea and the Adriatic Sea. This strip includes the following new member states: Montenegro, Albania, North Macedonia, Bulgaria, and Romania;
- After this wave of NATO expansion, NATO controls the space going from Tallinn to Tirana and from Split to Varna.

Nevertheless, the above-mentioned wave of NATO expansion was much less important than the preceding wave which covered the North-Eastern part of the post-Soviet space and a big part of the Northern part of the Black Sea area. From the neorealist point of view, the consequences of this later expansion were much less dramatic and disturbing. As a result, they were much less analysed and commented on by the leading theoreticians and analysts in Europe as well as the USA. And the same logic will be applied even on the pages of this book. The key attention will be paid to the consequences of the wave which included three post-Soviet states and two states of the Black Sea area.

In the light of all the above-mentioned facts, the following two chapters will analyse two profoundly different forms of greedy behaviour. The first of them, the NATO expansion, will be studied as a greedy behaviour started by a clear and incontestable invitation which happened within the existing and generally respected framework of the post-Cold War status quo. At the same time, this form of greedy behaviour will be analysed as a behaviour which fully respected the existing borders between states and was made without their military violation. Lastly, it will be studied as a strategy which fully respected all norms of the existing international law.

On the other hand, the security strategy of the RF in the post-Soviet space after the second wave of the NATO Expansion will be studied as a demonstration of another kind of behaviour. It will be analysed as an exemplary revisionist greedy behaviour imposed by a direct military coercion without respect for the territorial borders of one member state of the United Nations, and in contradiction to all basic norms of international law.

2.3.6 An "Expansion by Invitation"

The expression "expansion by invitation" will be analysed and explained in the light of the following basic concepts. First, there is Raymond Aron and his concept of expansion of ideological solidarity (Aron 1962). Second, there are five factors articulated by Stephen Walt, the main one of which is the "military level." Third, there is Michael Mandelbaum (1995) and his thesis that only strong states can expand, which means that every expansion is made to the detriment of weak states and/or states that are in decline. Lastly, there is Charles Glaser's above-mentioned theory of greedy intentions and greedy states (Glaser 1997, pp. 179–180).

The analysis of the NATO expansion after the end of the Cold War will be based on the following pillars:

(a) Since its beginning, NATO's expansion was presented as a necessary US involvement in Eastern and Central Europe, whose aim is to install/impose a new balance of power and a new international security order.
(b) The NATO expansion was interpreted as a necessary US measure with the aim to restructure this important part of the Old Continent according to the standards shared by the USA and its allies, and their strategic interests and requirements, regardless of the security interests and protestations of the former hegemon of this area.
(c) From the beginning of the process of NATO expansion, this part of Europe is witnessing a merciless competition between the former and the new hegemon, with all its dramatic and hardly predictable consequences.
(d) Features (a) and (b) have the four following common denominators:

- After the end of the Cold War, the USA has become an unchecked world hegemon without any competitor. It has gained a spectacular primacy in the post-Cold War international security relations.
- As a result, it has become an "indispensable nation" (Zenko 2014) which has not only the possibility but also the obligation to manifest its capacity as well as its willingness to shape and profoundly restructure the international order in all parts of the world.
- The USA's political and especially its military engagement in the post-Soviet space was conceived as a signalisation of the American primacy and superiority.
- At the ideological level, the NATO expansion is presented as an enlargement of the space of democracy, freedom, prosperity, and stability (Epstein 2005). As a result, the expansion agenda has become more available and desirable.

2.3.7 *Balancing Theory and Its Importance for the Study of NATO Expansion*

The neorealist school of thought puts a strong emphasis on balancing as a method of reinforcing military capability, and of strengthening the credibility of the deterrent (Nexon 2009). It is vitally important particularly for the states which are exposed to an imminent threat or feel disadvantaged (Elman 2002; Levy 2002). Balancing has two basic forms: internal and external. The first of them has two possible variants: arming and imitation.

Arming is aimed to raise the quantitative as well as qualitative parameters of the armed forces; thanks to them one state or coalition can attain an important superiority over or parity with its competitor. This form of balancing results in rises of military budgets and a high level of combat preparedness of the armed forces (Waltz 1979, p. 157). Imitation is based on a state adopting the successful methods of other states. The USSR as the predecessor of the RF has a long experience with imitation of the US arms systems (namely NW) during the Cold War. Arming and imitation are enormously important because they reinforce the aggregate capabilities of the competing states (Elman 2002; Levy 2002).

External balancing is much rarer than its internal counterpart (Waltz 1979, p. 167) because it contains a lot of risks resulting from the reliability (Beckley 2015) or unreliability of allies (Weitsman 2004). It is typical for interstate wars (namely WWI and WWII), but when the wars are finished, it can swiftly evaporate. The most typical example of this is the end of the cooperation between the USA and the USSR in the last days of WWII. In spring 1945, this brutal turn was provoked by two top secret plans codenamed Operation Unthinkable, which were identified in Moscow with the aim "to impose upon Russia the will of the USA and the British Empire" (Rzeševskij 1999).

The neorealist school of thought has three axioms for the study of strategies of balancing. First, the states which are behind must make big efforts (financial as well as political) if they want to get out from their position of inferiority. Second, parity is much more expensive for continental powers than for maritime powers. Lastly, maritime powers take a security risk when they approach the frontiers of continental powers, which can react with an active resistance (Parent and Rosato 2015).

Chapters 3 and 4 of this book will develop the neorealist argument that since the first wave of the expansion, NATO and especially the USA as its leading state, have two advantages of strategic importance. First, as a typical sea power, the USA is far away from the Eastern border of NATO, and thus it would not be harmed by the resulting damages in case of a direct conventional confrontation. And second, thanks to the invitations and even solicitations from the political and military élites of the former countries of the POW, it can profit from the external balancing.

Russia, on the other hand, is in a disadvantageous position. First, as a continental power, it has the new member countries on its Western border. This means that a possible direct military confrontation would damage its territory. Second, as a result of its brutal policy during the Cold War and the corresponding feelings of resentment of populations of Central and Eastern Europe, it has hardly any force of attraction. As a result, the RF has hardly any possibility of external balancing and it must rely only on internal balancing.

Of course, the neorealist school of thought has not only its defenders (including the author of this book), but also a wide range of its opponents and critics. They argue that the theory of balance of power is a weak theory (Nexon 2009) and that it should even be forgotten (Schroeder 1994). The neorealists are criticised particularly because they allegedly underestimate the roles of types of political regimes, and of the presidents and prime ministers in the ISR. This reproach has been repeated very often after the decision of the Russian president V. Putin to annex the Crimean Peninsula.

Nevertheless, neorealism has an incontestable potential in the research of the consequences of balancing behaviour (Waltz 2000). And these consequences have two basic forms. Intentional consequences arrive when a state or a coalition has the aim to weaken its competitor to obtain or even enhance its superiority. And the nonintentional consequences arrive when an actor does not have this aim, but its activities can negatively influence the structure of the ISR. Saying this does not mean that neorealists are structural determinists (Parent and Sorato 2015); it simply means that they give us the warning that even nonintentional consequences can destabilise the entire structure of the ISR (Jervis 1978). And this warning is enormously important and inspirational even for the study of the NATO expansion after the end of the Cold War and its consequences.

2.4 Positive and Negative Peace

And the above-mentioned distinction between intentional and nonintentional consequences is closely intertwined with the concept of "peace." On the pages of the following chapters, the word "peace" will be very often used, even if it is not a neorealist concept. But this word is accepted and conceptualised by all schools of thought. All theoretical approaches agree that this word represents the ideal state of the ISR as well as the most important value in the life of every person, social group, and state.

This paragraph will recall, very briefly, only a few realists and their approaches to the concept of peace. Thomas Hobbes, one of the so-called proto-realists (together with Thucydides, N. Machiavelli, and T. and J. J. Rousseau), as a typical structuralist thinker (Richmond 2008), underlined that peace is nothing more than a result of the balance of power which covers not only life without any direct armed international violence, but also the preparation for future possible wars. The classical realists are convinced that states are on an eternal quest for survival and security, that states always try to enhance their strength and power, and that, as a result, peace is always highly uncertain (Spykman 2007). Hans Morgenthau articulated three elementary goals of states which always weaken peace: to maintain the state's current position, strength and power; to become even stronger and more powerful, and to display the state's strength and power to enhance its prestige (Morgenthau 1948).

Realists, and especially neorealists, don't share the liberal approach to the peace which is based on three basic claims: domestic political opposition makes democratic states more risk-averse in some regime types (Morgan and Campbell 1991); economic interdependence reduces military conflict (Mansfield 1994) and can strengthen peace (Wallensteen 1973); and international organizations and regimes have the potential to achieve stabilization of international cooperation, confidence and peace (Oneal and Russett 2001).

Nevertheless, the following chapters will pay much attention to the theoretical concept of Johan Galtung, the founder of "Peace Studies," an interdisciplinary approach to peace. This approach differs profoundly from the realist school of thought, as it is not interested in describing the world as it is, but instead it poses the question of how it should be, or how it could be (Brown 1992). However, this does not mean that Peace Studies are absolutely incompatible with the neorealist analysis of the results and consequences of NATO expansion. On the contrary, they open a way to the concretisation of this dynamic process.

Peace Studies are critical towards militarism, one of the main threats to the international peace and security. It is necessary to remember that militarism is defined as a specific culture, and as a glorification of military discipline and values, armed violence, and, in extreme case war (Boulding 1992). At the same time, militarism is defined by the rising of military expenditures, growing numbers of soldiers and the build-up of new military bases (De Montbrial et al. 2000). And this fact means that the process of NATO expansion satisfies some criteria of this phenomenon.

Of course, it is not possible to say that the aim of this process is to provoke a war in Europe. Nevertheless, one of its consequences, no matter if intentional or non-intentional, is the rise of military tension in the space which covers the Eastern frontier of NATO and the Western frontier of the RF. This tension is manifested mainly by the growing military budgets, and the build-up of new military bases on the territory of new member states and, especially, in the Western part of the RF. At the same time, it is manifested by growing numbers of military exercises and of military incidents with a dangerous explosiveness. And all the above-mentioned phenomena represent an important inspiration for all the following chapters of this book.

Johan Galtung, an enormously enlightened Norwegian researcher and a convinced critic of militarism, enriched the social sciences with his inventive distinction between two basic variants of peace (Galtung 1964). Negative peace is typical for the regions or for the periods in human history where/when the international order is/was based on the existence of the structural violence which contained the seeds of future clashes of interest or armed conflicts (Galtung 1969). This variant of peace is very uncertain, and it is often used for the study of the basic causes of future crises and wars (Weber 1999). As a result, this form of peace is negatively defined as the absence of direct violence between states (Lindholm Schulz 2001). Some authors reproach Galtung by stating that his theory is simplifying and polarizing (Boulding 1977); nevertheless, his theory is widely accepted, respected, and appreciated and used for further research.

Negative peace was typical for the Euro-American area during the Cold War, namely during two extremely explosive periods. The first of them covers the 1950s, and it was started by the first doctrinal concept of the Cold War, NSC (National Security Council Report) 68 from 1950, written under the direction of Paul Nitze, the most influential proponent of the US's hard line policy (Thompson 2011). This strategy put the key emphasis on the long-term containment of the USSR (Nitze and Nelson 1994).

The second period of a dangerously negative peace was started with the deployment of the Soviet SS-20 nuclear missiles in 1977 and entered modern history under the label "the Euro-missile crisis" (Tatu 1983) because the above mentioned measure of the USSR was followed by a decisive answer of NATO in 1979 (Nuti et al. 2015). This period of negative peace swiftly ended in 1985 after the profound political

2.4 Positive and Negative Peace

change in Moscow when the relatively young General Secretary Gorbachev ended the long-term period of gerontocracy there.[8] This positive change is symbolised by the signature of the INF Treaty in 1987[9] and the following elimination of the enormously dangerous SS-20 missiles by the USSR and the corresponding elimination of Pershing II missiles by the USA (Klein 1988).

Positive peace is always a result of negation of structural violence; it is based on the non-confrontational structure of the ISR. Positive peace is characterised not only by the absence of direct violence, but also by the absence of structural violence. It is typical for security communities based on shared fundamental values and paradigms of their security culture and strategy. The most well-known example of this is NATO since its creation until today. But positive peace was also typical for the relations between NATO and the POW during the above mentioned second half of the 1980's thanks to the security cooperation between the presidents R. Reagan and M. Gorbachev. And the golden period of positive peace came just after the end of the Cold War and was symbolised by the so-called peace dividends: reductions of numbers of soldiers and their equipment, the cutting of military budgets and the process of denuclearisation (namely the START and SORT process) (Table 2.10).

Of course, Johan Galtung is not a neorealist thinker, and his distinction between two basic variants of peace is not a neorealist concept. Nevertheless, he offers us an excellent theoretical instrument for a systematic analysis of the results and consequences of the NATO expansion. The conclusions of all the following chapters as well as the conclusion of the entire book will specify the consequences, no matter if intentional or nonintentional, of the key analysed events, strategic decisions, and measures for the move from positive to negative peace.

The following chapters will use Galtung's concept as an excellent instrument for the analysis of the militarisation which came after the second wave of this process and which gradually increased after the military seizure of the Crimean Peninsula in 2014. The evaluation of the two waves of the NATO expansion will be based on an analysis of the most important symbols of this dangerous trend, namely the build-up of new military units at the Eastern frontier of the expanded NATO as well as in the territory of the Western part of the RF, and the intensive modernisation of their equipment and arms-systems. Particular attention will be paid to the new strategic and military doctrines of the USA, the build-up of the Western military district of the Russian armed forces and the military exercises near the new dividing line which has been drawn between the RF on one hand and the new member states on the other.

The most important attributes of Galtung's concepts open the way to an understanding of the security strategies of two antagonistic actors. Thanks to Galtung, we have an analytical instrument for the distinction between the modest short-term ambitions of the key actors: to avoid the outbreak of a direct military confrontation on the one hand and the courageous long-term ambition of a lasting peace without any international crisis on the other.

---

[8] It was symbolised by the reign of L. Brezhnev, J. Andropov, and K. Tchernenko.

[9] Treaty Between the United States of America and the Union of Soviet Socialist Republics on the Elimination of Their Intermediate-Range and Shorter-Range Missiles (INF Treaty).

Table 2.10 Basic differences between negative and positive peace

	Negative Peace	Positive Peace
Key aim	Elimination of the threat of war	A stable, long-term peace
Structural characteristics	Permanent international tension and mutual mistrust between states Strong influence of soldiers and military solutions	Structural integration of the key actors of the ISR Politicians, not soldiers, have a decisive influence on international politics
Key aims and measures	Rising military budgets Rising numbers of soldiers (in absolute as well as relative parameters) Rising numbers of military exercises Pre-emptive military actions	A long-term peace based on mutual communication between key actors, and on a long-term security cooperation Long-term preventive elimination of the negative trends which could lead to a crisis or even wars
Basic characteristics	Instead of the building of a long-term peace, key actors try to postpone mutual direct violence	International integration and a non-conflict structure of the ISR
Result	Conservation of the existing structure of the ISR	Positive changes of the ISR
Duration	The modest short-term ambition of key actors: to avoid the outbreak of war	The big long-term ambition: a lasting peace without any international crisis

Source Compiled by the author

2.5 Research Questions

All the research questions (RQ) of this book are non-normative because the main attention is not paid to an ideal world and the predictions or recommendations of what it should be like. On the contrary, all the RQ of this book are positive ones. They are aimed toward the existing world, which exists independently of our wishes and ideas (Malici and Smith 2013). This also means that the research is not dominantly quantitative, but primarily qualitative. Of course, however, a lot of phenomena of a quantitative character will be analysed, namely the military budgets of the key actors, the build-up of military bases and big military units, new arms systems, and the growing numbers of military exercises and incidents with a highly explosive potential.

Nevertheless, the qualitative approach is dominant (Barkin 2008). Firstly, the author of this book is not totally separated from the object of his research; he works under the influence of his values, convictions, and points of view. Second, he analyses a relatively modest sample of facts and events and he prefers an in-depth analysis of the consequences of the process of NATO expansion in the post-Soviet area. Third, all of this book is based on a content analysis of documents (namely doctrines) and the statements of the most influential decision makers. Lastly, decisive attention will be paid to the analysis of the values, attitudes, and convictions of the operative realists

2.5 Research Questions

Table 2.11 Research questions

RQ1	Why do the relations between the USA and the RF move from security cooperation (which was so typical for the first half of the 1990s) towards confrontation? Why are they moving from positive peace (PP) towards negative peace (NP)?
RQ2	What kinds of approaches were prevailing in, and which decisions were milestones of the process of NATO expansion?
RQ3	Why is the structure of the international security relations (ISR) at the Eastern border of NATO so confrontational?
RQ4	What are the consequences of this trend?

in NATO as well as in the RF. This means that this book will examine phenomena which exist not only in a real surrounding world, but also in the heads and brains of the key actors.

The research questions this book asks are the Table 2.11.

2.6 Methodology

In terms of methodology, the proposed book will be written as a theory testing and policy evaluative work (Van Evera 1997), which means that the following pages will test the potential of the neorealist theory to explain the complex phenomena of NATO expansion, and its key features and consequences. At the same time, the book will study the political motivations and measures of the key actors of this extraordinary dynamic process. In the light of recommendations of Umberto Eco (1977), the text will be based on primary resources (doctrines, speeches of presidents, statements of prime ministers and ministers, etc.) as well as secondary resources (monographs, essays, articles, journals). At the same time, this chapter explains the most important theoretical concepts and the most often used words in the book.

At the same time, the holistic approach[10] will predominate over individualism.[11] Also, the objective approach will be preferred before the subjective approach (Hermann 2012), and the "outside scoop" will be used rather than the "inside scoop". This specifically means that the author will not proceed as a political psychologist who is oriented toward the study of subjectivities and motives. On the contrary, the author will work as an investigative reporter piecing together a story of profound changes in the examined area during the post-Cold War period.

The expansion of NATO will be dominantly studied from the perspective of the institution and the status quo, and not from the position of particular people and their roles (Mearsheimer 2001). It is without a doubt that people (namely the most influential politicians like presidents, prime ministers, and general secretaries) identify

---
[10] It is aimed at the study of social structures.
[11] It is dominantly aimed at the study of the roles of the structure of the ISR after the end of the Cold War in regard to the role of NATO, even if the role of important personalities is not ignored in this approach.

and interpret problems in politics. They occupy important and influential roles in all institutions (e.g. the White House, the Kremlin, NATO, and the EU headquarters) and influence their decisions.

Nevertheless, the focus on institutions and their roles gives us a lot of information about constraints that impinge on the decision-makers in the field of foreign and security policy. Moreover, it opens the way to an understanding of the metamorphoses of the status quo in the examined area. In this particular case, the institutional lens opens the way to an understanding of the importance of the profound structural changes in the post-Soviet space during the last 25 years.

At the same time, the book is based on an equilibrium between materialism and idealism. The book will assign the same level of importance to the factors of a material character which constitute the so-called hard power, and the factors of a more subjective nature which form a state's soft power. The basic indicators of the hard power of the post-Soviet space are: the surface area, numbers of inhabitants, reserves of natural resources, and industrial might. An enormously important role here is played by military power, namely the bases, numbers of soldiers, and arms systems.

Finally, this book is built on an equal/balanced relationship between processes and outcomes (Hermann 2012). It will search for an answer to the question of *what* happened in the post-Soviet space as well as the reasons *why* it happened. The first question implies some following questions, namely, what were the reactions of the public, governments, and institutions to the expansion of NATO? And the second question continues with the following sub-questions: *Why* was this strategy chosen? Why did this strategy provoke the security fears of the Russian operational realists, and why did they react with the annexation of the Crimea? Why does the international military tension continue to grow in this area of Europe?

Sources

Aron, R. (1954). *The Century of Total War*. New York: Doubleday & Co.
Aron, R. (1962). *Paix et guerre entre les nations*. Paris: Calmann-Lévy.
Barkin, S. (2008). Qualitative Methods? In D. Prakash (Ed.), *Qualitative Methods in International Relations: A Pluralist Guide*. New York: Palgrave Macmillan.
Barrass, G. (2016). Able Archer 83: What Were the Soviets Thinking? *Survival, 58*(6), 7–30.
Bass, G. J. (2002, June 16). Days That Shook the World. *The New York Times*.
Beckley, M. (2015). The Myth of Entangling Alliances: Reassessing the Security Risks of U.S. Defense Pacts. *International Security, 39*(4), 17–22.
Blagden, D. W., Levy, J. S., & Thompson, W. R. (2011). Sea Powers, Continental Powers, and Balancing Theory. *International Security, 36*(2), 190–202.
Boulding, E. (1992). *New Agendas for Peace Research: Conflict and Security Reexamined*. Boulder, CO: Lynne Rienner Publishers.
Boulding, K. E. (1977). Twelve Friendly Quarrels with Johan Galtung. *Journal of Peace Research, 14*(1), 75–86.
Brown, C. (1992). *International Relations Theory: New Normative Approaches*. New York: Columbia University Press.

De Montbrial, T., Klein, J., & Jansen, S. (2000). *Dictionnaire de stratégie / publié sous la direction*. Presses Universitaires de France.
Eco, U. (1977). *Come si fa una tesi di laurea*. Milano: V. Bompiani.
Elman, C. (2002). Introduction: Appraising Balance-of-Power Theory. In J. A. Vasquez & C. Elman (Eds.), *Realism and the Balancing of Power*. Upper Saddle River: Pearson Publication.
Epstein, R. A. (2005). NATO Enlargement and the Spread of Democracy: Evidence and Expectations. *Security Studies, 14*(1), 63–105.
Galtung, J. (1964). An Editorial. *Journal of Peace Research, 1*(1).
Galtung, J. (1969). Violence, Peace and Peace Research. *Journal of Peace Research, 6*(3), 167–191.
Gilpin, R. (1981). *War and Change in World Politics*. Cambridge: Cambridge University Press.
Glaser, C. L. (1993). Why NATO Is Still Best: Future Security Arrangements for Europe. *International Security, 18*(1), 5–50.
Glaser, C. L. (1997). The Security Dilemma Revisited. *World Politics, 50*, 171–201.
Harper, J. L. (2012). The Kennan Century. *Survival, 54*(2), 157–166.
Hermann, M. (2012). The Study of American FP. In S. W. Hook & C. M. Jones (Eds.), *Routledge Handbook of American Foreign Policy*. New York: Routledge.
Hill, F., & Gaddy, C. (2015). *Mr Putin, Operative in the Kremlin*. Washington: Brookings Institution Press.
Huntington, S. P. (1958). Arms Races: Prerequisites and Results. *Public Policy, 8*(1), 41–86.
Jervis, R. (1978). Cooperation Under the Security Dilemma. *World Politics, 30*(2), 167–174.
Kegley, C. W., & Wittkopf, E. R. (2006). *World Politics: Trends and Transformation* (10th ed.). Belmont, CA: Thomson/Wadsworth.
Keohane, R. O. (1986). *Neorealism and Its Critics*. New York: Columbia University Press.
Keohane, R. O. (1988). Alliances, Threats, and the Uses of Neorealism: The Origins of Alliances by Stephen M. Walt. *International Security, 13*(1), 169–176.
Klein, J. (1988). Portée et signification du traité de Washington. *Politique étrangère, 1*, 47–63.
Levy, J. S. (2002). Balances and Balancing: Concepts, Propositions, and Research Design. In J. A. Vasquez & C. Elman (Eds.), *Realism and the Balancing of Power*. Upper Saddle River: Pearson Publication.
Lindholm Schulz, H. (2001). Structural Violence. In R. J. Barry Jones (Ed.), *Routledge Encyclopedia of International Political Economy* (pp. 1501–1502). London: Routledge.
Little, R. (2007). *The Balance of Power in International Relations: Metaphors, Myths and Models*. Cambridge: Cambridge University Press.
Malici, A., & Smith, E. (2013). *Political Science Research in Practice*. New York: Routledge.
Mandelbaum, M. (1988). *The Fate of Nations: The Search for National Security in the Nineteenth and Twentieth Centuries*. Cambridge: Cambridge University Press.
Mandelbaum, M. (1995). Preserving the New Peace: The Case Against NATO Expansion. *Foreign Affairs, 74*(3), 9–13.
Mansfield, E. D. (1994). *Power, Trade, and War*. Princeton: Princeton University Press.
Mearsheimer, J. (2001). *The Tragedy of Great Power Politics*. New York: Norton.
Mearsheimer, J. (2007). Structural Realism. In T. Dunne, M. Kurki, & S. Smith (Eds.), *International Relations Theories: Discipline and Diversity*. Oxford and New York: Oxford University Press.
Morgan, T. C., & Campbell, S. H. (1991). Domestic Structure, Decisional Constraints, and War: So Why Kant Democracies Fight? *The Journal of Conflict Resolution, 35*(2), 187–211.
Morgenthau, H. (1948). *Politics Among Nations*. New York: Knopf.
National Security Council Report, *NSC 68*, 'United States Objectives and Programs for National. Security', 14 April 1950.
Nau, H. (2012). Realism. In S. W. Hook & C. M. Jones (Eds.), *Routledge Handbook of American Foreign Policy*. New York: Routledge.
Nexon, D. H. (2009). The Balance of Power in the Balance. *World Politics, 61*(2), 330–359.
Nitze, P. H., & Nelson Drew, S. (Eds.). (1994). *NCS-68: Forging the Strategy of Containment* (p. 6). Washington, DC: National Defense University.

Nuti, L., Bozo, F., Rey, M.-P., & Rother, B. (2015). *The Euromissile Crisis and the End of the Cold War (Cold War International History Project)*. Stanford: Stanford University Press.

Nye, J. S., Jr. (2011). *The Future of Power*. New York: Public Affairs.

Oneal, J. R., & Russett, B. (2001). *Triangulating Peace: Democracy, Interdependence, and International Organizations*. New York: Norton.

Oren, M. (2002). *Six Days of War: June 1967 and the Making of the Modern Middle East*. Oxford: Oxford University Press.

Parent, J. M., & Rosato, S. (2015). Balancing in Neorealism. *International Security, 40*(2), 51–86.

Paul, T. V., Wirtz, J. J., & Fortmann, M. (Eds.). (2004). *Balance of Power: Theory and Practice in the 21st Century*. Stanford, CA: Stanford University Press.

Posen, B. R. (1984). *The Sources of Military Doctrine: France, Britain and Germany Between the World Wars*. Ithaca: Cornell University Press.

Richmond, O. P. (2008). *Peace in International Relations*. London: Routledge.

Ripsman, N. M., Taliaferro, J. W., & Lobell, S. E. (2016). *Neoclassical Realist Theory of International Politics*. Oxford: Oxford University Press.

Rzeševskij, O. (1999). Sekretnye voennye plany U. Xercillja protiv SSSR v mae 1945g [W. Churchill's Secret War Plans Against the USSR in May 1945]. *Novaja i novejšaja storia, 3*, 98–123.

Schmidt, G. (Ed.). (2001). *A History of NATO: The First Fifty Years*. Basingstoke: Palgrave Macmillan.

Schroeder, P. (1994). Historical Reality vs. Neo-Realist Theory. *International Security, 19*(1), 108–148.

Snyder, J. (1991). *Myths of Empire: Domestic Politics and International Ambition*. Ithaca: Cornell University Press.

Spykman, N. (2007). *America's Strategy in World Politics: The United States and the Balance of Power*. New Brunswick, London: Transaction Publishers.

Tammen, R., et al. (2000). *Power Transitions: Strategies for the 21st Century*. New York: Chatham House.

Tang, S. (2008). Fear in International Politics: Two Positions. *International Studies Review, 10*(3), 451–471.

Tatu, M. (1983). *La bataille des euromissiles*. Paris: Seuil.

Thompson, N. (2011). The Hawk and the Dove, Paul Nitze, George Kennan and the History of the Cold War. *Foresight, 13*(1), 77–78.

Van Evera, S. (1997). *Guide to Methods for Students of Political Science*. Ithaca: Cornell University.

Van Evera, S. (1999). *Causes of War: Power and the Roots of Conflict*. Ithaca: Cornell University Press.

Wallensteen, P. (1973). *Structure and War? On International Relations 1920–1968*. Stockholm: Raben and Sjorgen.

Walt, S. M. (1987). *The Origins of Alliances*. Ithaca, New York: Cornell University Press.

Waltz, K. N. (1959). *Man, the State and War: A Theoretical Analysis*. New York: Columbia University.

Waltz, K. N. (1979). *Theory of International Politics*. New York: McGraw-Hill.

Waltz, K. N. (2000). Structural Realism after the Cold War. *International Security, 25*(1), 5–41.

Weber, T. (1999). Gandhi, Deep Ecology, Peace Research and Buddhist Economics. *Journal of Peace Research, 36*, 349–361.

Weitsman, P. A. (2004). *Dangerous Alliances: Proponents of Peace, Weapons of War*. Stanford: Stanford University Press.

Wohlforth, W. (2010). Realism and Security Studies. In M. Dunn Cavelty & V. Mauer (Eds.), *The Routledge Handbook of Security Studies*. London: Routledge.

Yale Journal of International Affairs. (2010). Balancing Threat: The United States and The Middle East. An Interview Stephen M. Walt, Ph.D. *Yale Journal of International Affairs* (Spring/Summer). Available at yalejournal.org/wp-content/uploads/2010/09/105202walt.pdf.

Zenko, M. (2014). The Myth of the Indispensable Nation. *Foreign Policy*. Available at https://foreignpolicy.com/2014/11/06/the-myth-of-the-indispensable-nation/.

Chapter 3
From Hamburg and Munich to Tallinn and Burgas

This chapter covers a period of one and a half decades. During this relatively short period, the so-called Old Continent witnessed a profound change of the character of the ISR. Europe has moved from an unprecedented détente and positive peace towards negative peace and rising military tension. This substantial move resulted from two waves of the NATO eastward enlargement and from the Russian reactions to this process. It is the reason why this chapter will analyse key events which happened during this period. At the same time, it will analyse the role of the most influential operational realists as well as the attitudes of realist and neorealist thinkers.

3.1 The First Reflexions About the Expansion of NATO Under the Presidency of G. Bush Senior

Just after the end of the Cold War, all key operative realists of NATO countries began to discuss a new international security order (IO) (Westad 2017). The then US president George H. W. Bush presented his vision of a New World Order (New World Order 1991), which had a lot of common features with W. Wilson and his dream about a new era in international politics (Bush 1991). Among the most important questions, the one on the future of NATO and its role in the post-Cold War world gained a primordial importance. This question was discussed at several different levels, public as well as secret.

3.1.1 The Most Important Open Declarations

The first vision of a reunified European space after the end of the Cold War was presented in the speech of Francois Mitterrand from 31. 12. 1989. As his vision of a European confederation (Sarotte 2014, pp. 90–97) was to include the USSR, but

© The Author(s), under exclusive license to Springer Nature Switzerland AG 2021
J. Eichler, *NATO's Expansion After the Cold War*, Global Power Shift,
https://doi.org/10.1007/978-3-030-66641-5_3

without the USA (Mitterrand), it was categorically refused by the political elites of the USA and the FRG (Musitelli 2001–2002, pp. 18–28). A month later, on 31 January 1990, the so-called "Tutzing formula" of the West German Foreign Minister Hans-Dietrich Genscher was announced. According to this conservative vision (which included the condition that there would be no changes of the existing borders in Europe, including the borders of the USSR as well as those of NATO), the German unification process had not led to an "impairment of Soviet security interests," and NATO was to rule out an "expansion of its territory towards the east, i.e. moving it closer to the Soviet borders" (Genscher 1990).

On 9 February 1990, in Moscow, Mr James Baker presented to Gorbachev and Shevardnadze his famous formula "not one inch eastward" (Gorbachev and Baker 1990a). And during his negotiations with Shevardnadze, on 4 May 1990, he promised that the role of the CSCE would be strengthened and reassured him that the new international order would not yield winners and losers. Instead, it would produce a new legitimate European structure—"one that would be inclusive, not exclusive" (Gorbachev and Baker 1990b).

An emphasis on inclusiveness was typical also for M. Thatcher, who declared the following during her negotiations with Mikhail Gorbachev (MSG) in Moscow at the beginning of June 1990: "We must find ways to give the Soviet Union confidence that its security would be assured… CSCE could be an umbrella for all this, as well as being the forum which brought the Soviet Union fully into [the] discussion about the future of Europe" (Powell 2010, 411–417) and the same declaration was repeated and even reinforced by G. Bush during his phone communication with MSG in July 1990. "The US president promised an expanded, stronger CSCE with new institutions in which the USSR would play an honest role within a new Europe" (Gorbachev and Bush 1990).

And the dynamics of positive declarations continued at the beginning of 1991. In March British Prime Minister John Major made the following personal assurance to MSG: "We are not talking about the strengthening of NATO." Subsequently, he reassured the Soviet defence minister Marshal Dmitri Yazov that though the USSR might be concerned about a possible NATO enlargement, "nothing of the sort will happen" (Braithwaite 1991).

No change occurred in this regard after Gorbachev's replacement by B. Yeltsin. In July 1991, NATO Secretary-General Manfred Woerner said the following to Yeltsin and his collaborators: "We should not allow […] the isolation of the USSR from the European community." At the same time, "Woerner stressed that the NATO Council and he are against the expansion of NATO (13 of 16 NATO members support this point of view)" (Yeltsin 1991). And this approach continued even under the presidency of B. Clinton when W. Christopher gave Yeltsin a guaranty that his country would be included in the future international order in Europe (Goldgeier 2016) (Table 3.1).

All the above-mentioned promises had the potential to result in a remarkable reduction of defence expenditures and international tension, and in the enlargement of the space for balanced security cooperation and for the reinforcement of the mutual confidence so typical for positive peace.

3.1 The First Reflexions About the Expansion of NATO … 35

Table 3.1 Key publicly declared promises

Concrete promise	Author of the promise
The end of the CW will not yield winners and losers	Baker
The new international order will be based on inclusiveness	Baker, Hurd
The USSR will be a respected partner and its security interests will be respected	Genscher, Thatcher, Bush, Christopher
NATO will not expand eastwardly	Genscher, Baker, Kohl, Major, Woerner
The role of the OSCE will be reinforced	Thatcher, Bush, Baker

Source Compiled by the author

3.1.2 The Most Important Secret Negotiations

On the other hand, the secret negotiations continued, and of course, they took place behind the scenes. They were started on February 7, 1990, when James Baker, during his visit in Moscow, visited the German ambassador and gave him two secret letters for Helmuth Kohl. The first of these letters, written by President G. H. Bush, spoke about the possibility of NATO enlargement in the years to follow. Baker wrote the second letter and its aim was more modest—it proposed the conservation of NATO within its then existing borders as a face-saving measure for MSG.

In this situation, the Chancellor of the FRG H. Kohl, obsessed with the reunification of his country, opted for Baker's letter. But his decision making was framed by the "education" obtained from President Bush during their meeting in Camp David in the absence of the MFA H.-D. Genscher. Bush articulated the main idea in the following words: "To hell with that. We prevailed and they did not. We cannot let the Soviets clutch victory from the jaws of defeat" (Kohl and Bush 1990).

Following this attitude, James Baker completely changed his mind and underlined the argument that the OSCE was the biggest enemy of NATO (Itzkowitz Shifrinson 2016, pp. 7–44), which had to preserve and even reconfirm its exclusive character—of course, without the USSR (Nünlist 2017, p. 21). This approach was deepened at the end of October 1990, when the Office of the Secretary of Defense (OSD) proposed a new strategy (written under the key influence of D. Cheney [Dobbins 1990]) which is today known under the label "to leave the door ajar" (TLDA).

3.1.3 Key Common Denominators of the Proponents of the TLDA Strategy

The most influential proponents of the TLDA strategy shared the key principles of the so-called Reagan victory school, which was based on a hard-line approach to the USSR (Deudney and Ikenberry 1992, pp. 123–128, 130–138), and they actively supported its dismemberment with the aim to weaken the US's former competitor

Table 3.2 The key ideas of the most important secret negotiations and decisions

Key ideas	Key proponents of these ideas
The OSCE is a competitor of NATO, and its role must be marginalised	Bush
NATO will expand	Bush, Cheney
It is necessary to exploit the weakening of M. Gorbachev	Matlock, Bush
The support of the dismemberment of the USSR	Cheney
Pro-NATO education for Czech politicians	Bush, Wolfowitz

Source Compiled by the author

and create conditions for NATO's future eastward expansion (Nau 2012, p. 70) (Table 3.2).

The idea of the expansion of NATO has been a principal issue of controversy until today, the question being whether the 41st President of the USA gave the promise that NATO would not expand at the beginning of 1990. The four following answers continue to dominate the debate.

1. The USA gave no explicit promise in this regard: all conclusions that there was a promise that NATO would not expand are only political myths. Mark Kramer (Kramer 2009, pp. 7–44), who is neither a proponent nor an opponent of the NATO expansion, underlines that the leading Western politicians gave no categorical assurance, solemn pledges, or binding commitments in this respect (Kramer and Itzkowitz Shifrinson 2017, pp. 186–192). Nevertheless, the former CIA Director Robert Gates writes about "pressing ahead with [the] expansion of NATO eastward [in the 1990s], when Gorbachev and others were led to believe that wouldn't happen" (Gates 2000, p. 101).

2. There has been no implicit promise that if the USSR agreed with the German reunification, NATO would not expand (Sarotte 2019, pp. 7–41; Kimberly 2017, pp. 135–161). The eastward NATO expansion was, since the beginning, prepared and played as a long and complicated stalemate, which resulted in many waves of expansion (McGovern 2014). Particularly Joshua R. Itzkowitz Shifrinson from Texas A&M University holds this attitude (Itzkowitz Shifrinson 2016). If something was repeatedly promised, it is that there would be an inclusive international order, which would include even the USSR (Nünlist 2017, p. 20).

3. Nevertheless, some American researchers, like, for example, Gordon Hahn,[1] continue to repeat that the decision to start the NATO expansion was a broken promise with long-term consequences for the relations between the RF and the West. According to them, the NATO expansion opened a long period of maximal distrust, humiliated Russia's military and national security establishment, led to the hyper-cynicism of Putin and updatedthe Russian threat for the West (Hahn 2018).

---

[1] Senior Researcher at the Center for Terrorism and Intelligence Studies (CETIS), Akribis Group, San Jose, California.

4. The decision to expand NATO was a betrayal. This categorical conclusion is shared by all Russian operative realists (Putin and his entourage, Russian generals and diplomats) as well as by a large majority of Russian historians and experts on the field of ISR.

In the light of the above-mentioned facts, all the guarantees and promises have had only an oral form and character. The leaders of the USA and of the FRG managed to outmanoeuvre Gorbachev, who was increasingly weakened by the growing problems of his country.[2] Rarely does one country win so much in an international negotiation (Sarotte 2014).

3.1.4 Between Consistency and Hypocrisy

The negotiations waged between 1990 and 1991 are seen not only as a part of recent history but also in the light of their consequences for the ISR in the Northern Hemisphere. The leading Western politicians of that period are often celebrated as the respected winners and founders of a radically new international order. On the other hand, some critical authors see the above-mentioned behaviour of the West as cynical hypocrisy and a merciless egoism which sowed the seeds of many future problems, especially the great bitterness among the Russian elites, which resulted in their determination to get revenge for the unjust end of the Cold War. But in this regard, even James Baker concludes that "almost every achievement contains within its success the seeds of a future problem" (Sarotte 2017, p. 97). In addition, one could also reach the following sceptical conclusion: had Gorbachev understood that the former Warsaw Pact allies and parts of the Soviet Union itself would become parts of the Western military alliance, it is hard to imagine Russia would have retrenched so extensively (Deudney and Ikenberry 2009, pp. 9–62).

Within the large group of the Western politicians, the French president F. Mitterrand was much more coherent and consistent in his negotiations with Gorbachev and his successor Boris Yeltsin. Sharing the idea of the dissolution of both military blocs in favour of new European security structures, he did not hesitate to say to Gorbachev that in case of his refusal of the German reunification, he would be isolated from all his Western partners (Gorbachev and Mitterrand 1990). The openness and consistency were typical not only for the direct negotiations in Moscow on 25. 5. 1990, but also for Mitterrand's letter to his American partner, today known as "the Cher George letter." The French president did not hesitate to mention the possible negative consequences of a fait accompli politics and to advocate an approach that would dispel Gorbachev's worries and offer him several proposals (Mitterrand 1990).

On the other hand, a big difference between public declarations on one hand and secret attitudes and decisions on the other was typical for G. H. W. Bush and his entourage, including his Secretary of State, Mr J. Baker. This approach and behaviour

---

[2]These problems were the sharply rising crime rates, anti–regime demonstrations, the deteriorating economic situation, and separatist movements.

had immediate, but also medium-term and long-term motivations in regard to all the key issues: NATO expansion, and the roles of the OSCE and of Russia in the new international order.

3.2 The End of the USSR and Its Consequences

September 1991 saw a clash between the defensive realists (lead by B. Scowcroft) and the offensive realists (lead by D. Cheney) in the USA. The former preferred international stability and the preservation of the USSR; the latter took the decision to support the separatism and the following dismemberment of the US's former challenger from the period of the Cold War. The victory of the second approach was directly and closely connected with the subsequent decision to prepare and start the process of NATO expansion.

Besides the USA, there have been many secondary winners, namely all the former countries of the Warsaw Pact. Thanks to the so-called Sinatra doctrine of M. S. Gorbachev (Jones 2005), they received the possibility to close the period of their more than four-decades-long membership in the buffer zone of the USSR and to take into their hands the decision about their future, including their possible membership in Western organisations.

On the other hand, in international politics, there are no winners without losers. At the personal level, the key loser of the beginning of the 1990s has a concrete name: M. S. Gorbachev (Kaiser 1991, pp. 160–174). From the Russian point of view, he agreed to a lot of epochal changes, but he received no compensation. At the international level, the key loser was his country, which disappeared from the map to be replaced by the Russian Federation. And at the global level, the key loser was international communism, whose rule was based on the negation of the market economy and of political pluralism, on a brutal imposition of the Russian way of life, and on brutal Russian interventions in the politics of all the satellite states.

3.3 Bill Clinton as a Political Guarantor of the Second Wave of NATO Expansion

Since the beginning of 1993, the presidents of the Central and Eastern European (CEE) States solicited the 42nd President of the USA with their requests for security guarantees. The most active in this regard were V. Havel and L. Walesa, the presidents of the Czech Republic and Poland respectively. Considering the theory of Charles Glaser, the key arguments of these two important countries were formulated in a manner which is very typical for security seeking states. A few years after the dissolution of the Warsaw Pact, and after the outbreak of war in the former Yugoslavia, they looked for a new security provider.

3.3.1 Supporters of NATO Expansion

a. Prominent active politicians

Anthony Lake and his doctrine definition of the expansion of the stability
Anthony Lake, the National Security Advisor of President Bill Clinton between 1993 and 1997, was the first active politician to come forth with a doctrinal rationalisation of the NATO expansion. He argued by pointing to the necessity to enlarge the zone of stability (Lake 1993), which would help to expand American exports and create American jobs, improve living conditions and fuel demands for political liberalisation abroad. At the same time, the addition of new democracies would make the USA more secure because democracies tend not to wage war on each other or sponsor terrorism. On this basis, A. Lake proposed a move from the doctrine of containment, so typical for the period of the Cold War, towards the doctrine of enlargement of the world's free community of market democracies. He explained its substance as a security mission aimed at a peaceful enlargement of the "blue areas",[3] which would include market democracies.

The strategy proposed by Anthony Lake was based on four components. The first was the strengthening of the community of major market democracies, which constitutes the core of all strategies of enlargement. The second was the US help in the process of fostering and consolidating new democracies and market economies, especially in states of a special significance that offered special opportunities. The third component consisted of the countering of the aggression of states hostile to democracy and markets. Lastly, Lake underlined the necessity of a consistent humanitarian agenda everywhere where it was necessary.

Just after Lake's speech in which he made these points, Richard Holbrooke was charged by President Clinton with the mission to coordinate the long-term work of the US's leading diplomats and generals with the aim to start the so-called two-track policy, which was to cover NATO enlargement and enhancing the security cooperation with Russia (Goldgeier 1999).

Rühe and his deepening
The doctrinal definition of Anthony Lake was deepened a few weeks later by Volker Rühe, the minister of defence of the FRG (CDU) between 1992 and 1998, who came forth with the following declaration: if we will not export stability, we will import instability (Jackson 1993). He played a key role in placing NATO enlargement on the German political agenda (Hyde-Price 2000, p. 149). His emphasis on the export of stability was almost immediately adopted by all proponents of the idea of NATO expansion, especially by leading politicians of candidate countries.

Walesa and the liability of a new NATO
The arguments defined by Anthony Lake and deepened by Volker Rühe almost immediately became a big inspiration for the political chiefs of the two leading candidate

---

[3] It was a parallel with the period of the Cold War during which "blue" symbolised NATO, while "red" symbolised the Warsaw Pact.

countries, Lech Walesa and Václav Havel. The Polish president presented his solicitation during a meeting with President Clinton in the USA in June 1995. In the negative dimension, he underlined that if the USA helped his country, it would not alarm Russia—in this period, it was necessary to prevent any accusation of an anti-Russian strategy. And in the positive dimension, he argued that NATO expansion would facilitate the eastward flow of democracy and stability and, as a result, the new NATO states would become better and more reliable partners (Basken 1995). Poland's Ministers of Foreign Affairs repeated the same arguments (Cimoszewicz 1996), and they both repeatedly added that Poland would respect the existing frontiers in Europe (Yeltsin 1993).

Havel and the return to the West
The same logic of stability expansion was reprised and modernised by Václav Havel, the first president of the Czech Republic.[4] He repeatedly underlined a concrete interest of his country: its return to the democratic and stable West. He argued that the candidate countries of CEE had always belonged to the Western civilisation (Havel 1993). And during his visit to the USA in May 1997, he added another key argument: NATO expansion, conceived as an expansion of stability, has a great potential to eliminate the security threat that resulted from tribal passions and local conflicts fuelled by nationalism (Bearak 1997).

The Polish President entered the history of NATO expansion not only by his arguments, but also thanks to his "toast diplomacy" demonstrated on 24. 8. 1993, when he managed to manipulate B. Yeltsin to declare that Poland in NATO was not contrary to the interest of any state, including the RF. Even if the Russian President tried to sober up the next morning and go back on what he said, the genie of the first round of the NATO expansion was released from the bottle.

b. Prominent former policymakers

The first of the prominent policymakers in this matter was Henry Kissinger, who argued (Kissinger 1994a) mainly by referring to a possible worsening of the situation in Russia, which he said could lead to a no man's land between Germany and Russia, as such a situation had caused many wars in the history of the so-called Old Continent (Kissinger 1993). He warned that a delay of the NATO expansion could invite Germany and Russia to fill that vacuum between them, unilaterally or bilaterally, which was a scenario that everybody wanted to avoid (Kissinger 1994b).

Zbigniew Brzeziński, another widely respected and cited veteran of American foreign and security policy, supported the idea of NATO expansion since the beginning of this debate (Brzeziński 1994a). He spoke about the so-called Russian imperial impulse, which remained strong and appeared to be strengthening even after the enormous weakening of Russia after the end of the Cold War (Brzeziński 1994b, p. 72) and the implosion of the USSR. And in an article that he co-wrote together with Anthony Lake, he argued that NATO expansion was a creative response to three strategic challenges: to enhance the relationship between the United States and the

---

[4]The President of the Czech Republic between 1993 and 2003.

Table 3.3 Key arguments of supporters of NATO expansion

Argument	Author
Enlargement of the area of stability and prosperity = a basic argument of a doctrinal character	Anthony Lake
If we do not expand NATO, we will import instability	Volker Rühe
NATO expansion will "tame" nationalism as a cause of wars	Václav Havel
NATO expansion will fill the space between Germany and Russia	Henry Kissinger
NATO expansion will reinforce democracy and peace in Central Europe	Zbigniew Brzeziński

enlarging democratic Europe, to engage the still evolving, post-imperial Russia in a cooperative relationship with that Europe, and to reinforce the habits of democracy and the practices of peace in Central Europe (Brzeziński and Lake 1997)

c. Prominent academicians and opinion-makers

Out of the many relevant studies carried out by academicians, the most sophisticated study in favour of NATO enlargement was written by a trio of very influential opinion-makers from the RAND Corporation: Ronald Asmus, Richard L. Kugler, and Stephen Larrabee (Asmus et al. 1997). They argued that NATO enlargement would tie the new member countries to the West, and, as a result, stabilise all of the European security space. They presented the NATO enlargement as a necessary anchor for the new member states.

Common points of all the supporters
Thanks to Anthony Lake, the expansion of political stability was the key and the most often used argument in favour of the NATO expansion. In his time, it was a very sophisticated argument which helped to reduce the protests of Russia and eliminate reproaches that the enlargement had an anti-Russian motivation. The NATO expansion was largely presented as a necessary assurance that the former countries of the WTO would be integrated into Western structures, and that the positions of democratic reformers in these countries would be strengthened. At the same time, this process was presented as a necessary step toward the creation of a reliable deterrent against possible Russian aggression in Eastern and Central Europe, even if the Russian Federation was in an unprecedented decline (Table 3.3).

3.3.2 Sceptical and Critical Authors

Sceptical reactions were articulated mainly by the academicians. Out of these, it is necessary to recall especially Michael E. Brown, George Kennan (Kennan 1997), Johan Galtung, Amos Perlmutter and Ted Galen Carpenter, Bjorn Moller, John Lewis Gaddis (1998, pp. 145–151), and Michael McGwire (1998, pp. 23–42).

a. Prominent academicians and opinion-makers

Michael Brown and his structuralist arguments
Michael Brown, a prominent teacher from Harvard University, argued that at the beginning of the 1990s, the RF, namely its military force, was enormously weakened and posed no security threat for NATO, or for the PECO (Brown 1995, pp. 34–52). And he concluded the related article with a few arguments of a structuralist character. First, the NATO expansion would weaken the positions and influence of Russian reformers and democrats in favour of hardliners who would interpret this process as a dramatic change in the balance of power, as an extension of the American sphere of influence, and as a process with a strong anti-Russian dimension. Second, this process could provoke the Russian operative realists to adopt more assertive foreign and security policies that could diminish, not enhance, European and American security. He concluded that the process of NATO expansion represented since its beginning a big security risk for all the concerned actors (Brown 1995).

Brown's structuralist approach has also become enormously interesting from another point of view: it led him to reflections about the future of the post-Soviet space, namely that of Ukraine. According to him, NATO's eastward expansion could be acceptable as a reaction to aggressive Russian behaviour, namely, in case of Russia violating its pledges to respect international borders and the sovereignty of the former member states of the USSR. He concretely mentions scenarios of Russia's possible annexation of the Eastern part of Ukraine and its absorption of Belarus (Brown 1995, p. 45). The annexation of these two countries was imagined as a raison d'etre and as a possible justification of NATO expansion, but not as its possible consequence. Nevertheless, he was one of the first Western academicians who reflected on a possible interaction between NATO expansion and Ukraine. Today, we know that this was an enormously far-seeing approach.

George Kennan and his prognostic warnings
The decision to expand NATO was criticised even by *George Kennan*, one of the great American political leaders and thinkers of the twentieth century (Friedman 1998). He was exemplarily consistent since the end of the 1940s, when he opposed the creation of NATO and argued that it would lead towards an unnecessary militarisation of the ISR (Rutland 1998). At the beginning of 1997, Kennan published his warning that NATO expansion could become a risky strategy, namely if it would continue until it reached Russia's frontiers. He warned of the risk of an inflammation of nationalistic, anti-Western and militaristic tendencies in Russian opinions, which would weaken the rising Russian democracy. At the same time, he warned of a return of the Cold War atmosphere between the RF and the enlarged West, and about the negative movement of the Russian foreign policy. Kennan also manifested his worries about complications in the process of arms control (Kennan 1997). And sometime later, Kennan warned that NATO's expansion into former Soviet territory was a "strategic blunder of potentially epic proportions" (Skidelsky 2018).

Warnings of the CATO Institute
At the end of 1997, two American experts from the CATO Institute published their respective analyses in which they frontally questioned Lake's identification of NATO

expansion with the eastward expansion of stability (Eland 1997). They objected that the emphasis on the expansion of stability resulted from a large and premeditated overestimation of the political aspect to the detriment of the military aspect and also to the detriment of the possible geopolitical and security consequences (Bandow 1997).

In addition, Amos Perlmutter and Ted Galen Carpenter deepened this scepticism at the beginning of 1998. They argued that at the end of the 1990s, neither RAND nor the Pentagon published any serious analysis indicating the probability of strategic deployment of Russian military units within the critical 15-year period after the first round of NATO enlargement (Perlmutter and Carpenter 1998, pp. 2–6). They warned that if NATO expansion would continue, the growing military tension could return to Europe. Their conclusion was very clear: NATO enlargement is not a strategy, but a worrisome case of self-delusion that may cost the USA more than dollars and cents.

Johan Galtung and his comparison of NATO enlargement with the Versailles treaty
Among critical European authors, a prominent place belongs to Johan Galtung, the founding father of Peace Studies. He concluded that the decision to expand NATO was so bad that compared to it, the Versailles treaty from 1918 looks brilliant (Galtung 1997). In his critical analysis, he used four key arguments. First, the decision to expand NATO represents a continuation of the US global strategy of pincer movement, which was defined in the JCS 570/2 from 1943.[5] Second, it is dangerously exclusive, as this exclusiveness concerned the USSR and later the RF. Galtung criticised the fact that this country was not invited to join NATO even though it agreed to three changes of epochal importance.

The first of them was the dissolution of the WTO; the second was the RF's withdrawal of all its military units from all the USSR's former satellite states with no reciprocation, only reduction, on the part of the USA in Western Europe. Third, there was the peaceful dismemberment of the USSR without any misuse of force. This argument led Galtung to the conclusion that NATO expansion was "completely autistic" because it was not provoked by an urgent security threat from the RF. In addition, Galtung added a very sophisticated warning: in the perspective of continued expansion, NATO will eliminate neutral states with their bridge-building initiatives, which used to play such an important role during the Cold War, and which were so helpful during the periods of rising international tension.

Galtung also argued that the invitation to the first three CEE countries to join NATO was conceived as a reward for their anti-Soviet revolts: these revolts occurred in Hungary in 1956, in Poland in 1956 and the 1990's, and in Czechoslovakia in 1968. In addition, Galtung concluded this argument with a very disturbing prognosis: NATO expansion will provoke an unnecessary tension increase across a fault line in Europe, an arms race as well as a macro version of the Yugoslav micro-war.

---

[5]The study Joint Chiefs of Staff 570/2 from August 1943, which defined a black-bordered region in the far Southwest Pacific, Indochina, eastern China, Korea, and Japan.

Michael McGwire and his recommendation to stop the NATO expansion
This leading critical British author and internationally respected expert on international security and particularly the Soviet military strategy (McGwire 1987) came in 1998 with the warning that the NATO expansion process would disturb Russian elites, and provoke a return of military competitions, tensions and rising rivalry. He recommended not giving promises of NATO membership to any other countries, namely to the post-Soviet states, as such promises could have an enormously explosive potential. He also recommended producing a declaration that Central and Eastern Europe would forever be a zone without nuclear weapons.

Bjorn Moller and common security
This author remembered in 1997 that states have the predisposition to see their opponent's actions as hostile, which holds them in a dangerous spiral of malign interaction, as was previously brilliantly explained by Robert Jervis (1976). Moller argued that if NATO wants to invite new countries to join it, it should take into consideration the security interest of the RF, and thus it should make this country feel as secure as possible about NATO enlargement (Moller 1997). He concluded that in the light of the common security concept, NATO should transform from a hostile alliance against Russia into a collective security system which would encompass Russia as a partner (Moller 1997) (Table 3.4).

Common points of the sceptical and critical authors
All these authors argued that in the mid-1990s, Russia and particularly its armed forces were not on the rise, but on the contrary, in an unprecedented decline. According to them, Russia did not present any serious security threat, neither for the "old" NATO countries nor for the CEE. Second, they stated that expansion proponents overestimated political arguments (namely the expansion of stability) to the detriment of geopolitical and, especially, military consequences. They criticised the

Table 3.4 Key arguments of sceptical authors

Argument	Author
NATO expansion will inflame Russia's nationalism, anti-Western feelings and militarism and lead to a deterioration of the ISR	George Kennan
NATO expansion is a security risk for all the concerned actors	Michael Brown
NATO is exclusive towards the RF and demonstrates a distorted inclusiveness concerning new members	Johan Galtung
Emphasis on the expansion of stability–overestimation of the political aspect to the detriment of the military aspect and the possible geopolitical and security consequences	Authors from the CATO Institute
NATO expansion will provoke a return of military tensions, competitions and rivalry	Michael McGwire
NATO expansion is in contradiction with common security	Bjorn Moller

Source Compiled by the author

fact that the process of NATO expansion had, since the beginning, a hidden, but enormously anti-Russian motivation and that it opened the way towards the encirclement of this sensitive and complicated country.

This group of authors saw in it a dangerously explosive potential: they argued that the question was not whether, but when the Russian operative realists would adopt, under the security fears of Russia being an encircled country that were provoked by this zero-sum game, a confrontational strategy which would worsen the ISR in Europe. They also warned that the process of NATO expansion could result in a conservation of the dividing lines in Europe, a return of political and military tension, and a move from the security cooperation and positive peace towards confrontation and negative peace, which would be caused by the militarisation of the ISR in Europe. Nevertheless, it would be enormously wrong to label them as advocates of Russia because their referent object was not Russia, but the stability and security in the future Europe.

In the light of theory, all the sceptical and critical authors proposed freezing the ambitions of the active actor of the expansion (which had the advantage of the comfort of external balancing) with the aim to calm the passive actor of the expansion (which was, since the beginning, disadvantaged by the fact that it could rely only on internal balancing) and, most importantly, avoid a rise of military tension with a long range of negative and destabilising consequences.

3.4 The PfP as the First Step of NATO Expansion

The first years after the end of the Cold War were framed by some important external factors, namely by the continuing presence of the Soviet armed force in the FRG, uncertainties concerning the situation in the USSR, and the wars in the post-Yugoslav space. These factors were more and more disturbing for the leaders of the CEE states. In their eyes, the membership in NATO and its security guarantees became the best solution. Face to face with their growing interest and solicitation, NATO opted for a step by step strategy in regard to them.

3.4.1 Key Important Milestones

The first step was taken in January 1991, when the Brussels Council of NATO stated that the Alliance should become open to other European states that could satisfy the principles of the Washington Treaty (NATO 1991). It was a huge encouragement for the leaders of the CEE states. Among them, the Polish and Czech presidents had the most assertive approaches in this respect. They pushed leading American politicians to provide a full-guarantee expansion (FGE). They benefitted from the support of the most influential American opinion-makers (Asmus et al. 1993) and high-level diplomats, especially Strobe Talbott, with his arguments in favour of the expansion

(Talbott 1995) despite the Russian protests (Talbott 2002, pp. 99–101). Moreover, Talbott and other advocates of FGE received important support with the Republican Party's "Contract with America,"[6] which articulated the NATO expansion as a priority of the US foreign policy (Solomon 1998).

The second important turning point came with the programme Partnership for Peace (PfP), which was not conceived negatively as a reaction to a concrete security threat. Its aim was to serve as a platform of the security cooperation between former rivals and foes. PfP was conceived as a pragmatic compromise between two competing approaches: a pan-European security organisation (which is acceptable for the RF) and full-guarantee expansion (a dream of the leaders of the CEE states) (Sarotte 2019, p. 11).

The third important turning point came in August 1993, when L. Walesa, at the end of an official dinner in Warsaw, managed to manipulate Boris Yeltsin to declare that Poland being in NATO was not contrary to the interest of any state, including the RF. Even if the Russian president tried to sober up the next morning (Sarotte 2019, p. 7–41) and go back on his words, the process had been started. And it continued even despite an urgent letter send by Yeltsin to Clinton in which the Russian president did walk back his concession to Walesa after pressures from his ministers (Cohen 1993).

The fourth turning point happened on 12. 1. 1994 in Prague. During a meeting with the presidents of the V4 states, B. Clinton articulated his famous formula "Not whether, but when and how." It was a new important move towards the full-guarantee expansion. Nevertheless, it was necessary to take into consideration the continuing presence of the units of the Russian armed forces on the territory of the FRG. But this factor evaporated on 31. 8. 1994, just after the Berlin Ceremony, which crowned the process of the departure of all 546,200 Soviet soldiers that were previously stationed there. After this historical event, the last important barrier to NATO expansion fell. In this light, the exclamation of Yeltsin about the "Cold Peace" (Cold Peace 1994) during the Budapest Summit and the following fury of B. Clinton (Murphy 1994) was only an episodic parenthesis.

A year later, in September 1995, the fifth turning point came with the publication of the Study on NATO Enlargement. This document presented the basic principles for the NATO enlargement and the criteria for the countries looking for the Alliance's security guarantees (NATO 1995). On its pages, the logic of "spheres of influence" was categorically refused and NATO enlargement was presented as a contribution to the European stability and security in conjunction with other institutions. Concerning the deployment of armed forces, Paragraph 55 underlined that "for new members, the peacetime stationing of forces on other Allies' territory should neither be a condition of membership nor foreclosed as an option."

---

[6]The Contract with America was a legislative agenda advocated for by the United States Republican Party during the 1994.

3.4 The PfP as the First Step of NATO Expansion

Table 3.5 Kenneth Waltz and his critical arguments

NATO expansion will provoke growing security fears on the part of Russian operational realists and the revival of the mentality of a besieged country in Russia
It will result in a growing political as well as military tension in Europe
It will be perceived in Moscow as an approaching security threat
It will have large geopolitical consequences

Source Compiled by the author

3.4.2 The First Round of NATO Expansion in the Light of Kenneth Waltz

The first concrete decision of historical importance in this regard came with the Madrid Summit in July 1997, which was crowned by a formal invitation for Poland, the Czech Republic and Hungary,[7] three important CEE countries and former member states of the Warsaw Pact, to join NATO.[8] They received new security guarantees from the winner of the Cold War, which was seen as a leading country of the new international order. At the same time, the first round had some non-negligible benefits for NATO: in terms of hard power, the Alliance gained a territory of 485,000 km^2 and more than 483 million inhabitants, which means that it gained a new strategic depth to the detriment of its former enemy.

Even more important was the soft power, symbolised by the enormous gratefulness and helpfulness of the political elites of the new member countries. From the neo-realist point of view, all these factors opened new possibilities for the USA's external balancing towards its former competitor, which had been enormously weakened after the dismemberment of the USSR and the destabilising decade of the presidency of B. Yeltsin.

Just before the first round of the NATO expansion, Kenneth Waltz argued that the USA should not forget its commitments to its European allies, but he stated that the importance of NATO and of its role in world politics should decrease (Waltz 1993, pp. 75–76). He warned about some possible negative consequences of NATO expansion, namely about the temptation to act unilaterally and make capricious decisions. And after the first wave of this process, he warned about three possible dangerous consequences: the growing security fears of Russian operational realists, a growing political as well as military tension, and the negative consequences of the NATO expansion for the European security. He concluded that the process of NATO expansion would be perceived in Moscow as an approaching security threat and would have large geopolitical consequences (Waltz 2000, p. 36) (Table 3.5).

Today, we know that the first round of the NATO expansion enhanced the superiority of the USA and the inferiority of the RF (Neumann 2016). It opened a window of

---

[7] Madrid Declaration on Euro-Atlantic Security and Cooperation Issued by the Heads of State and Government.
[8] See Galtung and his argument about the distorted inclusiveness.

opportunity for the future installation of military infrastructure in case of a worsening of the security situation. It became a symbol of the so-called doctrinal expansion (in the light of Raymond Aron), which is conceived as the spread of the American military thought. Lastly, in the light of Stephen Walt, it enlarged the space of the North Atlantic ideological solidarity in the approach to the modernisation of military forces and the future cooperation in various military missions. No wonder that it provoked many protests on the part of Russian operative realists.

On the other hand, the consequences of the first round were not too dramatic. First, in accordance with M. Mandelbaum and his understanding of expansion, this round was not followed by a deployment of Western military units on the territories of the new member states. Second, it did lead to any changes in the distances between the military units of NATO and the RF. Third, in accordance with Stephen Walt, it did result in any dramatic change in the balance of security threats. Finally, yet importantly, this round did not lead to military incidents or to a growing risk of a direct military confrontation between NATO and the RF.

3.5 George W. Bush as a Political Guarantor of the Second Wave of NATO Expansion

The beginning of the twenty-first Century saw an unexpected and surprising rebirth of the hope of amelioration of the relations between the USA and the RF. In Washington and Moscow, two new young presidents, G. W. Bush and V. Putin, came to power. After the spectacular terrorist attacks of 11. 9. 2001, the latter offered the former a large set of help. Russia offered some of its arm systems to the Northern Alliance (mainly tanks) as well as its knowledge of the Afghan theatre (Rafiq 2017), namely of the structure and the activities of the Taliban (O'Flynn 2001). As a result, the world witnessed an exemplary productive security cooperation in the fight against global terror as a common security threat.

3.5.1 The Zero-Sum Game

After the successful overthrow of the Taliban regime, the Bush administration, influenced by the enormous superiority of the USA in contrast with the weakened Russia (namely in the economic, technological, geopolitical and military fields), did not resist the temptations of unilateralism. This behaviour was manifested by the following decisions of the first Bush administration (Deudney and Ikenberry 2009, pp. 39–62): the war in Iraq without the mandate of the UNSC (Freedman, L. (2006–2007), 52. the NATO expansion and engaging in rivalries over former Soviet republics, the withdrawal from the ABM Treaty, the deployment of missile-defence systems, and the controversial building of the oil-pipeline routes from the Caspian Basin.

All these unilateral decisions reinforced Russian fears that the United States was attempting to dominate areas with a historic Russian presence and generated Russian fears of encirclement and encroachment. The second wave of expansion as the first and the most important of the above mentioned decisions resulted in a new redefinition of the frontiers of the Old Continent. NATO entered two areas of strategic importance—the Baltic area and the Black Sea area.

3.5.2 The Baltic States as a New North-Eastern Frontier of NATO

To begin with, Estonia is the North part of the Baltic area, with 45,227 km^2 and 1,315,944 inhabitants. Its GDP is about 20.916 billion EUR (2016), its armed forces include only 6,000 soldiers Military Balance 2016), and its military expenditures at the beginning of 2000 were about 250 million USD; today, they amount to about 500 million USD, though the exact figure varies (*The Baltic Times* 2016). Latvia has an area of 65,000 km^2 with two million inhabitants, a current GDP of about 30 billion USD (Katz 2016), and 5,500 soldiers (Military Balance 2016, pp. 114–115). And Lithuania has 3 million inhabitants, and a GDP of about 40 billion USD; its military expenditures are comparable with those of Latvia. Out of these three states, it has the biggest armed forces: 16,000 soldiers (Military Balance 2016, pp. 116–117). The total number of soldiers in all three of the Baltic countries is only about 25,000, which is, from the strategic point of view, a negligible number.

However, much more important is the geopolitical position of these countries in the Southern parts of the Finland Bay (Estonia) and of the Baltic Sea (Latvia and Lithuania). This fact is enormously important in peace because their location covers many routes of the Russian maritime trade. And in case of war, this area has a strategic role because it offers a lot of possibilities for maritime operations and for the following eastward projections of military power. Their coasts and littoral landscapes represent an ideal terrain for extensive navy assaults.

The importance of the geopolitical changes of NATO's second wave of expansion was reinforced by the role of history as an important objective as well as subjective actor of the security policy of all states.[9] All three Baltic countries have had a long range of deeply rooted of negative experiences with Russia, namely those from the period of the USSR, which were rich in injustices, frustrations, and brutal Russification. As a result, these little countries share a negative perception of their Eastern imperial neighbour and perceive it as a security threat. They are determined to do the maximum for the elimination of this threat.

After their entry into NATO, these three Baltic States formed the Eastern border of this alliance, which has approximatively the same length as the frontier between the FRG and the states of the Warsaw Pact during the Cold War (Shlapak and Johnson

---

[9]History is objective in the sense that we cannot change what happened. At the same time, it is subjective in the sense that it is often interpreted very subjectively.

2016, p. 14), And 30 years after the end of the bipolar confrontation, the same tension moved some thousand kilometres eastward. Moreover, this tension has a controversial historical dimension, which provokes some disturbing reminiscences—NATO currently organises its military manoeuvres at a line which is almost identical with the line of combat of WW II at the beginning of 1942 (Shlapak and Johnson 2016).

3.5.3 The Black Sea Area as a New South-Eastern Border of NATO

The situation of this part of Europe dramatically changed just at the beginning of the 1990s (Brzeziński 1997). Russia lost its dominant position in the North (in the Baltic region) as well as in the South and the Black Sea area (Malek 2008). The common maritime manoeuvres of NATO and Ukraine, Georgia, Armenia and Azerbaijan (Antonopoulos et al. 2017) resulted in growing international tensions, and the pipelines from the Caspian region bypassed the territory of Russia. Lastly, this region witnessed the growing importance and role of Turkey, which started to balance the influence of Russia and reinforce its role as the Southern anchor of NATO. All these changes started a "geopolitical conflict between Russia and the West" (Black 2014). The first decade after the end of the Cold War saw not only a continuing reduction of the numbers of the Soviet armed forces but also their growing retardation and backwardness in contrast with the American RMA. Russia's conventional military, although vastly improved since its nadir in the late 1990s, reminds one of a shadow of its Soviet predecessor (Gates 2009).

The decision to expand into the Black Sea area was explained by four key arguments. At the geopolitical level, the necessity to anchor Ukraine in the framework of the Western civilisation was underlined (Flikke et al. 2011). At the level of the soft security, the General Secretary of NATO declared that NATO can no longer protect our security without addressing the potential risks and threats that arise far from our homes (de Hoop Scheffer 2004). In other words, he presented a new definition of the so-called forward defence of a new, expanded alliance (Freedman 1990). At the geo-economic level, the Black Sea area is in the centre of the axis between the Caspian area (with its rich resources of oil and natural gas) and the Mediterranean area (which opens the way towards the Atlantic Ocean) (Gallois 1990). This fact is strategically important in the era of the growing use of maritime routes (Chauprade and Thual 1999) when military forces play an important role in the protection of the continuity and security of transport of raw materials (Petersen 2004).

Lastly, at the military level, four arguments were underlined. The first of them is that the strategic level of NATO was moved from the FRG[10] to South-Eastern Europe. Second, the military force of the countries of this area plays an important role, and

---

[10]During the Cold War, the FRG was the hosting nation of two American armed corps (AC), one AC from France and one from Great Britain (the so-called British Army of Rhine).

US pilots enormously appreciate their common military manoeuvres with Romanian pilots with their Mig-21 and Mig-29 planes (MK Air Base). At the same time, maritime military bases also play an important role, especially those in Constanza (Romania) (RFE/RL 2003) and Sarafovo (Bulgaria), which were used during Operation Iraqi Freedom (Petersen 2004). Thirdly, the construction of anti-missile bases in the Black Sea region (Rozoff 2010), namely the U.S. Aegis Ashore Missile Defence System Romania (Deveselu Base), was hugely appreciated by the General Secretary of NATO (*Standard News* 2010). Fourth, Bulgaria and Romania have become new bases for the projection of the military force of this area towards the East, Southeast and South from the frontiers of NATO (Rozoff 2009). Their resources were used during many common military manoeuvres in the context of the task force called the Black Sea Rotational Force (Woyke 2016).

After the second wave of NATO expansion, the eastern border of NATO has played an important role. It has approximately the same length as the frontier between the former Federal Republic of Germany and its Eastern neighbours during the Cold War (Shlapak and Johnson 2016). Since the second wave of the NATO expansion, it has also been characterised by an enormously intensive military tension. This frontier is reminiscent of the situation in Central Europe in the first half of the Cold War, with one important difference: the line of tension has moved about 1,000 km eastward.

The above-mentioned US strategic gains were acquired to the detriment of the RF, a "strategic loser" (Friedman 2015). The USA and its allies obtained new possibilities of external balancing against their Eastern neighbour and challenger, which faces this situation without the possibility of external balancing. Even more important is the US military superiority in comparison with the Russian domains' backwardness, which pushes this country into internal balancing, namely into negative arming. Russia's efforts in terms of negative arming have been oriented towards A2/AD systems (Frühling and Lasconjarias 2016, p. 98) (Table 3.6).

From the theoretical point of view, the American external balancing during NATO's expansion after the end of the Cold War fully satisfies the criteria of another concept. It is the concept of the so-called "cheap hegemony" introduced by Fareed Zakaria (Zakaria 2019), who defined its pillars as follows: the U.S. policy makers still want to influence the globe, but they are unwilling to pay prices, make sacrifices, and bear burdens without a real commitment or engagement. Instead of the hegemony which was typical for the Cold War, they prefer to use advice, economic sanctions and airstrikes.

3.6 Russian Internal Balancing and Its Consequences

Since the end of the first decade after the end of the Cold War, the Russian operative realists have been stressed by the clear inferiority, qualitative as well as quantitative, of their armed forces. They are obsessed with the modernisation of their armed forces, and their efforts result in an intensive imitation of the US arms systems.

Table 3.6 Differences between the USA and the RF in the light of neorealism

	USA	RF
Power status	Sea power	Continental
Geopolitical position	Expansion: US military units have moved 1,000 km eastward	After the end of the CW, the RF left a space of 1 million km^2
Economic position	Superiority: The USA has a much higher GDP and a culture of innovation	Inferiority: The RF is behind in the qualitative as well as the quantitative dimension
Mode of balancing	External (its sphere of influence includes 9 countries of the former POW)	Internal (the RF can rely only on its internal resources)
Mode of Arming	Positive (qualitative as well as quantitative superiority)	Negative (the US advancement and superiority are largely stressed)
Military position	In the general balance, the US holds the position of superiority; it is in a position of inferiority only on the border with the RF	In the general balance, the RF holds the position of inferiority; its superiority is limited only to the space of its Western border

Source Compiled by the author

3.6.1 Historical Aspects

Russia's long tradition of imitating other countries' arms systems started with its imitation of the Prussian system in the 1870s (Boot 2006), and at the beginning of the twentieth Century, it continued with its imitation of the British naval system. Then in World War II, the Soviets imitated the doctrine of the Blitzkrieg (Mahnken 2003), particularly during their counteroffensive, which was crowned by the Berlin Operation (Glantz and House 2015). Some years after the end of WW II, the USSR took the decision to imitate the successful American and British systems of carrier aircraft and strategic bombers (Pape 1996). And at the beginning of the 1950's it started its long effort to develop nuclear weapons, being obsessed with the nuclear strategic parity.

3.6.2 Russian Balancing Face to Face with the First Two Rounds of NATO Expansion

The process of NATO expansion was seen as an act of Western disdain (Walker 2015) and as a symbol of the West's hypocrisy and refusal to take into consideration Russian security interests (Braithwaite 2014). This negative approach was articulated in the above mentioned Cold Peace speech by Yeltsin in Budapest in 1994 (Kempster and Murphy 1994), which reflected the fears of Russian operative realists that their country would become the key loser of the Cold War (Sakwa 2007) and be encircled by the enlarged sphere of influence of the USA, the key winner of the Cold War (Parry 2015). At the beginning of the second half of the 1990s, Russia started to manifest its so-called Weimar syndrome, interpreting itself as a humiliated, disrespected and ignored country (Krastev and Leonard 2015). The Russian military elites started to be intensively disturbed by the quick loss of Russia's former strategic depth and its lost status as a superpower.[11]

A new stage of Russian hostility towards the process of NATO enlargement came with the second Russian President V. Putin. He stopped the decline of Russian military budgets and inspired a new doctrinal thinking that was articulated in the so-called Governmental Rearmament Programs, which were oriented mainly towards the construction of new generations of tanks, armoured vehicles, artillery systems, and missiles (Klein 2016).

As a reaction to the second wave of NATO expansion, a new, enormously strong unit was created: it was the Western Military District in St. Petersburg (Ukaz Prezidenta 2010), which brings together one Guard tank army, two motorised brigades, two navy fleets, one army of navy infantry, two parachutist divisions, and a lot of specialised brigades and units (Military Balance 2017). In their build-up, a key emphasis was given to the A2/AD systems and the organisation of big manoeuvres (Frühling and Lasconjarias 2016, pp. 95–116). Putin personally chose its first commander, General Valery Gerasimov, and sometime later, he named him to the post of the Chief of the General Staff (Gerasimov 2012).

In the NATO countries, the Russian reactions are seen as a form of hysteria, an aggressive modernisation and an unnecessary sabre-rattling whose aim is to deter the new member states of NATO (Carter 2016–2017). The Russian operative realists object that the key mission of the Western Military District is not to wage an invasion into the territory of Russia's Western neighbours but to assure the defence against a possible invasion or incursion into the territory of the RF (Khodarenok 2015), which is seen by them as an imminent threat to the security of their country (Gerasimov 2017a). As a result, we are witnessing a classical dialogue of the deaf.[12] Russian as well as American operative realists continue to repeat their arguments: security fears vs. enlargement of the community of values and security guarantees for new member countries of NATO.

3.6.3 The Russian A2/AD Systems

On the pages of the American doctrinal documents, A2 is used an acronym for "Anti-Access", which concretely means preventing the movement of military forces to a theatre. The AD stands for "Area-Denial", a complex of action intended to slow the deployment of friendly forces into a theatre or cause forces to operate from distances farther from the locus of conflict than they would otherwise prefer (Freier 2012). The American approach is defined on two basic levels. On the positive one, the US strategists underline the necessity of free access for the US soldiers to areas where their challengers have their A2/AD systems. At the negative level, all countries

---

[11] It played a decisive role particularly during WW II.
[12] It is a phrase of French origin (*dialogue des sourds*) which refers to a discussion in which each party is unresponsive to what the others say and only continues to repeat its arguments.

which want to deny the projection of American military power over great distances are labelled as "challengers," as possible military adversaries.

The category A2 covers the following arms systems: surface-, air- and submarine-launched ballistic and cruise missiles, ballistic missiles with conventional heads, kinetic and non-kinetic anti-satellite weapons, submarine forces and anti-ship missiles, air-defence systems, and long-range reconnaissance and surveillance systems. All these systems are in the potential range of the Russian armed forces (Frühling and Lasconjarias 2016, pp. 95–116). In the RF, the A2/AD systems are represented by the SAM (surface-to-air missile) systems of high-quality air defence (Gordon and Matsumura 2013), especially their modernised version S-400 (SA-21) (Smura 2016), in the armament of 50 battalions on the territory of the RF (Gady 2018), namely in Kaliningrad and Crimea, but also in Syria (Gressel 2015).

The second pillar of Russian A2/AD systems is represented by the *littoral anti-ship capabilities*, concretely by the K-300 P Bastion mobile systems (MilitaryToday.com.), which have the capacity to destroy military ships as well as ground targets (Spiegel.de 2015). The third pillar is the armament of the Black Sea Fleet; it consists of a demi-dozen non–nuclear Kilo submarines (NavalToday.com 2017) which have the sobriquet Silent Killer (SecurityMagazin.cz 2016). Lastly, the Russian A2/AD systems include the modern systems of electronic warfare Krasucha 4, which are able to paralyse radar signals at a distance of 150–300 km (Zapfe and Haas 2016).

The above-mentioned systems are concentrated in several important areas called A2/AD bubbles (Lokshin 2016). The first of them is the area of Kaliningrad, an enormously militarised area (Forster 2016) on the borders with Lithuania and Poland in the Baltic area. The second is Crimea with a great quantity of K-300 P systems (Martinage 2014), which are able to destroy military planes not only in this area but also in some parts of Bulgaria and Romania (Burton 2016).

3.6.4 Russian A2/AD Systems in the Light of Neorealism

All Russian A2/AD systems were produced and deployed on the territory of the Russian Federation, namely in Moscow, areas of St. Petersburg and Crimea, with their key mission being to defend the North-West and South-West frontiers of the RF. They symbolise the internal balancing of the RF as the passive and continental actor that stands against the process of the NATO expansion. They represent a Russian instrument against external balancing. Representing the Russian reaction to the NATO expansion, they also became the symbol of a global clash between two contradictory forms of balancing: Russian internal balancing vs. American external balancing.

The Russian Chief of the General Staff underlined that these A2/AD systems represent a new qualitative level (Gerasimov 2017b), they do not shorten the distance between the USA and the RF, and they provide no possibility of attacking the territory of the USA, or of the so-called old member countries. They do not reinforce the invasive potential of the Russian military. They only strengthen the capacity to fight against any hostile invasive operations of another country's naval and air forces. In this light, these systems have an incontestable conventional dissuasive potential; they manifest that any possible adversary runs the risk of important losses (Sukhankin 2017). They are evaluated as a symbol of the determination of the Russian elites to deny any intervention into their near abroad (Kofman 2017).

The military value of the Russian A2/AD systems has been clearly explained by General H. R. McMaster, who said that they reduce the lethality and efficiency of the contemporary American arms systems by 40% (Tucker 2016). They represent a serious challenge for the American fighters of the 4th generation. This situation reinforces the calls of American military planners for the acceleration of the deployment of the military planes of the 5th generation (Baroudos 2016). As a result, we are, once again, witnessing a dangerous rise of the military competition and tension on the border between NATO and the RF (Rogovoy 2014).

In the light of Glaser's theory, Russian operative realists perceive the USA as a greedy state cumulating several new allies in Russia's former buffer zone. Their security fears were reinforced after the 2008 Bucharest Summit Declaration, whose paragraph 23 articulated the decision that two other post-Soviet countries, Ukraine and Georgia, would become members of NATO (Bucharest Summit 2008). These fears opened the way to two strategic decisions of the Russian operational realists. At the military level, they decides to deploy the A2/AD systems on their Western border and the Crimean peninsula, as this was their answer to the new misbalance of power. And at the political level, they started the preparations for the annexation of Crimea and for the large support for militant Russian separatists in Eastern Ukraine.

3.6.5 *A Security Controversy Between NATO and the RF*

From the military point of view, the deployment of the A2/AD systems gives the Russian operative realists new possibilities to make decisions and act very quickly to the detriment of NATO (Golts 2016), and to compensate for the military superiority of the USA by manifesting that the price of a possible military confrontation would be very high (Johnson and Long 2007). As a result, these systems provoked a new wave of the security controversy between NATO and the RF.

On the one hand, Russian elites continue to underline that these systems are not intended for the projection of the Russian military power, but for the protection of the territory of the RF. In addition, they add that their A2/AD systems serve not as instruments of expansion, but as instruments of defensive sufficiency. On the other hand, the leaders of both the USA and NATO argue that the Russian systems pose a direct security threat for their new allies, the new member countries of NATO. They underline that when faced with the Russian A2/AD, it is necessary to take new strategic approaches, namely in the Baltic and the Black Sea areas (Ülgen and Kasapoğlu 2016). The 2016 NATO Warsaw Summit condemned Russia for the strengthening of its military posture, the increase of its military activities, and the fact that it deployed new high-end capabilities and challenged the regional security (NATO 2016). This line of argumentation has been developed by Madeleine Albright, who underlined the necessity of an assertive deterrent against Russia (Golts 2016).

And a year later, the General Secretary of NATO announced that the Alliance would react to the Russian behaviour with two basic measures: the increasing of the numbers of soldiers in Poland and the three Baltic countries, and the building of two new Allied Commands—in Poland and Romania (Rettman 2017). NATO also reacted to Russia's activities by building the Very High Joint Readiness Task Force (VJTF), also called Spearhead (at the beginning, it had 5,000 soldiers under the command of Great Britain) (Lasconjarias and Nagy 2018). These measures followed the preceding deployment of the Aegis arms systems in the Spanish naval base Rota (Eckstein 2015).

3.6.6 A Clash of Perceptions and New Spirals of Security Dilemmas

Faced with the Russian arguments, NATO perceives the deployment of Russia's A2/AD systems as greedy behaviour, and as an expansive strategy. This vicious circle continues with the deployment of new Western units on the territory of the new member states of the expanded Alliance. Of course, the American expansion in the former zone of influence of the USSR has not been dominantly motivated by a desire for territorial gains. The US political elites were "only" determined to prevent the emergence of a dominant state that might control continental resources and use them to threaten the territorial integrity and global interests of the USA as the leading sea power (Blagden et al. 2011).

Nevertheless, the American behaviour in the post-Soviet space resulted in a dramatic reinforcement of the Russians' security fears and, especially, of their deeply rooted siege mentality (Bar-Tal 2004). As a result, our continent is witnessing a dangerous clash of perceptions: the American elites do not manifest enough empathy for the security perceptions of others and see the external world within the framework of their own deeply rooted ideas and prejudices, which can generate new problems (Pillar 2016). As a result, the structure of the security relations between the RF and NATO is increasingly controversial. We are witnessing new spirals of security dilemmas and of a dangerously growing military tension.

3.7 Conclusion

Thirty years after the end of the Cold War, the world is witnessing a profound change in the field of the ISR. Instead of the strategic parity that was present during the Cold War, the new world is characterised by a clear superiority of the West. The USA, as a typical sea power far away from the border between NATO and the RF, has a big advantage in its internal as well as external balancing against a typical continental power with great military tension on its western border. Its economic, financial and technological superiority was importantly reinforced by the recognition and helpfulness of the political elites of the new member countries of NATO.

In contrast, Russia is in a position of clear inferiority, particularly on the economic, financial and technological levels. As a typical continental state, it is exposed to a growing military tension just on its long western border. It has neither possibilities nor instruments for external balancing; it can rely only on its internal resources. Its arming has a negative character, and it is based on a modest imitation of the American RMA. At the beginning of the 2020s, Russia is in a double isolation and solitude, which has strategic as well as technological dimensions (Persson 2016, p. 191).

In this situation, our continent is witnessing a situation which is comparable with the first half of the 1980s when NATO pointed to the conventional and quantitative superiority of the POW, which tended toward a lower nuclear threshold. NATO's strategy did not rule out the first use of nuclear weapons in Europe with the aim to compensate for the conventional superiority of the POW. NATO was determined to avoid enormous losses of its territory and of its soldiers and to move the war to the territory of the adversary as soon as possible (Peters 1987). And sometime later, this strategic thinking resulted in the so-called Rogers Doctrine, which put the key emphasis on attacks on the second and third echelons of the adversary forces (Rogers 1985).

Today, this doctrine has become a strong inspiration for an important part of Russian security and military thinkers. But in comparison with the last two decades of the Cold War, the international situation profoundly changed. Today, it is the USA which has a clear conventional superiority, not only qualitative, but also quantitative. Confronted with such a situation, the Russian military thinkers deduce that a conventional conflict with the American units would result in a disaster and they pose the question of how to avoid it. And they are thinking about two possible solutions: a so-called non-contact warfare (Ven Bruusgaard 2016, pp. 7–26), or an engagement of non-strategic nuclear weapons (Ven Bruusgaard 2014). They have almost the same motivation as the American strategists 40 years ago: they try to deter their presumed adversary by a threat to harm its military forces and attack the territory of its new allies. At the end of the 2010s, these ideas were published particularly on the pages of the review *Vojennaja Mysl* (Military Thinking) (Kalinkin et al. 2015, pp. 18–22).

Even if nobody suspects that the Russians are preparing a nuclear war in Europe, and some experts admit that their conclusions about this result from the Russian fear of losing in a conventional conflict (Adamsky 2014), the evolution of their doctrinal thinking has a strongly controversial potential. The Russians' dissuasive discourse, whatever its motivation is (Kalinkin et al. 2015, pp. 34–37), should be perceived as an imminent security threat for the new European member states of NATO (Ven Bruusgaard 2016, p. 21).

Last, but not least, the confrontational structure of the post-Soviet space has important cultural consequences. In contrast to the westernisation ethos of the 1990s, Russian elites are increasingly critical towards the West, and especially towards the USA (Neumann 2016). The growing anti–Western dimension of the Russian patriotism and nationalism have become typical for the operative realists of this country and it is supported by the state and even by the Orthodox Church, particularly by

Table 3.7 American expansion in the former sphere of influence of the USSR

The USA's expansion into the territory of the former Warsaw Pact	Main forms of expansion	Consequences
The first wave of the NATO enlargement (1999)	Poland, the Czech Republic and Hungary (invited during the Madrid Summit in 1997) became new NATO member states	Protests of President Yeltsin; his slogan "Cold Peace"
The second wave of the NATO enlargement in 2004	Estonia, Latvia, Lithuania, Romania, Bulgaria, Slovakia and Slovenia (invited during the Prague Summit in 2002) became new NATO member states	Strong protests of Russian political and military elites Deployment of the Russian A2/AD systems
2008	Negotiations about the possibility of opening the EU and NATO for Ukraine and Georgia	Strong protests of Russian political and military elites The annexation of the Crimea

their narratives about a decadent West. All these events reinforce the mutual distrust and misunderstandings (Persson 2016) (Table 3.7).

Sources

Adamsky, D. (2014). Nuclear Incoherence: Deterrence Theory and Non-Strategic Nuclear Weapons in Russia. *Journal of Strategic Studies, 37*(1), 91–134.

Antonopoulos, P., Velez, R., & Cottle, D. (2017). NATO's Push into the Caucasus: Geopolitical Flashpoints and Limits for Expansion. *Defense & Security Analysis, 33*(4), 366–379.

Asmus, R. D., Kugler, R. L., & Larrabee, F. S. (1993). Building a New NATO. *Foreign Affairs* (September/October 1993), 28–40.

Asmus, R. D., Kugler, R. L., & Larrabee, F. S. (1997). Building a New NATO. *Foreign Affairs, 72*(4) (September/October 1993). Available at: https://www.rand.org/pubs/reprints/RP241.html.

The Baltic Times. (2016, October 20). *Think Tank: Baltic Defense Budgets Are Fastest-Growing Worldwide.* Available at: https://www.baltictimes.com/think_tank__baltic_defense_budgets_are_fastest-growing_worldwide/.

Bandow, D. (1997, July 30). *Any Alternatives to NATO Expansion?* Cato Institute. Available at: https://www.cato.org/publications/.../any-alternatives-nato-expansi.

Baroudos, C. (2016, September 21). *Why NATO Should Fear Russia's A2/AD Capabilities (and How to Respond).* Available at: https://nationalinterest.org/.../why-nato-should-fear-russias-a2-ad-capabil....

Bar-Tal, D. (2004, September). Siege Mentality. *Beyond Intractability.* Available at: http://www.beyondintractability.org/essay/siege-mentality.

Basken, P. (1995, June 26). *Clinton, Walesa Discuss NATO Expansion—UPI Archives.* Available at: www.upi.com. UPI Archives.

Bearak, B. (1997, May 15). For Havel, a NATO Open to All Democracies. *The New York Times.*

Sources

Black, E. (2014, March 26). Stephen Walt and a 'Realist' Take on NATO Membership for Ukraine. *MinnPost*.
Blagden, D. W., Levy, J. S., & Thompson, W. R. (2011). Correspondence: Sea Powers, Continental Powers, and Balancing Theory. *International Security, 36*(2) (Fall), 190–202.
Boot, M. (2006). *War Made New: Technology, Warfare, and the Course of History, 1500 to Today* (pp. 124–130). New York: Gotham Books.
Braithwaite. R. (1991). Ambassador Rodric Braithwaite's diary, 5. 3. 1991. Source: NATO Expansion: What Gorbachev Heard. *National Security*. Available at: https://nsarchive.gwu.edu/briefingbook/russia-programs/2017-12-12/....
Braithwaite, R. (2014). Russia, Ukraine and the West. *The RUSI Journal, 159*(2), 62–65.
Brown, M. E. (1995). The Flawed Logic of NATO Expansion. *Survival Global Politics and Strategy, 37*(1), 34–52.
Brzezinski, Z. (1994a, December 28). NATO—Expand or Die? *The New York Times*. Available at: https://www.nytimes.com/1994/12/28/.../nato-expand-or-die.html.
Brzezinski, Z. (1994b, March–April). Premature Partnership. *Foreign Affairs*, p. 72.
Bucharest Summit. (2008). Declaration Issued by the Heads of State and Government Participating in the Meeting of the North Atlantic Council in Bucharest on 3 April 2008.
Bush, G. (1991). The September 9, 1919 Speech to the University of Minnesota Armory in Minneapolis.
Brzeziński, Z. (1997). *The Grand Chessboard: American Primacy and Its Geostrategic Imperatives*. New York: Basic Books.
Brzezinski, Z., & Lake, A. (1997, June 30). For a New World, a New NATO. *The New York Times*.
Burton, L. (2016, October 25). *Bubble Trouble: Russia's A2/AD Capabilities*. Available at: https://foreignpolicyblogs.com/2016/.../bubble-trouble-russia-a2-a.
Carter, A. (2017). A Strong and Balanced Approach to Russia. *Survival: Global Politics and Strategy, 58*(December 2016–January 2017), 55–56.
Chauprade, A., & Thual, F. (1999). *Dictionnaire de géopolitique: États, Concepts, Auteurs* (p. 547). Paris: Éditions Ellipses.
Cimoszewicz, W. (1996). Building Poland's Security: Membership of NATO a Key Objective. *NATO Review* 3.
Cohen, R. (1993, October 2). Yeltsin Opposes Expansion of NATO in Eastern Europe. *New York Times*.
Cold Peace. (1994, December 6). Russia Warns NATO of a 'Cold Peace'. *The Independent*. Available at: www.independent.co.uk/news/russia-warns-na....
de Hoop Scheffer, J. (2004, June 18). *NATO's Istanbul Summit: New Mission, New Means*. Speech at the Royal United Services Institute.
Deudney, D., & Ikenberry, G. J. (1992). Who Won the Cold War? *Foreign Policy*, No. 87 (Summer), pp. 123–128, 130–138.
Deudney, D., & Ikenberry, J. I. (2009). The Unravelling of the Cold War Settlement. *Survival: Global Politics and Strategy, 51*(6), 39–62.
Deveselu Base. Available at: www.globalsecurity.org/space/facility/deveselu.htm.
Dobbins, J. F. (1990). State Department European Bureau, Memorandum to National Security Council: NATO Strategy Review Paper for October 29 Discussion, 25. 10. 1990. Source: George H. W. Bush Presidential Library: NSC Philip Zelikow Files, Box CF01468, Folder "File 148 NATO Strategy Review No. 1 [3]" [16].
Eckstein, M. (2015, May 1). *BMD-Equipped Destroyer USS Porter Arrives in Rota, Spain*. Available at: https://news.usni.org/2015/05/01/bmd-equipped-destroyer-uss-porter-arrives-in-rota-spain.
Eland, I. (1997, October 28). *The High Cost of NATO Expansion*. Cato Institute. Available at: https://www.cato.org/publications/.../high-cost-nato-expansion.
Flikke, G., Wigen, E., Blakkisrud, H., & Kolstø, P. (2011). *The Shifting Geopolitics of the Black Sea Region. Actors, Drivers and Challenges*. Norwegian Institute of International Affairs (NUPI).
Forster, K. (2016, October 28): *How a Tiny Pocket of Russian Land Next to Poland Could Soon Become...* Available at: https://www.independent.co.uk/.../russia-military-base-europe-puti....

Freedman, L. (2006–2007). Iraq, Liberal Wars and Illiberal Containment. *Survival, 48*(4), 52.
Freier, N. (2012, May 17). *The Emerging Anti-Access/Area-Denial Challenge.* Center for Strategic & International Studies.
Friedman, G. (2015). *Flashpoints: The Emerging Crisis in Europe.* New York: Doubleday.
Friedman, T. L. (1998, May 2). Foreign Affairs; Now a Word from X. *The New York Times.*
Frühling, S., & Lasconjarias, G. (2016). NATO, A2/AD and the Kaliningrad Challenge. *Survival: Global Politics and Strategy, 58*(2), 95–116.
Gaddis, J. L. (1998). History, Grand Strategy and NATO Enlargement. *Survival, 40*(1), 145–151.
Gady, F.-S. (2018, February 23). *Russia Upgrades Long-Range Air Defenses in Pacific Region.* Available at: https://thediplomat.com/.../russia-upgrades-long-range-air-defense.
Gallois, P. (1990). *Géopolitique. Les voies de la puissance.* Paris: Plon.
Galtung, J. (1997). *The Eastward NATO Expansion: The Beginning of Cold War II?* Copenhagen: COPRI.
Gates, R. (2000, July 24). Presidential Oral History Program. George H. W. Bush Presidency. University of Virginia, Miller Centrum, p. 101.
Gates, R (2009). A Balanced Strategy. Reprogramming the Pentagon for a New Age. *Foreign Affairs* (January/February), p. 32.
Genscher. H.-D. (1990). U.S. Embassy Bonn Confidential Cable to Secretary of State on the Speech of the German Foreign Minister: Genscher Outlines His Vision of a New European Architecture, 1. 2. 1990. Source: U.S. Department of State. FOIA Reading Room. Case F-2015 10829.
Gerasimov. (2012, November 9). Profile: Russia's New Military Chief Valery Gerasimov. *BBC News.*
Gerasimov, V. (2017a, March). The World on the Verge of War [in Russian]. *Voyenno-promyshlennyy kuryer.* Available at: http://vpk-news.ru/articles/35591.
Gerasimov, V. (2017b, April 20). *A World on the Brink of War.* Available at: blog. https://berzins.eu/gerasimov_brink_war.
Glantz, D. M., & House, J. M. (2015). *When Titans Clashed: How the Red Army Stopped Hitler* (pp. 286–289). Kansas: University Press of Kansas.
Goldgeier, J. (1999). The US Decision to Enlarge NATO. *Brookings Review* (Summer).
Goldgeier, J. (2016, September 12). Promises Made, Promises Broken? What Yeltsin Was Told about NATO in 1993 and Why It Matters. *War on the Rocks.*
Golts, A. (2016, July 11). *From Assurance to Deterrence: The Russia Question and NATO's Summit in Warsaw* (Vol. 13, Issue 124). Eurasia Daily Monitor. Available at: https://jamestown.org/.../from-assurance-to-deterrence-the-ussia-....
Gorbachev, M., & Baker, J. (1990a). Record of conversation between Mikhail Gorbachev and James Baker in Moscow, Excerpts, 9 February. Source: Gorbachev Foundation Archive, Fond 1, Opus 1.
Gorbachev, M., & Baker, J. (1990b). Record of conversation between Mikhail Gorbachev and James Baker in Moscow, 18. May 1990. Source: Gorbachev Foundation Archive, Fond 1, Opus 1.
Gorbachev, M., & Bush, G. (1990). Memorandum of Telephone Conversation between Mikhail Gorbachev and George Bush, 17. 7. 1990. Source: George H.W. Bush Presidential Library, Memcons and Telcons. Available at: https://bush41library.tamu.edu/.
Gorbachev, M., & Mitterrand, F. (1990). Record of conversation between Mikhail Gorbachev and Francois Mitterrand (excerpts), 25. 5. 1990. Source: Mikhail Gorbachev i germanskii vopros, edited by Alexander Galkin and Anatoly Chernyaev. Moscow: *Ves'mir*, 2006, pp. 454–466.
Gordon IV, J., & Matsumura, J. (2013): High-Quality Air Defenses. The Topic Is Discussed in Greater Depth In: *The Army's Role in Overcoming Anti-Access and Area Denial Challenges.* Available at: https://www.rand.org/content/dam/rand/.../RAND_RR229.pdf.
Gressel, G. (2015, October 12). *Russia's Quiet Military Revolution and What It Means for Europe.* Available at: www.ecfr.eu/.../russias_quiet_military_revolution_and_what_it_m....
Hahn, G. M. (2018, April 23). Broken Promise: NATO Expansion and the End of the Cold War UPDATE. *Gordonhahn.com Russian and Eurasian Politics.* Available at: https://gordonhahn.com/2018/04/23/broken-promise-nato-expansion-and-the-end-of-the-cold-war-an-update/.

Havel, V. (1993, October 28). We Really Are Part of the NATO Family. *International Herald Tribune.*
Hyde-Price, A. (2000). *Germany & the European Union: Enlarging NATO and the EU* (p. 149). Manchester: Manchester University Press.
Itzkowitz Shifrinson, J. R. (2016). Deal or No Deal? The End of the Cold War and the U.S. Offer to Limit NATO Expansion. *International Security, 40*(4), 7–44.
Jackson, J. O. (1993, November 8). Trying to Enlist in NATO. *Time.*
Jervis, R. (1976). *Perception and Misperception in International Politics.* Princeton: Princeton University Press.
Johnson, S. E., & Long, D. (Eds.). (2007). *Coping with the Dragon: Essays on PLA Transformation and the U.S. Military* (p. 73). Washington, DC: Center for Technology and National Security Policy.
Jones, J. (2005, July 6). The Sinatra Doctrine. Available at: https://hir.harvard.edu/article/?a=135.
Kaiser, R. G. (1991). Gorbachev: Triumph and Failure. *Foreign Affairs, 70*(2) (Spring), 160–174.
Kalinkin, D. A., Khryapin, A. L., Matvichuk, V. V. (2015, January). Strategicheskoye sderzhivanie v usloviakh sozdaniya SShA global'noy sistemy PRO i sredstv global'nogo udara [Strategic Deterrence in the Context of the US Global Ballistic-Missile Defense System and Means for a Global Strike]. *Voyennaya Mysl* (Vol. 1).
Katz B. D. (2016, October 19). Baltics States Have Doubled Arms Spending Since Putin's Advance. *Bloomberg.com.* Available at: https://www.bloomberg.com/news/articles/2016-10-19/baltics-states-have-doubled-arms-spending-since-putin-s-advance.
Kempster, N., & Murphy, D. E. (1994, December 6). Broader NATO May Bring 'Cold Peace,' Yeltsin Warns: Europe: Russian President Accuses U.S. of Being Power Hungry. Speech Comes as Nations Finalize Nuclear Treaty. Available at: articles. https://www.latimes.com/1994-12-06/news/mn-5629_1_cold-war.
Kennan, G. (1997, February 5). A Fateful Error. *New York Times,* p. A23.
Khodarenok, M. (2015, March 18). Scenario for the Third World War [in Russian]. *Voyenno-promyshlennyy kuryer.* Available at: http://vpk-news.ru/articles/24284.
Kimberly, M. (2017). Reconsidering NATO Expansion: A Counterfactual Analysis of Russia and the West in the 1990s. *European Journal of International Security, 3*(2), 135–161.
Kissinger, H. (1993, November 24). Not This Partnership. *Washington Post.*
Kissinger, H. (1994a, December 19). *Expand NATO Now.* Available at: https://www.washingtonpost.com/.../expand-nato-now/f1f0b4ed-5....
Kissinger, H. (1994b, August 16). It's an Alliance. *Washington Post.*
Klein, M. (2016). Russia's Military: On the Rise? *Transatlantic Academy Paper Series,* No. 2, pp. 11–12.
Kofman, M. (2017, February 16). *A Comparative Guide to Russia's Use of Force: Measure Twice, Invade Once.* Available at: https://warontherocks.com/.../a-comparative-guide-to-russias-use-....
Kohl, H., & Bush, K. (1990). Memorandum of Conversation between Helmut Kohl and George Bush at Camp David, 24. 2. 1990. Source: George H.W. Bush Presidential Library, Memcons and Telcons. Available at: https://bush41library.tamu.edu/.
Kramer, M. (2009). The Myth of a No-NATO-Enlargement Pledge to Russia. *The Washington Quarterly, 32*(2), 7–44.
Kramer, M., & Itzkowitz Shifrinson J. R. (2017). Correspondence: NATO Enlargement—Was There a Promise? *International Security, 42*(1), 186–192.
Krastev, I., & Leonard, M. (2015, May/June). Europe's Shattered Dream of Order. How Putin Is Disrupting the Atlantic Alliance. *Foreign Affairs.*
Lasconjarias, G., & Nagy, T. A. (2018, March 26). *NATO Adaptation and A2/AD: Beyond the Military Implications.* Available at: https://www.globsec.org/.../nato-intelligence-adaptation-challenge/.
Lake, A. (1993, September 21). *From Containment to Enlargement.* Available at: https://www.mtholyoke.edu/acad/intrel/lakedoc.html.
Lokshin, J. (2016, July). *Russia's Anti-Access Area Denial.* Available at: https://missiledefenseadvocacy.org/.../russia-anti-access-area-denial-comi.

Mahnken, T. G. (2003). Beyond Blitzkrieg: Allied Responses to Combined-Arms Armored Warfare During World War II. In E. O. Goldman & L. C. Eliason (Eds.), *The Diffusion of Military Technology and Ideas* (pp. 243–253). Stanford: Stanford University Press.

Malek, M. (2008). NATO and the South Caucasus: Armenia, Azerbaijan, and Georgia on Different Tracks. *Connections*, 7(3), 30–51.

Martinage, R. (2014). *Toward a New Offset Strategy*. Center for Strategic and Budgetary Assessments (CSBA).

McGovern, R. (2014, July 17). When the US Welched on Its NATO Promise. *Baltimore Sun*.

McGwire, M. (1987). *Military Objectives in Soviet Foreign Policy*. Washington, D.C: The Brookings Institution.

McGwire, M. (1998). NATO Expansion: 'A Policy Error of Historic Importance'. *Review of International Studies*, 24(1), 23–42.

Military Balance. (2016, February 9). *The International Institute for Strategic Studies (IISS)*. London: Routledge.

The Military Balance. (February 2017). IISS.

Military-Today.com. Bastion-P Coastal Defense Missile System.

Mitterrand. F. 53 discours historiques – Francois… Available at: https://www.lalibrairiesonore.com/catalogue/histoire/discours.

Mitterrand, F., & Bush, G. (1990). Letter from Francois Mitterrand to George Bush, 25. May 1990. Source: George H.W. Bush Presidential Library, NSC Scowcroft Files, FOIA 2009-0275-S.

MK Air Base—US Army Europe. Available at: www.eur.army.mil/21tsc/MKAB/about.html.

Moller, B. (1997). *Preconditions for NATO Enlargement from a Common Security Point of View* (p. 12). Copenhagen: COPRI.

Murphy, D. E. (1994, December 6). Broader NATO May Bring 'Cold Peace,' Yeltsin Warns. *Los Angeles Times*. Available at: https://www.latimes.com/archives/la-xpm-1994-12-06-mn-5629-story.html.

Musitelli, J. (2001–2002). «François Mitterrand, architecte de la Grande Europe: le projet de confédération européenne (1990–1991)». *Revue internationale et stratégique*, 82, 18–28.

NATO. (1991, December 20). NATO Mini. Comm. North Atlantic Cooperation Council Statement. Brussels. Press Communiqué M-NACC-1(91)111.

NATO. (1995, September 3). Official Text: Study on NATO Enlargment. Available at: www.nato.int.e-Library›Official texts (Chronological).

NATO. (2016, July 8–9). Warsaw Summit Communiqué. Issued by the Heads of State and Government participating in the meeting of the North Atlantic Council in Warsaw. Available at: https://www.nato.int/cps/en/natohq/official_texts_133169.htm.

Nau, H. (2012). Realism. In *Routledge Handbook of American Foreign Policy* (p. 70). London: Routledge.

Neumann, I. B. (2016). Russia's Europe, 1991–2016: Inferiority to Superiority. *International Affairs*, 92(6), 1381–1399.

NavalToday.com. (2017, August 11). *Russian Kilo-Class Submarine Krasnodar Joins Black Sea Fleet in…* Available at: https://navaltoday.com/…/russian-kilo-class-submarine-krasnodar.

New World Order. (1991, March 6). George Bush's Speech. Document.

Nünlist, C. (2017). Contested History: Rebuilding Trust in European Security. In *Strategic Trends 2017, Key Developments in Global Affairs* (p. 21).

O'Flynn, K. (2001, October 23). Russia in Multi-million Arms Deal with Northern Alliance. *The Guardian*.

Pape, R. (1996). *Bombing to Win: Air Power and Coercion in War* (pp. 276–283). Ithaca: Cornell University Press.

Parry, R. (2015, February 10). *'Realists' Warn Against Ukraine Escalation*. Available at: https://consortiumnews.com/…/realists-warn-against-.

Perlmutter, A., & Carpenter, T. G. (1998). NATO's Expensive Trip East: The Folly of Enlargement. *Foreign Affairs*, 77(1), 2–6.

Persson, G. (Ed.). (2016). *Russian Military Capability in a Ten-Year Perspective—2016*. FOI.

Sources

Peters, J. E. (1987). Evaluating FOFA as a Deterrent. *The RUSI Journal, 132*(4), 39–44.
Petersen, A. (2004, August 20). *Black Sea Security: The NATO Imperative*. Wilson Center. Global Europe Program. Available at: https://www.wilsoncenter.org/publication/black-sea-security-the-nato-imperative.
Pillar, P. R. (2016). *Why America Misunderstands the World: National Experience and Roots of Misperception*. New York: Columbia University Press.
Powell, C. (1990). Letter from Mr. Powell (N. 10) to Mr. Wall: Thatcher-Gorbachev Memorandum of Conversation, 8. 6. Source: *Documents on British Policy Overseas, Series III, Volume VII: German Unification, 1989–1990*. Foreign and Commonwealth Office. Documents on British Policy Overseas, edited by Patrick Salmon, Keith Hamilton, & Stephen Twigge, Oxford and New York, Routledge 2010, pp. 411–417.
Rafiq, A. (2017, January 12). Russia Returns to Afghanistan. *The National Interest*. Available at: https://nationalinterest.org/feature/russia-returns-afghanistan-19040.
Rettman, A. (2017, June 30). Nato's Russia-Deterrent Force 'Fully Operational'. *EUobserver*. Available at: https://euobserver.com/foreign/138399.
RFE/RL. (2003, March 14). "U.S. Base Commander Says Romanian Airport Used as 'Bridgehead' to Qatar" and "Bulgarian Government Offers U.S. Decommissioned Air Base". *Radio Free Evrope/Radio Liberty, 7*(49).
Rogers, B. (1985). Follow-On Forces Attack. *NATO Review, 1*, 1–9.
Rogovoy, A. V. (2014, December). *A Russian View of Land Power*. Cambridge, UK: Conflict Studies Research Center. Available at: http://amzn.to/2mJCS8l.
Rozoff, R. (2009, October 26). Bulgaria, Romania: US, NATO Bases for War in the East. *Novinite.com*. Available at: https://www.novinite.com/articles/109267/Bulgaria%2C+Romania%3A+US%2C+NATO+Bases+for+War+In+The+East.
Rozoff, R. (2010, May 21). U.S. And NATO Accelerate Military Build-Up in Black Sea Region. *Global Research*.
Rutland, P. (1998, July). NATO Old and New. *Prospect Magazine*. Available at: https://www.prospectmagazine.co.uk/magazine/natooldandnew.
Sakwa, R. (2007). *Russia Against the Rest. The Post-Cold War Crisis of World Order*. Cambridge: Cambridge University Press.
Sarotte, M. E. (2014). A Broken Promise? What the West Really Told Moscow About NATO Expansion. *Foreign Affairs*, pp. 90–97.
Sarotte, M. E. (2017, June 19). *Could German Unification Have Happened Today?* Available at: https://foreignpolicy.com/.../could-german-unification-have-happ....
Sarotte, M. E. (2019). How to Enlarge NATO: The Debate Inside the Clinton Administration, 1993–95. *International Security, 44*(1) (Summer), 7–41.
SecurityMagazin.cz. (2016, September 29). Tichý ruský zabiják: Černomořská flotila zařazuje nové... Available at: https://www.securitymagazin.cz/.../tichy-rusky-zabijak-cernomorska-flotila-zarazuje-n.
Shlapak, D. A., & Johnson, M. W. (2016). Reinforcing Deterrence on NATO's Eastern Flank. *Wargaming the Defense of the Baltics*. RAND Corporation. Available at: https://www.rand.org/content/dam/rand/.../RAND_RR1253.pdf.
Skidelsky, R. (2018, September). Kennan's Revenge: Remembering the Reasons for the Cold War. *The Guardian*.
Smura, T. (2016, November 27). *Russian Anti-Access Area Denial (A2AD) Capabilities—Implications for NATO*. Available at: https://pulaski.pl/.../russian-anti-access-area-denial-a2ad-capabiliti....
Solomon, G. B. (1998). *The NATO Enlargement Debate, 1990–1997: Blessings of Liberty*. Westport, CN.: Praeger.
Spiegel.de. (2015, March 15). *Russia Deployed Bastion Coastal Missile Systems on Crimean Peninsula*.
Standart News. (2010, May 16).

Sukhankin, S. (2017, August 2). Kaliningrad Oblast – Russia's Formidable A2/AD Bubble. Available at: https://neweasterneurope.eu/.../kaliningrad-oblast-russia-s-formidable-a2....

Talbott, S. (1995, August 10). Why NATO Should Grow. *New York Review of Books*. Available at: https://www.nybooks.com/articles/1995/08/10/why-nato-should-grow.

Talbott, S. (2002). *The Russia Hand: A Memoir of Presidential Diplomacy* (pp. 99–101). New York: Random House.

Tucker, P. (2016, May 19). *How the Pentagon Is Preparing for a Tank War with Russia*. Available at: www.defenseone.com/.../2016/...pentagon-preparing.../128460/.

Ukaz Prezidenta. (2010). Указ Президента Российской Федерации от 20 сентября 2010 года № 1144 «О военно-административном делении Российской Федерации».

Ülgen, S., & Kasapoğlu, C. (2016, June 10). *A Threat-Based Strategy for NATO's Southern Flank*. *Carnegie Europe*. Available at: http://carnegieeurope.eu/.../threat-based-strategy-for-nato-s-southern-fla....

Ven Bruusgaard, K. (2014). *Crimea and Russia's Strategic Overhaul* (pp. 84–87). Available at: http://www.strategicstudiesinstitute.army.mil/pubs/parameters/issues/Autumn_2014/11_BruusgaardKristin_Crimea%20and%20Russia's%20Strategic%20Overhaul.pdf.

Ven Bruusgaard, K. (2016). Russian Strategic Deterrence. *Survival: Global Politics and Strategy, 58*(4), 7–26.

Walker, E. (2015, April 13). *Between East & West: NATO Enlargement & the Geopolitics of the Ukraine Crisis*. Available at: https://www.e-ir.info/2015/04/13/between-east-west-nato-enlargement-the-geopolitics-of-the-ukraine-crisis.

Waltz, K. N. (1993). The Emerging Structure of International Politics. *International Security, 18*(2) (Autumn), 75–76.

Waltz, K. N. (2000). NATO Expansion: A Realist's View. *Contemporary Security Policy, 21*(2), 36.

Westad, O. A. (2017). *The Cold War: A World History*. New York: Basic Books.

Woyke, P. (2016, July 5). *Cautious and Rotational—US Military Engagement on NATO's Eastern Flank*. Available at: https://www.osw.waw.pl/.../cautious-and-rotational-us-military-en.

Yeltsin B. (1991). Memorandum to Boris Yeltsin from Russian Supreme Soviet delegation to NATO HQs, 1. July 1991. Source: State Archive of the Russian Federation (GARF), Fond 10026, Opus 1.

Yeltsin, B. (1993, August 26). 'Understands' Polish Bid for a Role in NATO. *The New York Times*. Available at: https://www.nytimes.com/.../yeltsin-understands-polish-bid-for-a-r....

Zakaria, F. (2019). The Self-Destruction of American Power: Washington Squandered the Unipolar Moment. *Foreign Affairs, 98*(4), 10–16.

Zapfe, M., & Haas, M. C. (2016). Access for Allies? *The RUSI Journal, 161*(3), 34–41.

Chapter 4
From the War Against Georgia to the Annexation of the Crimea and the Following Increase of Military Tension

The aim of this chapter is to analyse the period between the second wave of NATO expansion and the end of the 2010s. This analysis is based on the research questions of this book, namely RQ 3 (Why is the structure of the international security relations at the Eastern border of NATO so confrontational?) and RQ 4 (What are the consequences of this trend?). The following analysis has two dimensions. In the negative dimension, the aim is not at all to provide a defence of the RF and its policy (namely the annexation of the Crimea). And in the positive dimension, the chapter tries to explain the behaviour of the Russian political and military élites as a reaction to the second wave of the NATO expansion and to the publicly declared intention to invite two other post-Soviet states to join NATO. The aim of the chapter is to show that from the neorealist point of view, the strategy of a continued and gradually increasing NATO expansion shifted the relationship between NATO and the RF towards another important imbalance of security threats.

The chapter is divided into four sections. The fist of them starts with an analysis of an important speech that the Russian president V. V. Putin delivered in Munich in 2017, which manifested the negative attitudes of the political as well as military élites of his country towards the second wave of the NATO expansion and namely towards its consequences for the security of the Russian Federation. This section continues with an analysis of the key motives and causes of the Five Days War between the RF and Georgia. It examines the political, military and doctrinal consequences of this relatively short, but enormously significant war. The second section interprets the basic differences between the NATO and the RF after the second wave of the NATO expansion, namely the differences between the external and internal balancing of these two antagonistic actors. It continues with an examination of the annexation of the Crimean Peninsula, and its motives, aims and consequences. Despite the fact that Russia's decision to use its military power resulted from its deeply rooted security fears, and even if it was made in a covert, hybrid manner, it was in profound contradiction with international law and caused a strong shift towards a negative peace in Europe.

The third section analyses the growing military tensions at the Eastern frontier of NATO after 2014, namely the military exercises of NATO as well as those of the RF (namely Zapad 2017) and the growing numbers of mutual military incidents. Their common denominator is a dangerous increase of military tension in this explosive part of the so-called Old Continent. And the last section analyses the related academic debate in the USA and other NATO countries after 2014. It presents and compares the key arguments of two camps of thinkers. The first of them assembles a lot of authors who share a clearly critical attitude towards the RF and its hybrid war and assertive if not aggressive revisionist politics. The opposite camp includes not only academic neorealists, but also some liberal internationalists who interpret the annexation of Crimea as an answer of the Russian operative realists to the expansion of NATO towards its Western frontiers and as a signalling that any further eastward expansion of it will be opposed by military means.

4.1 From Munich 2007 to Georgia 2008

4.1.1 The First Negativist Speech by Putin

At the beginning of February 2007, the Bavarian capital witnessed the first open demonstration of the profoundly critical and negativist attitudes of the Russian operative realists towards the results of the second wave of the NATO expansion. This negativism was articulated in the speech of the Russian president Putin (2007) during the annual Munich Security Conference. His first substantial reproach in this vociferous and critical speech was addressed to the unilateral actions of the USA and its disdain for the basic principles of international law. In these words, Putin manifested the negative Russian reaction to OIF 2003, a large and massive war waged without a mandate of the UNSC and despite the open and strong protests of its three permanent members (France, China and Russia) (*The Guardian* 2003). Secondly, Putin criticised the USA because of its strategic determination to create a unipolar world in which it would become "the sole superpower, one single centre of power, one single centre of force and one single master" (Charbonneau 2007).

Thirdly, the main part of Putin's criticism was reserved for the second wave of the NATO expansion and its global strategic and military consequences. Putin openly and very strongly criticised the US plans to deploy elements of anti-ballistic missile defences in Europe, and the US construction of so-called forward operating bases in Romania and Bulgaria (Fidler and Sevastopulo 2007), two former WTO member countries which had joined the Alliance in the second wave of its eastward expansion. And he concluded with the statement that the US global strategy had had two basic negative consequences for the ISR. The first was that the US strategy undermined the global security, and the second was that the world had become more dangerous because of it. In other words, Putin used this occasion to present a strongly confrontational reaction of his country to the global strategy of the USA.

The historical importance of his speech lies in the fact that he openly declared the Russian categorical refusal of any other NATO expansion into the post-Soviet space, especially into the strategically important area of the Black Sea.

4.1.2 The Five Days War Between the RF and Georgia and Its Consequences

August 2008 witnessed the first decisive and massive military reaction of the Russian operational realists to the second wave of the NATO expansion. This reaction followed the decision of the Bucharest Summit to offer the MAP to two post-Soviet states: Ukraine and Georgia (NATO 2008). The second of these two invited countries became the first to enter into a direct military confrontation with Russia under the presidency of Vladimir Putin.

Georgia is a little country: it contains only 69,700 km^2 and 3,713,804 inhabitants. It represents, together with Armenia and Azerbaijan, an important part of the very complicated and explosive regional security complex (RSC) of the Southern Caucasus (Kuchins and Mankoff 2016). Its explosiveness results from religious and historical factors and also from the fact that Russia perceives it as its buffer zone (Chauprade and Thual 1999). But this fact provokes the strong security fears of Georgia's elites, which have their roots in 1920 when Russian Bolsheviks refused to respect the Treaty from 1920 which guaranteed Georgia's independence, militarily annexed this country and then brutally imposed the Soviet system there.

Just after the implosion of the USSR, the USA did not act in Georgia to any great extent. During the 1990s, Russia, as well as Georgia, went through a decade-long period of turmoil, wild privatisations, and social earthquakes. Nevertheless, the end of this decade saw a rise of Russian security fears which were provoked by the activities of the US oil companies Exxon a Chevron Mobil (Cornell 2017). And these fears were reinforced by the process of political cooperation between Georgia and the USA, which was symbolised by the signing of the military cooperation treaties between the USA and Azerbaijan (1997) and between the USA and Georgia (1998). The US president G. W. Bush tried to calm his Russian partner (Bush 2004) with the argument that new American military bases were necessary for the framework of his GWOT. This argument was accepted by the then-new Russian president Vladimir Putin, which created a hope for a security cooperation between the USA and the RF.

The Russian understanding for the US activities in this part of the post-Soviet region swiftly evaporated with the decision of NATO to offer the MAP to Ukraine and Georgia, which would be the third wave of the post-Cold War expansion. This offer was very disturbing for the Russian operative realists. They perceived it as another extension of the political and military presence of NATO in the strategically important Black Sea area and interpreted it as a new security threat. This perception continued to be reinforced by the growing security cooperation between the USA and Georgia, which passed three important milestones (Maco 2016). The first of them was the visit of President Saakashvili in Washington in 2004, which was followed by the second one, Georgia's participation in OIF 2003. The last one was the above mentioned NATO summit held in Bucharest in 2008, which approved the MAP for Ukraine and Georgia (NATO 2008).

In accordance with R. Keohane (1988), this decision meant that Georgia, together with Ukraine, became another target state (Keohane 1986) in the process of NATO expansion. The offer of the MAP to these two countries opened the way for the following changes of historical importance: another shortening of the distance between the enlarged NATO and Russia, another change in the balance of security threats, installations of new military bases which could raise the offensive strength of the enlarged NATO, and a dramatic change in the perception of security threats in this part of the Black Sea area.

Faced with this situation, the Russian president openly declared that this invitation was perceived by Russia as a direct security threat for it (Mankoff 2009) because the security of states is not based on promises (Tsygankov 2010). His answer was based on the neorealist perception of threats, and particularly on the geographic dimension of the MAP offer for the two important neighbour states. This general declaration was immediately followed by two important measures of Russian operative realists. The first of them was the augmentation of the staff of the Russian peacekeeping units in Abkhazia. And it was followed by a large manoeuvre called "Caucasus 2008" with the participation of the divisions and regiments of the 58th Army, which represents an important part of the North Caucasus Military District (Finn 2008).

A short parenthesis: the debate about the parallels with Czechoslovakia in 1968
The 58th Army units operated near the frontiers of Georgia, and this activity was reminiscent of the "Dunaj" (Danube) manoeuvres of the Soviet armed forces near the northern frontier of Czechoslovakia in summer 1968. This fact provoked a discussion in the Czech Republic. The then Prime Minister Mirek Topolánek (Vláda 2008) made an emotive argument drawing parallels between the two events with the aim to give full support to Georgia, and his attitude was strongly supported by the MFA Karel Schwarzenberg (Týden.cz 2008a). But, on the other hand, the President Vaclav Klaus did not hesitate to openly declare that there was a strong difference between the two cases—it was in the behaviour of the chiefs of the two states that were exposed to the threat of a Soviet or Russian military intervention (Lidovky. cz 2008). While the Czechoslovak leader Alexander Dubček relied only and strictly on political arguments and negotiations in dealing with the Soviet threat in 1968, the Georgian President Saakashvili opted for a direct use of military power in the later case. And Klaus concluded his statement with a categorical refusal of a comparison between the two cases and articulated the following argument: "In 1968, Czechoslovakia did

not invade Carpathian Russia,[1] and the Soviet intervention was not an answer to our attack. Dubček was not Saakashvili" (Týden.cz 2008b).

During the night of 7 August 2008, Saakashvili gave the order to inflict a military attack on Tskhinvali, the capital of South Ossetia. He presented it as an answer to the preceding attacks of the South Ossetia artillery on his country (Nichol 2009). Georgia engaged some brigades of its light infantry, its special forces and one light artillery brigade in the attack (Military Balance 2009, p. 211). During the battles, Saakashvili argued that this military incursion was an unavoidable answer to the Russian support of the South Ossetia separatists (Saakashvili 2008a). And four months later, he used the argument of the presence of thousands of Russian soldiers on the territory of South Ossetia to justify his actions (Saakashvili 2008b).

The decisive importance of the night from the 7th to the 8th of August 2008 was underlined even in the Report of the Independent Commission of the EU, led by Heidi Tagliavini.[2] This report recalled (Tagliavini 2014) many military provocations between the two hostile countries and their mutual military incidents (Traynor 2009). Nevertheless, it identifies the outbreak of the then present war with the operation of the Georgian units against Tskhinvali (BBC 2009) and the surrounding areas (Manchanda 2009) which had been ordered by Saakashvili. He presented himself as being in the role of a tragic hero who nevertheless offered his declared enemy an irresistible opportunity to react with the use of a military force which was much more massive and destructive then that of Georgia.

Today, we know that the Russian military answer was very well prepared thanks to the "Caucasus 2008" manoeuvre, and that it was overwhelming as well as devastative. The most important operations were assumed by the units of the 19th and 42nd Motor Rifle Divisions (Thornton 2011). By their side, the 7th and 76th Airborne Divisions were engaged as well. At the same time, the Black Sea Fleet was engaged with the aim to transport the assault units and block two ports of Georgia (Military Balance 2009, p. 212). It mainly used the vessel Cesar Kunikov in this operation (Felgenhauer 2008; Muchin 2008; Shanker 2008).

From the long-term military perspective, Russia managed to exploit this short war so as to install a new naval base for its Black Sea Fleet in Ochamchire (Simonian 2009a) and it gained a new sea base for its aircraft—the former Soviet airbase in Gudauta in Abkhazia (Simonian 2009b). As a result, this short war made the Russian military presence on Georgian territory as large if not even larger than it was before Russia withdrew from its three remaining military bases in Akhalkalaki, Batumi and Vaziani (Vendil Pallin and Westerlund 2009).

---

[1] Carpathian Russia was the extreme western part of the USSR, which had belonged to Czechoslovakia in the period between 1918 and 1939, which was the golden period of this region. But after the end of WW II it was rendered to the USSR following a request of J. Stalin. Within the framework of the philosophy of Václav Klaus, this fact could hypothetically be used as an argument for a military inclusion comparable with that made by Saakashvili 40 years later.

[2] An excellent Swiss diplomat who is internationally appreciated for her long-term outstanding engagement on the field of international aid and peacekeeping missions. She led the European Union investigation into the causes of the 2008 South Ossetia War, and represented the OSCE in the 2015 negotiations about the Minsk II agreement concerning the war in Donbass.

The Five Days War resulted in an indisputable victory for Russia, but the value of this victory is questionable simply because the Georgian armed forces were too weak, poorly armed, and badly trained. This victory was obtained mainly thanks to Russia's quantitative supremacy. At the same time, this war revealed the qualitative backwardness of the Russian military, namely in comparison with the USA and other member states of NATO. Only one-fifth of the Russian systems satisfied the parameters that a modern military should have, and the rest were obsolete. This was typical especially for the C4ISR systems, which are also called Glonass,[3] and which are much less reliable and efficient in comparison with the US systems of this category (Mukhin 2010). Lastly, such backwardness was typical even for Russia's T-62 and T-72 tanks (Baranets 2009).

4.1.3 Doctrinal Reactions of the Russian Operational Realists

Russian doctrinal reflections of the war with Georgia were articulated at two levels: political and military. The political reflections were articulated three weeks after the end of this war by the Russian president D. Medvedev[4] in his "five points" speech about the foreign and security policy of his country, which received the label "the Medvedev doctrine" Matthews (2008). This doctrine is characterised by a strong emphasis on the role and interests of the Russian state and civilisation (Fedorov 2008). He concretely underlined that all states have the obligation to respect the principles of international law and to build a multipolar, not unipolar, world that would include good relations of the RF with the USA and the EU with the aim to avoid mutual conflicts. This part of the Medvedev speech was motivated by the fears that the USA would not only continue but even intensify and escalate its unilateralism (Neumann 2006).

The most important ideas were declared in points 4 and 5 of the speech. Medvedev declared that the RF would protect the lives and interests of Russians everywhere in the world, especially on the territory of its so-called near abroad (Medvedĕv 2008). By using these words, Medvedev explicitly stated that interventions of other states in this area would be interpreted as a threat to the vital interests of the RF (Friedman 2008). This statement reflected the fact that the Russian victory in the Five Days War reinforced the self-confidence of the Russian operative realists and their determination to protect their interests and influence in the post-Soviet space, even at the price of a military action.

But at the military level, it was not possible to hide the weaknesses of the Russian military. The shortfalls and backwardness of the Russian military led the operative realists in Moscow to a profound doctrinal reflexion. This reflexion was anchored in three important doctrinal documents which will be analysed in-depth in the following

---

[3]*Globalnaya Navigatsionayya Sputnikovaya Sistema* [GLONASS], or, in English, Global Positioning System.

[4]He held the post of the President of the Russian Federation between 7 May 2008 and 7 May 2012.

part of this chapter. The first of them is the Strategy of National Security (SNB) until 2020 (Strategija nacionalnoj bezopasnosti 2009). Sometime later, the other two documents, the Conception of Foreign Policy and the Military Doctrine, were published. All these documents have a common denominator: the statement that the Russian Federation will not hesitate to use military force, even unilaterally, against events which would be perceived as threats for the security of the RF (Eichler and Tichý 2013). Last but not least, all these documents have a clear anti-NATO expansion message. They have been articulated as a strong warning that the RF will not hesitate to use force against another neighbouring post–Soviet country which would obtain NATO membership.

The above mentioned Five Days War as well as the cited doctrinal documents have had a symbolic importance. They came twenty years after the so-called lost decade (the 1990s) and one decade after the introduction of two strategic measures of the Russian operative realists. The first of them was the Russian negative arming. The doctrinal basis of the conception of this long-term strategy was articulated in the Russian governmental arming programme (Klein 2016), which put the main emphasis on the above mentioned A2/AD system.

And the second was that in 2010, only two years after the war with Georgia, the Russian President V. Putin ordered the creation of the Western Military District in St. Petersburg. Since the beginning, this colossal military unit has been armed with all new A2/AD systems that are accessible. These two measures were immediately mirrored in the USA. The Chief of the Department of Defence labelled them as a form of sabre-rattling, and as an aggressive conventional as well as nuclear threat for Russia's Western neighbours (Carter 2016–2017, pp. 55–56).

4.2 Basic Differences Between NATO and the RF After the Second Wave of the NATO Expansion

In the light of the neorealist theory of balancing, the second wave of the NATO expansion accentuated the differences and imbalances between the Russian Federation and NATO (and particularly the USA as its hegemon). The following Table 4.1 shows that these misbalances have been based on seven important criteria: balancing, geography, preferred means, arming, imitation, alliance behaviour, and costs. This comparison explains two key factors: the large international context of the growing tension between the two compared actors of the contemporary ISR, and the big differences in the geopolitical and security positions of NATO and the RF. All these criteria will help us to answer RQ 3 and RQ 4 of this book.

Table 4.1 Differences between NATO and the Russian Federation after the second wave of the NATO expansion

	RF	NATO
Dominant forms of balancing	Exclusively internal balancing	Dominantly external balancing, particularly thanks to the helpfulness of the political élites of the new member states
Geography	Land-power; It would be directly touched by a mutual clash; The RF has more to fear from its close continental competitors (its former satellites, which are currently close allies of the US)	It has the advantage of an insular power which is far from the area of possible military incidents or confrontations.
Preferred military means	Dominantly land forces (70%) + 2 fleets	Dominantly Sea and Air forces
Arming and its concrete measures	Transfers of units, the build-up of new military units, particularly the Western Military District	Transfers of units to the territories of its new allies, which are strongly anti-Russian The build-up of new military bases far away from the USA and as near as possible to the frontiers of the RF
Imitation	New accents articulated in the doctrinal documents Emphasis on A2/AD systems near the Western and South-Western borders of the RF	The USA does not need to imitate other countries; it can rely on its 3 strategic advantages: • A high GDP as well as a high GDP per capita, • An innovative culture, and scientific as well as technological superiority, • Strategic and military experiences from the wars waged from 1991 until today (ODS 1991, OAF 1999, OEF 2001, OIF 2003)
Alliance behaviour	In this area, the RF operates by itself, without allies	The USA can exploit the large military as well as political potential of its new client states (especially Poland and the three Baltic States)
Costs	The competition with the USA and its allies is increasingly expensive for the RF	The competition is much less expensive for the USA than for the RF

4.2.1 External vs. Internal Balancing

The most important factor of the NATO expansion between 1990 and 2002, including the absorption of the former DDR, concerns the geography involved. In total, the new NATO members at this time represented 1,2 million km^2 with more than 120 million inhabitants.[5] In the light of geopolitics and military strategy, the NATO Expansion is a zero sum game which includes an enormously large and deep buffer zone or a strategic depth which plays a vital role in every war as well as in times of peace. And in the light of modern history, we cannot forget the fact that this enormous space of strategic depth played a decisive role on the Eastern Front during WW II.

Far behind the geopolitical importance of the area of the then new member states is its economic strength. After the second wave, their military budgets rose about 20 billion USD, which represented about 28% of the military budget of the RF, less than one third of the military budget of the United Kingdom, less than one half of the military budget of Germany, and only 3% of the military budget of the USA. In other words, the military budgets of the then new NATO member countries did not play any important role. At the same time, their resources of oil and gas are relatively modest and strategically unimportant. For example, Romania has 600,000,000 barrels of oil (out of all the countries in the world, it is the 44th in this respect), but with a daily production of 96,470 barrels and a daily consumption of 200,000, it has a daily deficit of 103,530 barrels.

From the neorealist point of view, the geopolitics and namely the immensity of the strategic depth are the basic factor of the second wave member countries of NATO. There is also the basic pillar of the external balancing. Within its framework, the shortening of the distance between NATO and Russia's Western frontier plays an important role. Lastly, the territory of these member countries offers the possibility to use their military bases for the operations of land, air and navy forces. This possibility has its strategic importance particularly in the cases of Poland, the Baltic States, Bulgaria and Romania with their almost 850,000 km^2.

4.2.2 Virulent Reproaches of Two Presidents

Since the decision of the second wave of the NATO expansion, Russian operative realists perceived the new international order as a result of the so-called asymmetrical end of the Cold War (Sakwa 2015). Their profound disillusionment was articulated in two important speeches that were cited all over the world. The first of them was

---

[5]The DDR had 108,000 km^2 with 20 million inhabitants, the Czech Republic 79,000 km^2 with more than 10.6 million inhabitants, Poland 313,000 km^2 with 39 million inhabitants, Hungary 93,000 km^2 with 10 million inhabitants, Lithuania 65,000 km^2 with 2.8 million inhabitants, Latvia 64,500 km^2 with 2 million inhabitants, Estonia 45,300 km^2 with 1.3 million inhabitants, Slovakia 49,000 km^2 with 5.5 million inhabitants, Slovenia 20,200 km^2 with 2 million inhabitants, Bulgaria 111,000 km^2 with 7 million inhabitants, and Romania 240,000 km^2 with 20 million inhabitants.

Table 4.2 Critical arguments of Russian political elites

Putin	Gorbachev
The triumphalism of the USA	The triumphalism of the USA
Unilateralism	Unilateralism
The US withdrawal from the ABM Treaty	The US withdrawal from the ABM Treaty
Destruction of the strategic parity The US/NATO's active support of the so-called colour revolutions The US/NATO political interventions in Ukraine The abuse of the framework of the Global War on Terror for military interventions	Destruction of the strategic parity

Putin's speech in Valdai on 18 March 2014, pronounced just after the annexation of the Crimea. The second was given by M. S. Gorbachev on 14 November 2014, on the occasion of the 25th anniversary of the fall of the Berlin Wall (Shakarian 2014). Sometime later, the last Soviet president developed and deepened his key arguments in an article published in France (Gorbachev 2015). The basic points of the two speeches are presented in the following Table 4.2.

The speeches of the former President of the USSR and the second President of the Russian Federation were based on a very critical evaluation of the security behaviour of the USA after the end of the Cold War and they had some important common denominators. First, Mikhail Gorbachev as well as Vladimir Putin strongly criticised the triumphalism as well as the unilateralism of the administrations of B. Clinton and his successor G. W. Bush. According to them, these two phenomena had been manifested by the eastward expansion of NATO, especially by its second wave, after which NATO was present even on an important parts of the post-Soviet space. Second, they clearly disapproved of the American withdrawal from the ABM Treaty, which was signed by the USA and the USSR in 1972. This crucial decision of the 43rd President of the USA provoked the Russian fears of a complete implosion of the heritage of the complex system of arms control in the nuclear field. These fears were underlined especially in Putin's speech in Munich. And the third common denominator of their criticism was pointing to the destruction of the strategic parity in favour of the USA.

As Vladimir Putin represented a much more influential politician than Gorbachev, it is necessary to underline that his Valdai speech has been much more critical and offensive to the West than the attitudes of the last president of the USSR. Putin openly criticised the behaviour of the so-called 'winners' in the Cold War for their tendency to put pressure on events, reshape the world to suit their own needs and interests and present their view as the view of the entire international community. At the same time, he did not hesitate to use an allusion to the domination of the post-Cold War world by one country and its allies, or its satellites rather, and he argued that the search for global solutions often turned into an attempt to impose their own "universal" recipes. There is no doubt that these arrows were aimed at the USA and its supporters within NATO. Furthermore, he criticised the escalation of international conflicts, the growing spread of chaos and the drawing of new dividing lines. It was a frontal criticism of the USA as a leading state of NATO.

Lastly, a very important part of Putin's criticism was aimed at the behaviour of his American counterpart. He particularly mentioned the abuse of the atmosphere of the Global War on Terror as a framework for arbitrary military interventions in the Islamic word and overthrows of hostile regimes. Before his speech in Munich, a long range of negative consequences of wars in Afghanistan and Iraq were very well known over all the world. This context offered to Putin an irresistible opportunity to condemn the US and NATO for their military activities leading to human victims, immense human suffering and damages for the next generations. In comparison with his Munich speech, in his Valdai speech Putin enlarged the list of his reproaches directed toward the USA. These reproaches concerned three concrete engagements of the USA: its active support of the so-called colour revolutions in the post-Soviet space, its large political support of the anti-Russian nationalist movements in Ukraine, and, much more importantly, its abuse of the framework of the Global War on Terror for military interventions in and long-term occupations of strategically important countries in the Islamic world.

Russia's profound criticism was based on the canons of the neorealist school of thought. It was articulated in the form of two categorical phenomena which reflected the principle of the zero sum game. Two presidents, each of them in his own words, reproached NATO for its post-Cold War triumphalism accompanied by an open and ostensible disrespect for the Russian security interests. At the same time, they condemned NATO's expansion in the post-Soviet area, which had been obtained at the price of a continued pushing of Russia to the East. Furthermore, they criticised the enlargement of the Black Sea coastline controlled by NATO, which had been paid for by a dramatic diminution of the coastline controlled by the RF. Their fourth reproach condemned the movement of NATO infrastructure directly towards the Russian borders, which contrasts with the continuing expulsion of Russia from its former border areas. Lastly, these reproaches are summarised by the conclusion that NATO and especially the USA as its hegemon profited from the profound post-Cold War changes to impose its growing control on the immense former zone of influence of the USSR area with all its resources, which is in a big contrast with the substantial decrease of the Russian presence and control in this area.

4.2.3 The Annexation of the Crimean Peninsula and Its Consequences

Since the dismantlement of the former Soviet Union, Russian political and military elites continued to underline the geopolitical importance of Ukraine as a necessary buffer zone which should be a no-go zone, especially for the expanding NATO (Allison 2006). Accordingly, the territory of the Crimean peninsula continued to be presented as a vitally important area. First, it provides excellent possibilities for the projection of military power for anybody who controls it. Second, from the Russian security point of view, it is invaluable for the defence of its Southern border (Melvin 2014, pp. 70–76).

There is no doubt that the Yanukovych regime[6] was enormously kleptomaniacal, authoritarian, arbitrary, and revengeful. Nevertheless, in the light of the neorealist school of thought, its overthrow in late February 2014 provoked a panic and a worst-case scenario thinking in Moscow. The decision making of the Russian operative realists confirmed the value of the neorealist canon that the regime type plays only a secondary role, while the primordial role is reserved for geopolitics, namely for the position of every state in the structure of the ISR. In the spring of 2014, the military seizure of Crimea became a primordial strategic option for Moscow, and this decision was, since the beginning, conceived as a signalisation of its determination to actively oppose any further NATO military engagement in Ukraine, indeed in all of the post-Soviet space.

Crimea as a clash of two hybrid wars?
The aim of this section is not to describe the surprising and enormously swift annexation of the Crimean peninsula in March 2014. There is a long range of monographs and articles consecrated to this subject. In the light of all four RQs of this book, especially RQ 4 (What are the consequences of NATO expansion in the post-Soviet space?) this section only recalls that the Russian operative realists came forth with their vision of two hybrid wars. According to Lavrov, the first of these wars had the form of a long-term and systematic Western (namely American) support of the so-called "colour revolutions" in the post-Soviet area (Lavrov 2007). And the seizure of Crimea was presented as a Russian reaction to it. In other words, we were witnessing a clash of two irreconcilable antagonistic narratives (Neumann 2016) that resulted in a military form (Persson 2016, pp. 194–195).

The historic and strategic importance of the Crimean Peninsula is based on the role of the town of Sevastopol, a colossal naval base with a typical military architecture and an enormously strict military discipline. This town played a pivotal role in the security of Russia, the USSR (especially during WW II) and the contemporary RF. No wonder that the leading British military historian Mungo Melvin underlines that from Potemkin to Putin, Russia has demonstrated an implacable resolve to hold this strategic town (Melvin 2014, pp. 70–76). And he continues by stating that the history of this town, strongly marked by many invasions of other powers during the preceding centuries, strongly influenced the decision making process of the leading Russian operative realists, who feared that Sevastopol might become a NATO base (Melvin 2017). After the decision of the Bucharest summit of NATO, these fears took the form of a panic and an obsessive security complex. The Russians feared that in case of a continuing NATO expansion, their country would be confronted with a seizure of the Sevastopol naval base by the USA and its allies. For the Russian military and political élites, such a scenario was absolutely unacceptable.

---

[6] Viktor Yanukovych was the Prime Minister of Ukraine between 4 August 2006 and 18 December 2007, and the President of Ukraine between 25 February 2010 and 22 February 2014.

The Russian annexation of the Crimea and Russia's support of the self-proclaimed military leaders of the Eastern Ukrainian separatists, has generally been defined as a "hybrid, ambiguous, or non-linear warfare" (Hybrid Warfare 2015, p. 17). Here, it is necessary to remember that until today, we have had no universally accepted definition of hybrid warfare, but it is commonly described as a war against a non-standard, complex, and fluid adversary (Fleming 2011). Every hybrid war has three fundamental elements (Hybrid Warfare 2015, p. 18). First, the use of conventional as well as unconventional forces is combined with information operations whose aim is to intimidate. Second, attacks of military units are accompanied by cyber-attacks. Lastly, new political structures are established with the aim to consolidate gains and prevent reversals. And the Russian version of hybrid warfare in 2014 has been defined as a quick mobilisation of military forces with the aim to intimidate the target nation while the attacker shields its own forces that are employed on the foreign territory (Hybrid Warfare 2015, p. 19). No wonder that in the USA, the Russian hybrid warfare was, since the beginning, perceived as a manifestation of the Russian determination to escalate the security competition with the West (Schadlow 2014).

Key motives of the annexation of Crimea
The seizure of Crimea was motivated not only by the losing of the Black Sea Fleet base, but also by a desire to coerce Kiev into accommodating broader Russian demands (Military Balance 2015, p. 169). From the military point of view, it was preceded by the deployment of the so-called local self-defence forces, which took control of the parliament building in Simferopol. They were composed of unidentified, but nevertheless very professional and highly trained Russian military units. They even managed to block the runway of the Balbek Air Base (near the navy base of Sevastopol), eliminate its Mig 29 combat aircraft and swiftly disarm the Ukrainian soldiers there. It is without a doubt that this whole operation was illegal, but on the other hand, the so-called little green men achieved all the fixed objectives without bloodshed, and without any victims. Their engagement opened the way towards the organisation of the plebiscite held under their control on 16 March, which was followed by the annexation of the Crimean peninsula on 21 March 2014.

In its hybrid war, Russia has been using all accessible economic, political, diplomatic, and military means, and its operative realists mobilised enormously large and assertive informational and propagandistic campaigns, electronic and cyber instruments, and forms of psychological pressure (Galeotti 2019). In the military field, the Russians particularly used special forces, open as well as covert engagements of their military force, non-contact war, a low level of fighting, controlled escalation, and practices intended to cause the destruction of the adversary's will and determination to fight (Berzins 2014). Lastly, eastern Ukraine became a victim of a non-standard hybrid war waged by a strong state actor against a weak state actor.

Even from the military point of view, the annexation of the whole peninsula of Crimea became the answer of the Russian operative realists. First, this operation was carried out as a surprising covert deployment of Russia's special forces, which swiftly took control of the key points on the peninsula, disarmed the Ukrainian forces, and seized objects of strategic importance. Second, the Russian leadership switched between the utilisation of covert and open operations, and deployment of armed forces according to then-current needs. Third, there was an emphasis on the so-called non-contact warfare; both sides to the conflict attempted to marginalise direct violence and control its potential escalation as much as possible. Fourth, a new military method evolved, whose goals were the subversion of the enemy and the weakening of his morale and resistance rather than his direct destruction (Berzins 2014).

The Russian hybrid warfare had an enormously important informational dimension. It was devised as a usage of subversive measures aimed at triggering a feeling of defeat on two main fronts. One of its goals was to persuade the Crimean public that it should not fear a Russian occupation. At the same time, however, there was a "hidden message" for the people in it—that any potential resistance would be futile and counterproductive, as it would only lead to significant losses and damage (Thornton 2015). The informational war has had an important scope and therefore the main emphasis was placed on the quantity and intensity of the broadcasted information (Pomerantsev and Weiss 2014) while its quality and veracity were only secondary factors (Pomerantsev 2014).

Doctrinal reflections
Despite the successful military annexation of the Crimean peninsula and indirect backing of self-declared combatants in Eastern Ukraine, Russian operative realists did not succumb to the temptation of triumphalism. It was absolutely clear that the units of the so-called little green men had been assembled from members of the absolutely best Russian units while the combat readiness of the majority of the Russian armed forces had been far behind them. These facts have been mirrored in the diction of the updated military doctrine from December 2014 (Military Doctrine of the Russian Federation 2015), which confirmed that the deeply rooted security fears continued to play the decisive role. These fears have been articulated in the following order: the fear of the strengthening of global military competitions, that of the build-up of NATO's military capabilities, that of the process of bringing the military infrastructure of NATO member countries near the borders of the Russian Federation (Military Balance 2016, p. 164), that of regime changes and that of big military exercises of foreign forces in the neighbourhood of the RF.

On the level of geopolitics, these fears had been generated by the profound changes in two post–Soviet countries: Ukraine and Georgia. And on the military level, a particular attention of this doctrine has been paid to the threat posed by the PGS (Prompt Global Strike) systems. This category includes the arms systems with the capability to deliver a precision-guided conventional weapon airstrike anywhere in the world within one hour, in a similar manner to a nuclear ICBM (Grossman 2006). These systems represent an impressive advantage of the USA (gained particularly thanks to its RMA—Revolution in Military Affairs) and its allies. At the same time, they are one of the most acute symbols of the Russian backwardness in the field of military technology.

A new security dilemma, a new vicious circle

The official Russian argumentation for the seizure of Crimea has been articulated in Putin's 45 min long speech addressed to both chambers of the Federal Assembly of the Russian Federation in the Kremlin on 18 March 2014 (Putin 2014). This speech presented a doctrinal framework concerning not only this historically and strategically important peninsula and the potential NATO expansion to it, but also any other expansions of NATO in the post-Soviet space. First, Putin did not avoid the suffering of Crimean Tatars in his speech, but he recalled the following complete rehabilitation of this nation. Second, he remembered that a significant amount of the historical Russian southern land was transferred to the Ukrainian SSR in 1954, and that this decision was made by the Bolsheviks without taking into account the national composition of its population. Third, he emphasised that the decision[7] was taken in violation of constitutional norms, behind the scenes, and in a totalitarian state. At the same time, he condemned the West's reaction to the 2014 annexation and the following sanctions, and concluded by reproaching the West by arguing that in 1989, the USSR supported the Germans' sincere desire for national unity.

It is no surprise that Putin's speech provoked enormously critical reactions. Hillary Clinton, the former US Secretary of State, made a parallel with the German annexation of the Sudeten part of Czechoslovakia in 1938 (Clinton 2014a) and did not hesitate to compare Vladimir Putin to Adolf Hitler (Clinton 2014b). This argumentation was immediately repeated by various important American politicians and journalists (Burns 2014). And Barack Obama underlined in his speech on March 26, 2014 that the historical relations between Ukraine and Russia did not give Russia the right to dictate Ukraine's future (Obama 2014).

In summary, Putin manifested the determination of the Russian operative realists to hold the Crimean peninsula forever, even at the price of a military action. From the neorealist point of view, his message was very clear: the RF will allow no other shortening of the distance between the armed forces of NATO (as an active actor) on one hand and its own forces (as a passive actor) on the other, and it will actively resist any other military expansion which is perceived by it as a greedy security behaviour (regardless of the distinction between Russian suspicions based on security fears, and the real intentions of the USA and its allies in this space). And the following categorically negative reactions from the US resulted in a new degree of the bipolar confrontation.

From the geopolitical point of view, the Russian operative realists had unilaterally redrawn Russia's frontiers with Ukraine and presented it as a reaction to the challenge represented by the continuing NATO expansion into the post-Soviet space. And the following US-led sanctions were presented as a necessary answer to the challenge represented by the Russian action. As a result, Europe became the theatre of a new and very dangerous security dilemma and of the beginning of a new vicious circle of measures and counter-measures.

---

[7]The political annexation of the Crimea to the Ukrainian SSR was decided upon and imposed by Nikita Khrushchev during his reign as the General Secretary of the Communist Party of the Soviet Union.

Western reactions to the annexation of Crimea

At the global level, the Russian annexation of Crimea in 2014 was condemned by the Resolution of the General Assembly of the UN which was approved on 27 April 2014. Its text, titled "Territorial Integrity of Ukraine", was approved by a vote of 100 in favour to 11 against, with 58 abstentions, by the Assembly. It called on states, international organisations and specialised agencies not to recognise any change in the status of Crimea or the Black Sea port city of Sevastopol, and to refrain from actions or dealings that might be interpreted as such (UN 2014). An enormously critical condemnation of the annexation was approved by the summit of NATO in Wales (September 2014)—it used the expression "breach of international peace and security" in connection with this event (NATO 2014a).

Sometime later, France and the USA started to coordinate their efforts within the framework of the so-called Normand format, concretely within the context of the Minsk-1 and Minsk-2 agreements (from 5 September 2014 and 12 February 2015, respectively). A much more radical attitude was formulated by Lech Walesa, the former president of Poland, who surprised the entire world with his declaration that it was necessary that his country deploy nuclear arms on its territory.

No wonder that the annexation of the Crimea and the support for the separatists in eastern Ukraine provoked a lot of resolute criticism and condemnations. Since the annexation of the Crimea, Putin has been presented as a wrecker of the established international order (Conradi 2018). Critical attitudes towards the annexation were also presented by the General Secretary of NATO (North Atlantic Treaty Organization 2014a), and the Alliance's answer was expressed in the Readiness Action Plan (RAP) and a long-term operation with the participation of the Very High Readiness Joint Task Forces.

The Ukraine Support Act (H.R. 4278) from March 2014 defined a framework for the resulting political and economic sanctions against Russia and for concrete financial help for Ukraine (Ukraine Support 2014). And the Ukraine Freedom Support Act (UFSA) of 2014 (113th Congress 2014) underlined the importance of freedom as a fundamental value in the conflict (Ukraine Freedom Support Act 2014). Furthermore, the US Minister of Defence Ashton Carter and General Martin Dempsey underlined their "absolute support for the deliveries of lethal arms to Ukraine". And last, but not least, a large manoeuvre organised by General Philip Breedlove (SACEUR) became a NATO military answer to the growing militarisation of Crimea (particularly the deployment of new Russian military units with their systems of arms there).

The above mentioned American documents have three important common denominators. First, there was a large economic support of Ukraine which was accompanied by hard economic and commercial sanctions against the RF. Secondly, the support of Ukraine even had its military dimension, though of course it was a non-lethal assistance provided to the government of Ukraine. Nevertheless, this direct engagement of the US was immediately followed by the mirror measures of Russian operative realists, namely the support of the pro-Russian separatists operating in Eastern Ukraine.[8] They have received an intense support, both indirect and direct, from the Russian political and military leaders, whose basic motivation is a desire to destabilise Ukraine (Bowen 2017). Lastly and the most importantly, this part of Eastern Europe witnessed a growing militarisation of an enormously long (2,063 km, including 1,974.04 km by land and 321 km by sea) frontier between Ukraine and Russia. The post-Soviet space "received" a new dividing line which is extraordinarily confrontational and explosive.

After the Crimea annexation, all the discretion and tactfulness which had been typical for the US doctrinal documents was forgotten. All the leading US operational realists condemned this act in a very categorical manner. They started to openly mention the RF as a serious and imminent security threat for the USA and its allies. The Chairman of the Joint Chiefs of Staff (CJCS) described the Russian Federation as an "existential threat for the USA, their allies and [the] international order" (Ferdinando 2016) And his political chief, the Secretary of Defence, did not hesitate to underline the government's determination to "ensure the United States can deter, and if necessary win, a high-end conventional fight." In contrast to the doctrinal documents, he directly mentioned Russia as a military threat which must be countered by the new generation of arms systems (Carter 2016–2017, p. 58). This approach profoundly influenced the navy manoeuvres of NATO member countries (Giuliani 2015).

Concrete US measures after the Crimea annexation
The year 2014 started a strategic shift in the relations between the USA and the RF (Rynning 2015). The USA and its allies decided to increase their military presence and visibility in the post-Soviet space from the Baltic to the Red Sea. This increased presence is visible on three important levels. *At the top political level*, the Allies suspended all cooperation with the RF within the framework of the NATO-Russia Council (NRC), which was established at the NATO-Russia Summit in Rome on 28 May 2002 by the Declaration on "NATO-Russia Relations: a New Quality" (NATO 2002). The NRC replaced the Permanent Joint Council (PJC), a forum for consultation and cooperation created by the 1997 NATO-Russia Founding Act. Since the beginning, the NRC assumed the role of a mechanism for consultation, consensus-building, cooperation, joint decision-making and joint action. But in April 2014, in reaction to Russia's illegal military intervention in Ukraine and its violation of Ukraine's sovereignty and territorial integrity, NATO took the decision to stop all practical cooperation between itself and Russia, including the cooperation within the framework of the NRC.

At the doctrinal level, the response of the Alliance was articulated in two key decisions approved with the aim to augment the level of its ambitions related to

---
[8]The separatist movement includes a long range of self–proclaimed commanders of battalions, deputies and ministers.

the Eastern frontier. First, during the 2014 Wales Summit NATO, the leaders of the Alliance approved the decision to create the Very High Readiness Joint Task Force (VJTF) (SHAPE NATO), a high-readiness "Spearhead Force" able to be deployed with the aim to face threats that could menace the NATO sovereignty (NATO 2015a). At the same time, it was decided that this force would consist of a land brigade numbering around 5,000 troops, and that, in case of battle operations, this force would be supported by air, sea and special forces. In case of a major crisis, the VJTF would be supported by two more land brigades as a "rapid reinforcement capability". Altogether, the enhanced NATO Response Force could amount to around 30,000 troops (NATO 2015b).

Second, NATO approved the Readiness Action Plan, which is based on the following important measures: the deployment of four multinational battalions to Latvia, Lithuania, Estonia and Poland, and the enlargement of the existing NATO Response Force (NRF) (SHAPE NATO), which has been created in 2002 as a technologically advanced, multinational force made up of land, air, maritime and special operations forces components, which are rapidly deployable. This force is able to provide collective defence and a rapid military response in case of an emerging crisis. In addition, it can perform peace-support operations, provide protection to critical infrastructure and support disaster relief.

This force counts 13,000 personnel, which are members of a brigade of five manoeuvre battalions with air, sea and special-operations support. The numbers of the NRF could, at best, rise to a level of 40,000 personnel, including supportive elements, as well as a command structure (Bialos and Koehl 2012). At the same time, a decision was made to augment the readiness of the Very High Readiness Joint Task Force (VJTF) by around 5,000 troops, significantly increase the size and number of exercises, pre-position equipment in the Baltics and Eastern Europe, establish small headquarters in Baltic and Eastern European states, and accelerate the decision-making for the Response Force (Brooke-Holand 2016).

At the operational level, NATO took the decision to enhance its presence in the eastern part of its territory, with four multinational battle groups in Estonia, Latvia, Lithuania and Poland (NATO 2019). These four forward-deployed battalion-sized battle groups are multinational and trained with the aim to satisfy the criteria of combat-readiness and a credible demonstration of their military strength. They are led the United by Kingdom, Canada, Germany and the United States, and with the participating states, they represent the Enhanced Forward Presence (EFP), whose mission is to strengthen the Connecting Forces Initiative. Their key mission is to protect and reassure NATO's Central and Northern European member states on NATO's eastern flank, and to ensure their security in the new geopolitical situation.

Enormously important is the fact that each of these battle groups includes soldiers from other member states of NATO. It concretely means that in the battle group in Estonia, which is led by the United Kingdom, soldiers from Denmark and Iceland are trained. The battle group in Latvia, led by Canada, includes soldiers from Albania, the Czech Republic, Italy, Montenegro, Poland, Slovakia, Slovenia, and Spain. The Lithuanian battle group, which is led by Germany, is composed of soldiers from Belgium, Croatia, the Czech Republic, Iceland, Luxembourg, the Netherlands, and

Norway. And, lastly, the battle group in Poland, the largest new member country, is led by the United States and coordinates the training of soldiers from Croatia, Romania, and the United Kingdom.

As a result, at the Eastern frontier of the recently expanded NATO, soldiers from 19 participating Alliance countries are deployed and trained. Of course, their numbers and their armaments are far more modest in comparison with the period of the Cold War, particularly when considering the number of Soviet soldiers on the territory of these 4 states—3 former member states of the USSR and Poland as a former satellite state of the POW—in the Cold War era. Nevertheless, their presence and their military training (especially in the case of the USA, Canada and the "old states of NATO") is a factor of the rising military tension on the frontier between the RF and NATO.

The existence of the Western military circuit of Russian forces in St. Petersburg on the one hand, the concentration of military units of the USA and its allies on the other and their activities result in a dangerous rise of military tension on the Eastern flank of NATO and high numbers of military incidents.

4.2.4 Russian Doctrinal Documents Approved After the Annexation of Crimea

The Russian security fears and feelings of humiliation were articulated not only in speeches but also on the pages of two doctrinal documents published during the last decade. The following Table 4.3 presents the key ideas and arguments of these documents. In them, the expansion of NATO is evaluated as a threat for the national security of the RF, which requires the strengthening of all instruments of the Russian deterrent, including a massive build-up of the conventional forces at the Western frontier of the RF.

Table 4.3 Russian doctrinal documents published after the outbreak of the war in/over Ukraine

Doctrinal document	Key ideas
The National Security Strategy of the RF (2015)	Expansion of NATO is a threat to the national security of the RF; The strategic deterrent; Modernisation and reorganisation of Russian armed forces
The Foreign Policy Strategy of the RF (2016)	*Priorities of the FP of the RF*: To actively face the American political interventions' destabilisation of the post-Soviet space; To eliminate the resulting augmentation of the threat of nuclear war; To assert the national interests of the RF in the post-Soviet space itself, including Ukraine

4.3 The Academic Debate After the Annexation of the Crimea

Since its beginning, the process of NATO expansion and particularly its consequences have become the subject of a largely academic debate. This debate is very intensive and confrontational, but it especially became so after the Russian annexation of Crimea. In this sub-chapter, the most well-known authors in the debate will be divided into three groups: those with strongly critical attitudes, those with non-critical attitudes, and those with impartial attitudes.

4.3.1 The Strongly Critical Authors

The first group includes the authors with strongly critical attitudes toward Russia and its behaviour in Ukraine. These authors articulated two sets of arguments: the political and military ones.

a. *Political arguments*

One of the most respected authors of this group, Walter Russell Mead (Mead 2014), argued that the Crimean annexation signified a return of an unscrupulous and highly cynical geopolitics which could lead to a complete change of the international order. He labelled Russia as one of the revisionist countries (together with Iran and China) and concluded that Vladimir Putin humiliated President Obama with his unilateral and power-based political decision and that he destroyed the whole philosophy of the "reset" formed by the Prague Treaty of 2010.

Mead's argument was deepened by another leading American author, Michael McFaul, a Professor of Political Sciences and the Ambassador of the USA to the RF between 2012 and 2014, who was especially critical toward Putin's unilateralism, which, according to him, strengthened the internal unity of the Northern Alliance, weakened the Russian economy, and damaged Putin's international reputation (McFaul et al. 2014). Sometime later, McFaul strongly condemned the Russian president for his cynical political style which led him to a serious error in the form of the annexation of Crimea (McFaul 2018).

Nevertheless, such critical attitudes were typical not only for the American authors, but also for a lot of their European colleagues. First of all, it is necessary to remember Roy Allison from Oxford University, who brilliantly argued (Gehring et al. 2017) that the Russian intervention in Crimea and Eastern Ukraine represents a frontal challenge to the post-Cold War European regional order with long-term negative impacts (Allison 2014). Nevertheless, he confirmed the military value of Crimea as an ideal platform for power projection into the Black Sea region and beyond. Two other famous British authors (MacFarlane and Menon 2014), Neil MacFarlane and Anand Menon, concluded that the annexation of the Crimea represented the most dangerous security crisis in Europe after the end of the Cold War (MacFarlane and Menon 2014). And in relation to the annexation, Lawrence Freedman (2014) remembered the grave demographic problems of Russia: its chronic corruption, technological backwardness, and dependency on the exportation of raw materials; and the large discrediting of its political elites.

b. *Military arguments*

Matthew Kroenig from Georgetown University articulated three radical propositions in connection with this matter: a hard-line policy towards the RF, reinforcement of NATO military units in Eastern Europe and a growing emphasis on nuclear weapons and the nuclear deterrent of Russia (Kroenig 2015). And Kroenig's emphasis on a military answer to Putin's policy was shared by Ashton Carter (the US Secretary of Defence in the period between 2015 and 2017), who did not hesitate to present the RF as an imminent security threat for the new allies of the USA (namely for the Baltic states). And he concluded that after Crimea, the aim of his country is not only to deter but also, if necessary, to win a conventional fight with Russia (Carter 2017, p. 58).

Moreover, Carter's article represented an important move from a deterrent to the possibility of a direct confrontation that could happen not only on land but also on the sea, in the air, in space and in cyberspace. His argumentation had a strong neorealist dimension: it reflected the emphasis on the reinforcement of the American military presence in the post-Soviet space. As a result, it confirmed the productive consequences of the annexation of Crimea; it was followed by the return of American war scenarios whose aim is to transfer, as soon as possible, the fights in the territory of the RF.

Carter's arguments were not only discussed by academicians, but they became the key inspiration for the political élites of the USA. They were shared and cited even by Vice President Joseph Biden, who did not hesitate to label Russia as an authoritarian kleptomaniac regime which is aggressive towards its neighbours, develops its subversive operations, and supports the extreme right parties in European countries. Moreover, Biden fully shared the belief that the US and its allies must deter and, if necessary, defeat Russia in case it attacks any NATO member country (Biden and Carpenter 2018).

All the above-mentioned critical authors reproached Putin for the following key faults: unilateralism, disrespect for international law, militarism, aggressiveness, and the negative and counterproductive consequences of his actions for the international security relations 25 years after the end of the Cold War.

4.3.2 The Non-Critical Authors

On the other hand, many Western authors articulated much less critical attitudes towards Russia. Moreover, some of them did not hesitate to express some understanding of the Russian security fears provoked by the process of the expansion of NATO.

The North American discussion
In the USA, in 1993 Kenneth Waltz, the founder of neorealism, recommended that the USA avoid the temptations of isolationism. Nevertheless, he added that after the end of the bipolar confrontation, the importance and the role of NATO should permanently decrease. And sometime later, after the first round of NATO enlargement, he added that in case of its continuing expansion, NATO would act with the aim to fully satisfy the wishes of the USA as the key winner of the Cold War (Waltz 2000, p. 35).

At the same time, he warned of three possible counter-productive impacts of the end of the bipolar world order: an international imbalance, an enormous dominance of the USA and growing costs of the NATO enlargement. With his typical emphasis on the geographic dimension of the security threats, he warned that the new member countries would require the security guaranties of the USA, which would lead to the growing engagement of the USA and its old allies in the instability and conflict potential east of their frontiers.

And in the conclusion, K. Waltz did not hesitate to pose a disturbing hypothetical question: What would be the reaction of the USA if the USSR won the Cold War and then expanded into Central America while justifying it with the necessity to expand the area of stability (Waltz 2000, pp. 31–32)? Finally, Waltz warned of the risk that NATO expansion could provoke a growing security cooperation between Russia and China, which would be perceived as a security threat by India, an enormously important actor of ISR at the global level.

Stephen Walt, the second most important and often cited American neorealist, criticised the deterrent model of the US behaviour towards the RF by arguing that Russia is not a rising power but a declining one (Walt 2015). At the same time, he clearly refused the idea to arm Kyiv with the argument that such a strategy would certainly reinforce the spiral model between the USA and the RF, with all the expected negative consequences for all of Europe, including Ukraine (Parry 2019). He thus recommends abandoning the dangerous and unnecessary goal of endless NATO expansion and changing Ukraine into a neutral buffer state (Walt 2015).

John Mearsheimer (Mearsheimer 2014), another American neo-realist, reproached Washington's elites for their refusal to understand the Russian security fears provoked by the NATO expansion in the post-Soviet space, particularly in the case of Ukraine, which represents Russia's doorstep. In full accordance with H. Kissinger, he recommends the transformation of this country into a neutral state that would not threaten Russia and thus allow the West to repair its relations with Moscow.

Almost the same arguments have been used even by some American liberals; for example, such arguments were made by Daniel Deudney and G. John Ikenberry

(2009–2010). In their common analysis, they recounted the historically unprecedented geopolitical retrenchment of the former Soviet empire made by M. Gorbachev and criticised the disdain of the American elites when they stood face to face with the security fears and phobia of encirclement and encroachment which were shared by Gorbachev's Russian followers (Ikenberry 2014).

The neorealist arguments are shared by Michael O'Hanlon, another very important American author. He warns in the diagnostic part of his 2017 analysis that the relations between the USA and the RF are in a dangerous state. He openly writes that NATO expansion is the key cause of this disturbing state. And in the therapeutic part of his text, he recommends a disavowal of NATO's 2008 public promises to Ukraine and Georgia that they would someday be invited into the Alliance. He does not hide that such a step could give Putin some degree of vindication, but he underlines that it would be a far less injurious outcome than running an unnecessarily heightened risk of war (O'Hanlon 2017).

The strategy of NATO expansion was criticised even by *Michael Brenner*, a professor of international relations at the University of Pittsburgh, and the author of an often cited book about the history of NATO (Brenner 1998). He writes that all the contemporary problems in this area result from the fact that the American elites were convinced that Russia would never surpass its decline of the Yeltsin decade, but its renewal under Putin provokes a strong nostalgia accompanied by a high decibel hysteria in the USA (Brenner 2016). Lastly, an open understanding for the Russian behaviour was demonstrated by *Julian Lindley French*. After a profound analysis of the international and historical context of the Crimea annexation, this author concluded that Russia's invasion of Crimea was an inherently defensive operation (Lindley French 2014) which was conceived as an answer to the process of NATO expansion.

The West European discussion
In Western Europe, a non-critical approach to the Crimea annexation was expressed particularly by General Mungo Melvin, the president of the Association of Military Historians of Great Britain. He underlined that Crimea and, particularly, the military port of Sevastopol have no parallel in Europe as far as placement, depth and strategic importance are concerned. He argued that Sevastopol is not a simple military base, but, above all, a bastion of vital importance for the defence of the entire Russian territory. Moreover, Melvin did not hesitate to compare the town of Sevastopol with Norfolk in the USA and Portsmouth in Great Britain in this respect (Melvin 2017).

And he continued by remembering the first separation of the Crimean Republic from Ukraine in 1992, which had been fully ignored by Kyiv even though this separation had been approved by the Supreme Council of the Crimean Republic. And Melvin concluded that in the light of modern history, Russia did not conquer Crimea, but simply absorbed it (Melvin 2014) by a non-lethal action which happened without victims, which is in huge contrast with the long wars in the Islamic world, namely in Afghanistan and Iraq. His rational, non-emotional and non-ideological argumentation attracted a large worldwide attention (Kent 2017).

A non-confrontational point of view regarding the matter was held by another important and respected author—Egon Bahr (Bahr and Neuneck 2015), the father of the Ostpolitik of German Chancellor Willy Brandt and a co-author, with Olaf Palme, of the idea of zones without nuclear weapons (Blechman and Moore 1983). After 2014, he became a leading figure of a group of critics who refused (Pifer 2015) the radical proposals of Matthew Kroenig (which underlined the necessity to strengthen the emphasis on nuclear weapons) with the key argument that Europe does not need a nuclear déjà vu of the 1970s and 1980s.

Finally, an important and influential French author, Renaud Girard (2017), published a strong critique of the Ministers of Foreign Affairs of Poland, France and Germany, who visited Kyiv in 2017. Girard argued that these three ministers had failed to reassure Putin that his country would have its military base in Sevastopol as a point of defence of vital importance. They should have, according to Girard, also given him guarantees that NATO would build no military bases on the territory of Ukraine, which would be in full conformity with the fact that France and Germany vetoed the proposal to invite Ukraine into NATO during the Bucharest Summit. And Girard's third point is that they missed the opportunity to assure Putin that the Russian language would be an official language in Eastern Ukraine.

Girard then concluded with the statement that Europe should have avoided the two following very negative events. The first of them is the sanctions because they would have large disturbing consequences not only for the RF but also for the West. And second, Girard recommended avoiding the growing military presence of NATO on its so-called Eastern front because it could result in a growing military tension in Europe. And on the positive level, Girard recommended that the EU accept the fact that Crimea will be a part of the Russian Federation, a country which has an enormous potential to help the West in its fight against global terrorism (Girard 2015).

Common attitudes of this group of authors

All the authors of this group (in the USA as well as in Western Europe) share some common approaches and conclusions. First, according to these authors, three decades after the end of the Cold War, the so-called Old Continent is witnessing a dangerous degree of political and military tension between NATO and the RF. Second, the main cause of this tension results from the process of NATO expansion, particularly from its unilateral character and the disregarding of Russian security fears. Third, all the authors in this group disagree with the dramatisation of the annexation of Crimea. Fourth, and maybe most importantly, all these authors recommended stopping the process of NATO expansion with the aim to avoid any further unnecessary political and military tension in Europe and its future growth. Lastly, it is remarkable that in the analyses of the Ukrainian crisis, some arguments were shared by both neorealists and liberals.

4.3.3 Authors with Impartial Attitudes

George Friedman, a leading American expert in geopolitics, underlines that after the second wave of the NATO enlargement, the distance between NATO naval forces and the historical town of St. Petersburg is only 100 miles, and also that the distance between Ukraine and Kazakhstan is only 300 miles (Friedman 2015). He concludes that in the Northwest as well as in the Southwest and the South, the Russian frontiers are hardly defensible, and this fact provokes and deepens new Russian security fears, and that it is necessary to take these fears into consideration.

Also, Friedman argues that Ukraine represents a vitally important buffer zone and that in case of its entry into NATO, the distance between the forward military units of NATO countries and the strategically important Russian town Volgograd[9] would only be 200 miles. Friedman writes this not with an aim to justify the Russian fight against the entry of Ukraine into NATO, but with the aim to understand the historical and geopolitical foundations of the Russian security fears (Friedman 2015). In his latest book, Friedman confirmed his anchor in the realist theory of BoP (balance of power) (Friedman 2020).

Kristin Ven Bruusgaard,[10] another author of this stream, based her argumentation on the recent history of wars (Ven Bruusgaard 2016, pp. 22–23). She recalled that the wars waged during the first 25 years after the end of the Cold War manifested a large and crushing military supremacy of the Armed Forces of the USA, which was in huge contrast with the backwardness of the Russian Armed Forces. This situation deepened and strengthened the traditional fears on the part of Russian military and security experts. They deduced that a conventional military conflict with the USA would be a catastrophe for their country. According to them, such a catastrophe could be avoided by two possible methods. The first of them is a non-contact war without a great numbers of victims. But the second is much more grave and dangerous: it is a threat of the use of non-strategic nuclear weapons (Nedelin et al. 1999). This does not mean that the Russians strategist are preparing for nuclear war; it only means that they are afraid of the possible and highly probable debacle that would occur in case of a conventional war. But their deterrent discourse, based on the possibility to wage a limited nuclear war at the frontier between Russia and NATO, could provoke a misunderstanding in the West (Nedelin et al. 1999) which would have disastrous consequences (Ven Bruusgaard 2016, p. 21).

Since the beginning of the Ukrainian crisis, this situation on the frontier between Russia and NATO is perceived as a negative zero-sum game within which all parties suffer net losses (Pleshakov 2017). The confrontational structure of the post-Soviet space after the second wave of NATO expansion and the resulting security fears of

---

[9]Volgograd is one of the 13 "Town–Heroes" from WW II; this fact that plays an enormously important role in the mentality of Russians.

[10]Kristin Ven Bruusgaard is a teacher and researcher at the University of Oslo, where she does work on Russia and nuclear strategy affairs.

Russian operative realists have negative consequences even in the cultural domain. Russian elites are currently leaving the westernisation discourse, which was so typical for the 1990s, and instead underline their anti-Western and, particularly, anti-American attitudes (Neumann 2015).

4.4 The Conclusion of the Chapter

The beginning of the twenty-first Century saw the most massive wave of NATO expansion. During this period, the Alliance entered the post-Soviet space in the Baltic area as well as the Black Sea space in the South. As in the case of the preceding wave, it was an expansion by invitation. From the neorealist point of view, this wave deepened and enlarged the imbalance between NATO and the RF, particularly in terms of internal and external balancing. It is no wonder that it provoked very strong and intensive security fears on the part of the Russian élites.

The above-mentioned fears resulted in a strong securitisation of their discourses and of the new doctrines of the RF, which are based on typical neorealist arguments, especially the emphasis on the geographic dimension of the security threats. At the same time, the expansion of NATO into the Baltic and the Black Sea areas resulted in a strong militarisation of the security policy of the RF. Moreover, the Five-Day War with Georgia in 2008 showed that this militarisation became the key instrument of Russia's signalling that every other wave of NATO expansion into the post-Soviet space would face a very determined active resistance, including the use of military force. The above-mentioned Five-Day War manifested not only the Russian determination to resist another wave of NATO expansion, but also the backwardness of the conventional forces of the RF. It opened the way to the modernisation and professionalisation of the Russian military which has continued until today.

The culmination of the tension between NATO and the RF came in 2014 after the Russian military annexation of Crimea. This use of force (even if it resulted from exacerbated security fears) provoked the gravest and the most dangerous international crisis after the end of the Cold War. It was immediately condemned by the most important international organisations, namely by NATO, the EU, and the OSCE, and by a special resolution of the 68th General Assembly of the UN. And these condemnations were accompanied by enormously strong and large economic sanctions against the RF.

The most disturbing consequence of this crisis is the growing military tension at the frontier between the new NATO member states and Russia, whose security behaviour is strongly predestined by its strategic solitude as it stands face to face with the expanded NATO. The new NATO units in the area between the Baltic and the Black Sea, and the opposing Western Military District of the RF are the most palpable symbols of this tension. The exercises are characterised by growing numbers of units and their equipment and by a dangerous explosiveness of the related military incidents. As a result, these exercises represent a new form of spirals of security dilemmas: NATO's exercises are interpreted as a challenge for the RF, while the

Russian exercises are presented as a direct threat to the security of the new member states, indeed to the expanded NATO. As a result, three decades after the end of the Cold War, we are witnessing a highly disturbing move from positive towards negative peace.

Sources

Allison, R. (Ed.). (2006). *Putin's Russia and the Enlarged Europe*. London: Chatham House.
Allison, R. (2014, November). Russian 'Deniable' Intervention in Ukraine: How and Why Russia Broke the Rules. *International Affairs, 90*(6), 1255–1297.
ANAKONDA 14. (2014, September 10). ANAKONDA 14—The Largest Exercise of Polish Army. Available at: https://defence24.com/anakonda-14-the-largest-exercise-of-polish-army.
Bahr, E., & Neuneck, G. (2015, April–May). Against Renuclearising Europe. *Survival: Global Politics and Strategy*.
Baranets, V. (2009, August 6). Lessons from the Caucasus: One Year Later. Website of *Komsomolskaya Pravda*, quoted on *BBC Mon FS1 FsuPol iu/osc*.
BBC. (2009, September 30). Georgia 'Started Unjustified War'. *BBC*.
Berzins, J. (2014, October 14). Russian New Generation Warfare: Implications for Europe. *European Leadership Network*.
Bialos, J. P., & Koehl, S. L. (2012, June 25). *The NATO Response Force—Facilitating Coalition Warfare Through Technology Transfer and Information Sharing*. CreateSpace Independent Publishing Platform.
Biden, J. R. Jr., & Carpenter, M. (2018, May 10). How to Stand Up to the Kremlin. *Foreign Affairs*.
Biggest Ever National Exercises. *Biggest Ever National Exercises UK and US Biggest Outside Participants*. http://www.icds.ee/blog/article/hedgehog-estonias-biggest-military-exercise-of-all-time-does-everyquill-really-count/; https://www.gov.uk/government/news/raf-typhoons-intercept-russian-aircraftnear-estonia.
Blechman, M. M., & Moore, M. R. (1983, April). A Nuclear-weapon-free Zone in Europe. *Scientific American, 248*(4), 37–43.
Bowen, A. (2017). Coercive Diplomacy and the Donbas: Explaining Russian Strategy in Eastern Ukraine. *Journal of Strategic Studies, 42*(3–4), 312–343.
Brenner, M. J. (Ed.). (1998). *NATO and Collective Security*. London, UK: Palgrave Macmillan.
Brenner, M. (2016). Washington's Putin Obsession. *Défense et Stratégie, 40* (Autumn), 5.
British Army. (2016, April 21). *16 Air Assault Brigade and 11e Brigade Parachutiste—British Army*. Available at: www.army.mod.uk›NewsandFeatures.
Brooke-Holand, L. (2016). *NATO's Military Response to Russia*. Available at: https://commonslibrary.parliament.uk/research-briefings/cbp-7276.
Burns, N. (2014, March 26). Three Myths About Putin's Russia by Nicholas Burns. *Globe Columnist*.
Bush, G. W. (2004). *Remarks Following Discussions with President Mikheil Saakashvili of Georgia and an Exchange with Reporters*. Available at: http://www.presidency.ucsb.edu/ws/?pid=62702.
Carter, A. (2016–2017). A Strong and Balanced Approach to Russia. *Survival: Global Politics and Strategy*. December 2016–January 2017.
Charbonneau, L. (2007, February). Putin Says U.S. Wants to Dominate World. *Reuters*.
Chauprade, A., & Thual, F. (1999). *Dictionnaire de géopolitique (Dictionary of geopolitics)* (2nd ed.). Paris: Ellipses.

Clark, N. (2012, February 10). *10 Years on, Putin's Munich Speech Continues to Resonate.* www.rt.com›Op-ed.
Clem, R. (2018, November). Military Exercises as Geopolitical Messaging in the NATO-Russia Dynamic: Reassurance, Deterrence, and (In)stability. *The Strategist, 2*(1), 133–136. Available at: http://dx.doi.org/10.26153/tsw/865.
Clinton, H. (2014a, March 6). *Hillary Clinton Says Vladimir Putin's Crimea Occupation…* Available at: https://www.theguardian.com/world/2014/mar/06/hillary-clinton-says-vladimir-putins-crimea-occupation-echoes-hitler.
Clinton, H. (2014b, March 5). *Hillary Clinton Says Putin's Actions Are Like 'What Hitler Did…* Available at: www.washingtonpost.com›news.
Cockburn, H. (2017, September 15). Zapad 2017: Russia Kicks off Huge Military Exercises on Europe's Border. *The Independent.* Available at: https://www.independent.co.uk/news/world/europe/zapad-2017-russia-milita….
Conradi, P. (2018). Who Lost Russia? How the World Entered a New Cold War. *Oneworld.*
Cornell, S. E. (2017). The Raucous Caucasus. Available at: https://www.the-american-interest.com/2017/05/02/the-raucous-caucasus/.
Deudney D., & Ikenberry, G. J. (2009–2010). The Unravelling of the Cold War Settlement. *Survival: Global Politics and Strategy,* December 2009–January 2010.
Eichler, J., & Tichý, L. (2013). *Lukáš Tichý: USA a Ruská federace: komparace z pohledu bezpečnostní a strategické kultury.* Praha: Ústav mezinárodních vztahů.
Emmott, R. (2017, September 7). Germany Disputes Size of Russian Wargames, Predicts 100,000 Troops. *Reuters.*
Fedorov, Y. E. (2008). *The Sleep of Reason: The War on Georgia and Russia's Foreign Policy.* Asociace pro mezinárodní otázky, Research Paper, 5/2008, 19–21.
Felgenhauer, P. (2008, July 31). Russian Rail Road Troops Complete Mission in Abkhazia. *The Jamestown Foundation.*
Ferdinando, L. (2016, February 25). Breedlove: Russia, Instability Threaten U.S., European Security Interests. Available at: https://dod.defense.gov/News/Article/Article/673338/breedlove….
Ferris, E. (2017, October 4). *The True Purpose of Russia's Zapad Military Exercises. Why Moscow Wanted to Send a Message to Minsk.*
Fidler, S., & Sevastopulo, D. (2007, February 10). Putin Rails Against US Foreign Policy. *Financial Times.*
Finn, P. (2008, August 9). Russian Air, Ground Forces Strike Georgia. *The Washington Post.*
Fleming, B. P. (2011, May 5). *Hybrid Threat Concept: Contemporary War, Military Planning and the Advent of Unrestricted Operational Art* (pdf). United States Army Command and General Staff College.
Frear, T. (2015, August 12). *Anatomy of a NATO Exercise.* Available at: www.europeanleadershipnetwork.org›commentary.
Frear, T., Kulesa, L., & Kearns, I. (2014, November). Dangerous Brinkmanship: Close Military Encounters Between Russia and the West in 2014. *European Leadership Network.*
Friedman, G. (2008, September 2). *The Medvedev Doctrine and American Strategy.* Stratfor Global Intelligence.
Friedman, G. (2015). *Flashpoints: The Emerging Crisis in Europe.* New York: Doubleday.
Friedman, G. (2020). *The Storm Before the Calm: America's Discord, the Coming Crisis of the 2020s, and the Triumph Beyond.* New York: Doubleday.
Freedman, L. (2014, June–July). Ukraine and the Art of Crisis Management. *Survival. Global Politics and Strategy, 56*(3), 7–42.
Galeotti, M. (2019). *Russian Political War: Moving Beyond the Hybrid.* London: Routledge.
Gehring, T., Urbanski, K., & Oberthür, S. (2017). The European Union as an Inadvertent Great Power: EU Actorness and the Ukraine Crisis. *JCMS: Journal of Common Market Studies, 55*(4), 727–743.
Girard, R. (2015, May 12). Pourquoi donc humilier la Russie? *Le Figaro.*

Sources

Girard, R. (2017). *Quelle diplomatie pour la france: prendre les réalités telles qu'elles sont*. Paris: Les Éditions du Cerf, 2017, 22–24.
Giuliani, E. (2015, March 11). *NATO and Russia Simultaneously Stepping Up Military Presence in the Black Sea Region*. Politics.
Gorbatchev, M. (2015, January). De la chute du mur de Berlin au risque d'une nouvelle guerre Froide. *La Revue internationale et stratégique*, 17–22.
Gordon, M. R., & Schmitt, E. (2017). *Russia's Military Drills Near NATO Border Raise Fears of Aggression*. Available at: www.nytimes.com›2017/07/31world›europe.
gov.pl. (2015). Available at: http://mon.gov.pl/aktualnosci/artykul/2015-10-02-dragon-15-najwieksze-tegoroczne-cwiczeniewp/.
Grossman, E. (2006, April 8). Air Force Proposes New Strike Missile. Military.com.
Hooker, R. D. (2015, June). Operation Baltic Fortress, 2016: NATO Defends the Baltic States. *The RUSI Journal, 160*(3), 26–36.
Hybrid Warfare. (2015). Challenge and Response. In *The Military Balance* 2015.
Ikenberry, G. J. (2014, May/June). The Illusion of Geopolitics: The Enduring Power of the Liberal Order. *Foreign Affairs*.
Kent, N. (2017, October 3). Book Review: Sevastopol's Wars: Crimea from Potemkin to Putin. *The RUSI Journal*, 75–77.
Keohane, R. O. (Ed.). (1986). *Neorealism and Its Critics* (p. 378). New York: Columbia University Press.
Keohane, R. O. (1988, Summer). Alliances, Threats, and the Uses of Neorealism: The Origins of Alliances. *International Security, 13*(1), 169–176.
Kissinger, H. (2014, March 5). *To Settle the Ukraine Crisis, Start at the End*. Available at: https://www.washingtonpost.com/…/.
Klein, M. (2016). Russia's Military: On the Rise? (*Transatlantic Academy Paper Series*, no. 2), 11–12.
Koncepcija vnešnej politiky. (2008). Ministerstvo inostrannych del Rossijskoj federacii 2008. *Koncepcija vnešnej politiky Rossijskoj federaci*. Utverdena prezidentom Rossijskoj federacii D. A. Medvedevym, 12 июля 2008 г. http://www.mid.ru.
Kroenig, M. (2015, February–March). Facing Reality: Getting NATO Ready for a New Cold War. *Survival: Global Politics and Strategy, 57*(1), 49–70.
Kucera, J. (2015, March 13). NATO Picks Site for Military Training Center in Georgia. *EurasiaNet*. Available at: www.eurasianet.org/node/72526,&#x200E.
Kuchins, A. C., & Mankoff, J. (2016). *The South Caucasus in a Reconnecting Eurasia: U.S. Policy Interests and Recommendations*. Available at: https://csisprod.s3.amazonaws.com/s3fs-public/publication/161007_Kuchins_SouthCaucasusReconnectingEurasia_Web.pdf.
Lavey, A. M. (2015, May 14). *US, Georgian Soldiers Train Together on Close Quarters Techniques*. Available at: www.army.mil/…/U_S___Georgian_Soldiers_train_together_on_close_quarters_techniques/.
Lavrov, S. (2007, September 3). *2007 Speech at MGIMO University on the Occasion of the Start of a New Academic Year*. http://www.mid.ru/brp_4.nsf/e78a48070.
Lidovky.cz. (2008, August 18). https://www.lidovky.cz/domov/za-valku-muze-gruzie-mysli-si-klaus.A080818_104236_ln_domov_bat.
Lindley-French, J. (2014). Ukraine: Understanding Russia. *The RUSI Journal, 159*(3), 36–39.
Maco, J. (2016). *Beyond Positive Attraction: Russia's Soft Power Projection in Georgia*. St Andrews: University of St Andrews. Available at: https://www.linkedin.com/in/jakubmaco/detail/treasury/education:365550826/?entityUrn=urn%3Ali%3Afs_treasuryMedia%3A(ACoAAB9d9NIB98kTT03Z2X6E_BX84H1XT5TdxII%2C1502806622647.
MacFarlane, N., & Menon, A. (2014). The EU and Ukraine. *Survival. Global Politics and Strategy, 56*(3), 95–101.
Manchanda, S. (2009, September 30). Report Blames Georgia for Starting War with Russia: Newspapers. *EarthTimes*. Archived from *the original* on 2 October 2009.

Mankoff, J. (2009). *Russian Foreign Policy: The Return of Great Power Politics*. Lanham: Rowman & Littlefield.
Marchis, S. (2014, June 18). *Lithuanian President, Dignitaries Visit Saber Strike 2014*. Available at: http://www.army.mil/article/128187/.htm.
Matthews, O. (2008, November 21). Dmitry Medvedev's Grand Strategic Ambitions. *Newsweek*.
McFaul, M. (2018). Russia as It Is. A Grand Strategy for Confronting Putin. *Foreign Affairs*, July/August 2018 Issue, 81–92.
McFaul, M., Sestanovich, S., & Mearsheimer, J. J. (2014). Faulty Powers. *Foreign Affairs*, November/December 2014 Issue.
Mead, W. R. (2014). The Return of Geopolitics. The Revenge of the Revisionist Powers. *Foreign Affairs*, May/June 2014 Issue.
Mearsheimer, J. J. (2014). Why the Ukraine Crisis Is the West's Fault. The Liberal Delusions That Provoked Putin. *Foreign Affairs*, September/October 2014 Issue.
Medveděv, D. A. (2008, November 5). Address to the Federal Assembly of the Russian Federation. Grand Kremlin Palace, Moscow.
Melvin, M. (2014). Sevastopol: Crimean Citadel from Potemkin to Putin. *RUSI Journal*, 159(3), 70–76.
Melvin, M. (2017). *Sevastopol's Wars: Crimea from Potemkin to Putin*. Oxford: Osprey Publishing.
Military Balance. (2009–2016).
Military Doctrine of the Russian Federation. (2015). *English Translation*. Available at: https://rusemb.org.uk/press/2029.
Muchin, V. (2008, August 4). V armii: Voenno-ekonomicheskie manevry. *Nezavisimaia Gazeta*.
Mukhin, V. (2010, January 18). Catastrophic Look of the Russian Army. *Nezavisimoye Voyennoye Obozreniye*, 2.
NATO. Available at: www.nato.int.
NATO. (2002). *NATO-Russia Relations: A New Quality*. Declaration by Heads of State and Government of NATO Member States and the Russian Federation. Available at: https://www.nato.int/cps/en/natohq/official_texts_19572.htm.
NATO. (2008). *Bucharest Summit Declaration*. Available at: http://www.nato.int/cps/en/natolive/official_texts_8443.htm.
NATO. (2014a, September 5). Wales Summit Declaration Issued by the Heads of State and Government Participating in the Meeting of the North Atlantic Council in Wales. Available at: https://www.nato.int/cps/en/natohq/official_texts_112964.htm.
NATO. (2014b, May 16). *Nato's Steadfast Javelin I Exercise Underway in Estonia*. Available at: http://www.nato.int/cps/en/natolive/news_109929.htm.
NATO. (2014c, September 8). *NATO Exercise Steadfast Javelin II Tests Allied Interoperability*. Available at: http://www.nato.int/cps/eu/natohq/news_112999.htm.
NATO. (2015a, March 9). *NATO Response Force/Very High Readiness Joint Task Force: Fact sheet*.
NATO. (2015b, February 6). *Defence Ministers Agree to Strengthen NATO's Defences, Establish Spearhead force*. nato.int (Press release). Brussels, BE: North Atlantic Treaty Organization.
NATO. (2015c, September 6). *'Spearhead' Force Deploys for First Time, Exercise Noble Jump Underway*. https://www.nato.int/cps/en/natohq/news_120512.htm. June 2015–19 June 2015.
NATO. (2015d, October 20). Available at: *News: Alliance Kicks off Live Military Exercise Trident* … NATO.https://www.nato.int/cps/en/natohq/news_123995.htm.
NATO. (2015e, October 20). *News: Alliance Kicks off Live Military Exercise Trident* …—NATO. Available at: https://www.nato.int/cps/en/natohq/news_123995.htm.
NATO. (2019). NATO's Enhanced Forward Presence. nato.int, May 2017. Available at: https://www.nato.int/nato_static_fl2014/assets/pdf/pdf_2019_04/20190402_1904-factsheet_efp_en.pdf.
NATO SHAPE. shape.nato.int›nato-response-force… Available at: https://shape.nato.int/nato-response-force--very-high-readiness-joint-task-force.

Sources

Nedelin, A.V., Levshin, V. I., & Sosnovsky, M. E. (1999). O primenenii iadernogo oruzhiya dlya deeskalastii voennikh dyestvii [On the Use of Nuclear Weapons for the de-Escalation of a Military Conflict]. *Voyennaya Mysl, 3*(May–June), 34–37.

Neumann, I. B. (2006). Russia as a Great Power. In Hedenskog, Jakob et al. (Eds.), *Russia as a Great Power: Dimensions of Security Under Putin* (pp. 13–28). London and New York: Routledge.

Neumann, I. B. (2016). Russia's Europe, 1991–1996: Inferiority to Superiority. *International Affairs, 92*(6), 1381–1399.

Nichol, J. (2009, March 3). *Russia-Georgia Conflict in August 2008: Context and Implications for U.S. Interest* (pdf). https://fas.org/sgp/crs/row/RL34618.pdf, 4.

Obama, B. (2014, March 17). Statement by the President on Ukraine—Obama White House… oba mawhitehouse.archives.gov.

O'Hanlon, M. E. (2017). *Beyond NATO: A New Security Architecture for Eastern Europe.* Washington, DC: Brookings Institution.

Operation Atlantic Resolve. United States Department of Defense. Available at: www.defense.gov/…atlanticresolve/FactSheet_Operat….

Parry, R. (2019, December 10). *Cheering a 'Democratic' coup in Ukraine.* consortiumnews.com.. Available at: https://consortiumnews.com/2019/12/10/cheering-a-democratic-coup-in-ukraine/.

Persson, G. (Ed.). (2016). Russian Military Capability in a Ten-Year Perspective—2016, FOI.

Pifer, S. (2015, April–May). Nato's Response Must be Conventional, Not Nuclear. *Survival: Global Politics and Strategy, 57*(2), 120–124.

Pleshakov, C. (2017). *The Crimean Nexus: Putin's War and the Clash of Civilizations.* New Haven: Yale University Press.

Pomerantsev, P. (2014, May 6). How Putin Is Reinventing Warfare. *Foreign Policy.*

Pomerantsev, P., & Weiss, M. (2014). The Menace of Unreality: How the Kremlin Weaponizes Information, Culture and Money. *The Interpreter.* Available at: http://www.interpretermag.com/wp-content/uploads/2014/11/The_Menace_of_Unreality_Final.pdf.

Putin, V. (2007, February 10). Speech and the following discussion at the Munich Conference on Security Policy. kremlin.ru.

Putin, V. (2014, March 18). *Address by President of the Russian Federation. President of…* Available at: kremlin.ru›events›president›news.

Putin, V. (2017a, November 20). Владимир Путин проводит серию совещаний с руководством Минобороны и ВПК. *Regnum.Ru.*

Putin, V. (2017b, November 22). Совещание с руководством Минобороны, оборонно-промышленного комплекса, главами министерств и регионов. *Kremlin.ru.*

Putin, V. (2017c, November 22). Путин приказал предприятиям готовиться к войне. *Nezavisimaya gazeta.*

Reuters. (2017, October 12). Russia Accuses U.S. of Illegally Building Up Eastern Europe Forces. *Reuters.*

Rynning, S. (2015, May). The False Promise of Continental Concert: Russia, the West and the Necessary Balance of Power. *International Affairs, 91*(3), 539–552.

Saakashvili, M. (2008a, August 11). The War in Georgia Is a War for the West. *The Wall Street Journal.*

Saakashvili, M. (2008b, December 2). Georgia Acted in Self-defense. *The Wall Street Journal.*

Sakwa, R. (2015, February 4). Dangerous Plan to Arm Ukraine. Letters: Professor Richard Sakwa and… *The Guardian.*

Schadlow, N. (2014, August 18). Peace and War: The Space Between. *War on the Rocks.*

Shakarian, P. (2014, November 14). Gorbachev's Landmark Berlin Speech. *Russia Direct.* https://russia-direct.org/opinion/gorbachevs-landmark-berlin-speech.

Shalal, A. (2017, July 20). U.S. General Says Allies Worry Russian War Game May Be 'Trojan Horse'.

Shanker, T. (2008, August 16). Russians Melded Old-school Blitz with Modern Military Tactics. *The New York Times.*
Simonian, Y. (2009a, January 27). Chernomorskii flot dreifuet v Ochamchiru [The Black Sea Fleet Is Drifting Towards Ochamchire]. *Nezavisimaia Gazeta.*
Simonian, Y. (2009b, January 30). Moskva prikroet Abkhaziiu s vozdukha. [Moscow Covers Abkhazia from the Air]. *Nezavisimaia Gazeta.* http://www.ng.ru/politics/2009-01-27/1_flot.html.
Stewart, P. (2016, August 12). U.S. General Calls on Russia to Allow Observers at Military Drills. *Reuters.*
Stoltenberg, J. (2017, June 20). Joint Press Point with NATO Secretary General Jens Stoltenberg and Lithuanian President Dalia Grybauskaitė. *NATO.*
Strategija nacionalnoj bezopsansoti. (2009). Sovet bezopsansoti Rossijskoj federacii 2009. *Strategija nacionalnoj bezopsansoti Rossijskoj federacii do 2020 g.*, 12 maja 2009 g., no 537. http://www.scrf.gov.ru/documents/99.html.
Tagliavini, H. (2014, November 20). Address by the Special Representative of the Chairperson-in-Office Ambassador Heidi Tagliavini to the OSCE Permanent Council. Vienna.
The Economist. (2017, August 10). Russia's Biggest War Game in Europe Since the Cold War Alarms NATO. *The Economist.*
The Guardian. (2003, March 10). *Iraq: Russia and France Threaten to Use Veto.*
Thornton, R. (2011, June). *Military Modernization and the Russian Ground Forces.* https://ssi.armywarcollege.edu/pdffiles/PUB1071.pdf, 16–20.
Thornton, R. (2015, August). The Changing Nature of Modern Warfare: Responding to Russian Information Warfare. *The RUSI Journal, 160*(4), 40–48.
Traynor, I. (2009, September 30). Russia and Georgia Set to Share Blame for South Ossetia Conflict. *The Guardian.*
Tsygankov, A. P. (2010). *Russia's Foreign Policy: Change and Continuity in National Identity* (2nd ed.). Lanham: Rowman & Littlefield.
Týden.cz. (2008a, August 18). Available at: https://tyden.cz/knize-se-pustil-do-klause-kvuli-gruzii-76181.html.
Týden.cz. (2008b, August 18). Available at: https://www.tyden.cz/rubriky/domaci/postoje-ceskych-politiku-k-valce-na-kavkaze-se-ruzni_76195.html.
Ukraine Freedom Support. (2014). S.2828—Ukraine Freedom Support Act of 2014 113th. Available at: https://www.congress.gov/bill/113th-congress/senate-bill/2828.
Ukraine Support. (2014, March 27). H.R.4278, Ukraine Support Act 113th Congress (2013–2014). Available at: www.congress.gov›bill›house-bill›4278.
UN. (2014, March 27). *General Assembly Adopts Resolution… United Nations.* Available at: https://www.un.org/press/en/2014/ga11493.doc.htm.
U.S. Army. (2014, October 20). *U.S. Army Europe Conducts Exercise Saber Junction.* Available at: http://www.army.mil/article/132332/U_S__Army_Europe_conducts_exercise_Saber_Junctio/.
Ven Bruusgaard, K. (2016). Russian Strategic Deterrence. *Survival. Global Politics and Strategy, 58*(4), 7–26.
Vendil Pallin, C., & Westerlund F. (2009). Russia's War in Georgia: Lessons and Consequences. *Small Wars & Insurgencies, 20*(2), 400–424.
Vláda, Č. R. (2008, August 26). Premiér M. Topolánek: Rusko nemůže omezovat svobodu svých sousedů. Available at: https://vlada.cz/scripts/detail.php.
Walt, S. M. (2015, February 9). Why Arming Kiev Is a Really, Really Bad Idea. *Foreign Policy.*
Waltz, K. N. (2000). NATO Expansion: A Realist'S View. *Contemporary Security Policy, 21*(2): Explaining Nato Enlargement, 35.
Worley, W. (2017, August 21). Russia Causes Alarm with 'Largest Ever' Military Drills in Belarus. *The Independent.*
www.aco.nato.int. (a). Available at: http://www.aco.nato.int/-nato-warships-participate-in-exercise-breeze-2014-.aspx.

Sources

www.aco.nato.int. (b). Available at: http://www.aco.nato.int/nato-allies-begin-naval-exercise-baltops-in-the-baltic-sea.aspx.

www.agerpres.ro. (2015). Available at: http://www.agerpres.ro/english/2015/04/20/mircea-dusa-and-general-bradshaw-to-participatein-wind-spring-15-multinational-exercise-18-27-15.

www.jfcnaples. (2015). Available at: www.jfcnaples.nato.int/page11122031/2015/jfc-naples-commander-announces-exercise-increased-nato-capability-in-romania-.aspx.

www.worldbulletin. (2015). Available at: http://www.worldbulletin.net/balkans/161780/bulgaria-hosts-breeze-2015-naval-exercise.

Chapter 5
The Growing Militarisation of the Baltic and Black Sea Areas After the End of the Cold War

This chapter analyses five important subjects. The first of them is the smoothly growing militarisation of the Baltic and Black Sea areas which has started in the first years after the end of the Cold War. The Second is the doctrinal development of NATO before the annexation of Crimea. This section is based on an analysis of the Lisbon Summit 2010. Third, the key features of the new Eastern frontier of NATO, namely the military doctrines of the new member states and the modernisation of their military bases, are examined. Fourth, a large amount of attention is paid to the military consequences of the Russian annexation of Crimea, and particularly to the European Deterrence Initiative (EDI, formerly the ERI). Lastly, two important doctrinal documents by leading US thinkers will be analysed.

5.1 The Smoothly Growing Militarisation After the End of the Cold War

5.1.1 The U.S. NGSPP as a Forerunner of a Future Expansion

The military cooperation between the USA and the Baltic states was started in 1993, when these states participated in the U.S. National Guard State Partnership Program (NGSPP). Estonia's armed forces formed a partnership with units from the Maryland National Guard, Latvia's armed forces entered into a partnership with the Michigan National Guard, and Lithuania's armed forces became a partner of the Pennsylvania National Guard (National Guard State Partnership Program 2019). And the entry of these three countries into NATO in 2004 gave the Alliance access to an area of strategic importance. They became a new referential object of the security strategy of NATO, which then immediately launched the Baltic Air Policing mission based on rotating four-month deployments of four aircraft.

The move of the Eastern frontier of the Alliance towards Moscow and the following intensification of the military cooperation between NATO was mirrored six years later, in 2010, when the Russian President V. Putin ordered the creation of the Western Military District (WMD) in St. Petersburg, which has been analysed and explained in the preceding chapter. This district has been, since the beginning, built as a colossal military unit armed with all the new A2/AD systems that have been accessible since 2010.

5.1.2 The Baltic Military After the End of the Cold War

5.1.2.1 Estonia

Between the years 1993 and 2010, Estonia created and applied the National Defence Concept based on the principles of total defence and territorial defence. Two important doctrinal documents have been approved by its government: the National Security Concept 2010 and the National Defence Strategy 2011. They concluded that the most serious potential threats to the country's security resulted from the combination of internal and external developments which could no longer be addressed primarily by military means, but by the application of the principles of total defence (TD). In this regard, Estonia has the most developed TD, UW, and resistance plans and capabilities of the three Baltic governments (RAND 2019).

5.1.2.2 Latvia

The security strategy of this country was based on "comprehensive" defence. The National Armed Forces (NAF) of Latvia were established in 1994. In 2007, the government ended conscription and gave its preference to the build-up of a small, professional force with 6500 professional soldiers, 8000 members of the National Guard (600 active professionals), and 3000 reserve soldiers. The Latvian Land Forces are organized on the basis of one infantry brigade which has a mechanized infantry battalion, a light infantry battalion and an SOF (Kristovskis 2016).

5.1.2.3 Lithuania

With a population of 2.8 million, Lithuania possesses the largest armed forces of the three Baltic States, with almost 20,000 soldiers: about 7500 in the Land Forces, with a peacetime organization of one mechanized infantry brigade, one motorized infantry brigade, and an engineering battalion. In wartime, trained personnel and reservists would form another infantry brigade. There are about 600 personnel in the Navy and 1000 in the Air Force (Ministry of National Defence, Republic of Lithuania 2018).

5.1.3 The Black Sea Military After the End of the Cold War

Only a year after the second wave of the NATO enlargement, U.S. Secretary of State Condoleezza Rice signed the Defense Cooperation Agreement (DCA) with Romania in 2005,[1] and in 2006 the same DCA was signed with Bulgaria[2] (Embassy of the United States, Sofia, Bulgaria). The cooperation with the new Black Sea area member states is oriented toward bilateral, long-term investment in both Romania and Bulgaria, the presence of U.S. forces and other host nation-invited NATO forces on their territories, and the build-up of the rotational forces operating out of sites in Romania (up to 1700 personnel) and Bulgaria (up to 2500 personnel) within the framework of the "shift east" conceived as a move to forward operating bases (Shift That Esper Says Will Strengthen NATO Against Russia 2020).

The DCA confirmed, once again, the emphasis on the invitation manifested by the top political elites of the two Black Sea states and addressed to the USA. These Agreements also opened the way for the creation of an important international unit named the Eastern European Task Force (EETAF) in two phases. During phase I (November 2004–June 2007), the USAREUR prepared the necessary host nation agreements and constructed all the necessary facilities (Moldovan et al. 2009). Phase II was started by the first "Proof of Principle" battalion-sized rotation in June 2007 with the aim to build a full brigade combat team in this area. The key attention was paid to the modernization of the Mihail Kogălniceanu Airfield (MKAF or MKAR) in Romania and of the Novo Selo Training Area (NSTA) in Bulgaria. It was decided that these bases would be completely modernized with the aim to create the structure of the Permanent Forward Operating Site (PFOS).

All the above-mentioned initiatives created a framework for a long-term military program called the Black Sea Area Support Team (BS-AST), which is executed by U.S. Army Europe (USAREUR) with the aim to strengthen the relationships between the USA and its new allies. It is a part of the Theater Security Cooperation program, whose aim is to enhance partner capacity, foster the regional cooperation and provide Romania and Bulgaria with necessary training facilities, and also to introduce the following long-term process of combined training and military exercises.

5.2 The Doctrinal Development of NATO Before the Annexation of Crimea

The summit of NATO held in Lisbon in 2010 approved the "Strategic Concept for the Defence and Security of the Members of the North Atlantic Treaty Organisation adopted by Heads of State and Government in Lisbon" (Active Engagement 2010).

---

[1] Embassy of the United States, Bucharest, Romania. Archived 2009-09-05 at the Wayback Machine.
[2] Embassy of the United States, Sofia, Bulgaria. Archived 2008-08-20 at the Wayback Machine.

5.2.1 Lisbon 2010

The chapter of this document called "Core Tasks and Principles" underlined the strategic importance of three basic pillars of the long-term strategy of NATO: collective defense, crisis management, and cooperative security. This doctrinal document can be read and interpreted in two different manners: a non-controversial and a controversial manner.

5.2.1.1 Non-Controversial Paragraphs

The section called "Partnerships", particularly its article 33, underlined the strategic importance of the NATO-Russia cooperation whose aim is to contribute to the creation of a common space of peace, stability and security. The document repeated that NATO poses no threat to Russia, that the allies want to see a true strategic partnership between NATO and Russia, and that they will act with the expectation of reciprocity from Russia. The following article 34 repeated that the securities of NATO and Russia are intertwined and that they could develop a security cooperation in missile defence; counter-terrorism, counter-narcotics, and counter-piracy operations; and the promotion of wider international security. These articles had no potential to provoke a controversy with Russia.

5.2.1.2 Controversial Paragraphs

On the other hand, some statements of this doctrinal document had a potential to cause controversy because they presented some conditions for the security and strategic culture of the RF for the years to come. First, the section called "Security through Crisis Management" articulated some attitudes with an explosive potential. Its article 26 clearly formulated the determination "to seek [a] Russian agreement to increase transparency on its nuclear weapons in Europe and *relocate these weapons away from the territory of NATO members.* Any further steps must take into account the disparity with the greater Russian stockpiles of short-range nuclear weapons." From the neorealist point of view, the active actor solicits the passive actor to move its weapons so that they would not be perceived as a threat for the security of its new allies.

And second, article 35 underlined NATO's determination to develop partnerships with two strategically important post-Soviet states: Ukraine and Georgia. The basic framework for their invitation had been defined by the NATO-Ukraine and NATO-Georgia Commissions, and based on the NATO decision approved at the Bucharest Summit 2008.

5.3 The New Eastern Frontier of NATO

5.3.1 NATO in the Black Sea Area

5.3.1.1 NATO in Bulgaria: The Historical and Political Framework

Bulgaria has a long history of close relations with Russia and the USSR. During the Cold War, particularly during the autocratic reign of Todor Zhivkov (Zhivkov),[3] it acted as a loyal and reliable member state of the POW. In 1968, it actively participated in the military intervention in Czechoslovakia. After the end of the Cold War, its new political elites opted for a pro-Western orientation and membership in NATO. The 2006 Defense Cooperation Agreement (DCA) defined the conditions of the shared use of several military facilities on Bulgarian territory (Embassy of the United States, Sofia 2008). The central aim of this strategy is to promote the NATO armed forces in this geopolitically important area.

The "Strategic Partnership" between the USA and Bulgaria relies on three pillars. First, four shared military bases in Bulgaria have been created and they will host 2500 American soldiers deployed in this strategic area (Rey and Groza 2008) within the framework of the so-called "rotational deployments" (Bulgarian and US Military 2020)—the US units each spend about 6 months in Bulgaria before being replaced by other units. Second, the brigades are the main units sent to this country from the USA. Third, this framework gives Bulgaria the status of a "reliable ally in an area of strategic importance" (The Way Ahead 2017).

The entry of Bulgaria into NATO has had a decisive doctrinal impact—the year 2012 saw the publication of a white paper on defence, and in February 2011, the National Assembly adopted a 10-year national security strategy (Bulgarian Ministry of Defence 2010) which emphasized a decrease of the risk of a major war and stated that none of Bulgaria's neighbouring countries were seen as a direct military threat (Dikov 2012).

Four Important Bases

Thanks to the above mentioned DCA, the USA and other NATO member states have at their disposal four important military bases with all their facilities. Nevertheless, no foreign land forces are permanently based in Bulgaria (Wezeman and Kuimova 2018, p. 9), and all Bulgarian military bases are fully controlled by the Bulgarian government. The US Armed Forces have the possibility to deploy to Bulgaria 2500 troops and military equipment for such military activities as security cooperation exercises and joint operations involving NATO and NATO partner states (The Agreement). Moreover, from the military point of view, all these bases play a strategically important role (Widome 2006).

---

[3] Zhivkov, T. Bulgarian political leader. *Encyclopedia Britannica*.

5.3.1.2 The GRAF Ignatievo Air Force Base

This air base is a perfect example of the dramatic military history of all of Bulgaria. It was constructed in 1940 by the German aviation industry, it was used in the air war against the USSR, and its military planes scrambled from the West towards the East. After WWII, this base fell under the control of the USSR as an important part of its military potential against NATO in the Black Sea area. It hosted the Soviet Ilyushin planes and its pilots were prepared to scramble from the East to the West. And after the second wave of NATO expansion, it is largely modernised thanks to important US investments and its pilots are again preparing to scramble from the West to the East.

5.3.1.3 The Bezmer Air Force Base in Yambol

This base is enormously appreciated by the US strategists thanks to its proximity to the Black Sea, Russia and the Middle East. It benefits from relatively hot summers and mild winters. During WWI, the German zeppelins of this base dropped bombs on targets in Russia, Malta, Romania and Sudan. And after its end, the Soviet Su 25 aircraft and Su 22 M4 planes (intended for reconnaissance missions) were moved here with the aim to prepare attacks against the Western enemy.

After the end of the Cold War, the USA has invested in the modernisation of this base with the aim to improve and upgrade its navigational and communication systems (Ivanov 2007). Thanks to these efforts, the Bezmer Air Base is considered as the sixth most important and advanced US military facility outside the US territory (Bulgaria: Bezmer and Adjacent Regions). The possibility to store long range aircraft there is highly appreciated. No wonder that this base has been largely used by the armed forces from Romania, Turkey and France during the Immediate Response manoeuvres in 2005 and 2006.

5.3.1.4 The Novo Selo Range Army Base (NSTA)

The relatively short history of this facility started in 1962, when Bulgaria was a member state of the POW. During the whole period of the Cold War, this base played a very important role in the strategic plans of the USSR. First, it was located relatively close to the Soviet Union, and second, it was situated in the proximity of the Black Sea. It offered a large portfolio of military operations that could be conducted from it. It was used especially by the Bulgarian Army as a training area for tank and armoured units that were to be used in combat operations against the forces of NATO.

Since the beginning of the twenty-first Century, the importance of this base increased because of the rising international and military tension in the entire Black Sea area. Being located near the Black Sea and the Sliven area, it represents a highly important military facility on the map of the US military bases in the contemporary world (US Plans 2018). Its location in the proximity of the Bezmer Air Base facilitates the transport of military units and their arms systems after their landings. The US strategists took the decision to invest about 80 million USD in the base, namely in a wide variety of upgrades and improvements in the infrastructure and technologies installed and used on this site (US Military Chief to Land in Novo Selo 2008).

This base offers a large portfolio of exercises, particularly for the training of tank units and reconnaissance troops, and can be used for various tests of chemical and biological weapons. In times of peace, this base is intended for use by temporary tenant units that can use it for training; it is not authorised for housing a permanent unit. Thanks to the DCA 2006, US soldiers can be deployed there only for limited periods of time, and in continuous rotations. But despite this limit, in the hypothetical case of a war, this base would be used at full capacity and it would play a decisive role in this part of Europe. It is appreciated as one of the best military areas NATO has at its disposal in the eastern part of Europe (MilitaryBases.com).

5.3.1.5 The Aitos Logistics Center Air Force Base

This base is situated in the south-eastern part of the country, close to the Black Sea, the Middle East and the post-Soviet space. It can be used for the projection of military forces to the west and south, and in case of war, it could play a very important role. This base stores a large quantity of ammunition for the US military forces established in the area and for the NATO forces planted in nearby regions. It is divided into multiple segments, each of them responsible for different types of weapons or hardware (Table 5.1).

5.3.2 NATO in Romania

During the Cold War, this country was a member of the POW, but this membership was imposed on it despite its traditions and the wishes of the political elites. It was symbolised by the clash between the Prime Minister *General Nicolae Rădescu* (Vladimirov 2018) and the Soviet Deputy Foreign Minister Andrey Vishinski (who was strongly supported by J. Stalin). This clash led to the former being forced to resign and, some time later, go into exile. Romania was the most independent member of the Warsaw Treaty Organization (WTO), sometimes going against general WTO and Soviet policies (Wezeman and Kuimova 2018, p. 2).

Its specific orientation was symbolised by its emphasis on its own autonomous policy choices without interference from outside, which was typical for the Romanian leader Gheorghe Gheorghiu-Dej and his successor Nicolae Ceausescu (Deletant), who refused to participate in the military intervention in Czechoslovakia in 1968. He boldly denounced the invasion in a public address before 100,000 people in Palace Square in Bucharest, and declared that it was a "grave error and constituted a serious danger to peace in Europe and for the prospects of world socialism" (Coondonator

Table 5.1 Military bases in Bulgaria

Name	Type	Its importance in times of peace	Its importance in case of war
Bezmer	*Air Force Base*	Excellent weather conditions It can store long-range aircraft The sixth most important and advanced US military facility outside the US territory	An important platform for NATO air combat operations
GRAF Ignatievo	*Air Force Base*	It is used not only by Bulgarian and US units, but also by other NATO countries	An important platform for air combat operations in this part of Europe.
Novo Selo Range (NSTA)	*Army Base*	Exercises of tanks units and reconnaissance troops Tests of chemical and biological weapons	It would play a decisive role in this part of Europe
Aitos	*Logistics Center Air Force Base*	It stores ammunition not only for Bulgarian and US units, but also for other NATO units located around Europe	A strategically important platform for the projection of military forces to the west and south

Source Compiled by the author

2009). The dissolution of the POW was cordially welcomed by the whole country, and its new political elites unequivocally opted for a pro-Western orientation and the security guaranties of the USA. The DCA from December 2005 opened the way to a joint use of Romanian military facilities by US troops.

The Campia Turzii Air Base

This base was built in the beginning of the Cold War and hosted the Soviet-made Ilyushin Il-10 attack aircraft. In 1969, an air defence unit was created there with the mission to provide protection against air attacks. During the second half of the 1980's, this base became fully operational and served as a base for MiG-21 fighters.[4] But the end of the Cold War opened the way for a long-term westernization of this important facility. On 1 July 2002, within the framework of the Romanian Armed Forces reorganization and modernization program, the 71st Air Base was officially founded. Since this date, this base was involved in many multinational military exercises and training missions and hosted, during different rotations, the planes of many NATO member states, like, for example, six United States Air Force McDonnell Douglas F-15E Strike Eagle fighters during the NATO 2008 Bucharest

---

[4] History of the 71st Air Base, archived on 2008-03-27 at the Wayback Machine; the Romanian Air Force official site. Retrieved on 27 March 2008.

Summit, or four McDonnell Douglas CF-18 Hornets of the Royal Canadian Air Force detachment (Airmen Augment Romanian Security for NATO Summit 2008).

The month of December 2005 saw the beginning of the implementation of the "Agreement between Romania and the United States of America" (Ballistic Missile Defense Systém in Romania 2016). This document stipulated the conditions of the presence of American troops on Romanian territory and plays an important role in the US long-term strategy called "lily pad," a concept developed for basing US troops overseas (Chandler 2005). It opened the access of the U.S. forces to Romanian military facilities for a broad range of activities, including training, transit, staging and deploying of forces and materials, and prepositioning of defense equipment.

Nevertheless, the intentions to apply this concept provoked a controversial discussion in Romania. Even its president Traian Basescu felt the necessity to articulate a clear attitude with the aim to calm the passions (Tudoroiu 2008). He stated that the U.S. would not be able to launch an attack from Romanian territory without the approval of the government of Romania. He condemned as "exaggerated" press reports saying that the U.S.-Romanian DCA had given to the U.S. the possibility to attack a third country from Romanian territory without a clear parliamentary ratification. He categorically excluded the possibility that the DCA could open the way to the "placement of nuclear arms on Romanian territory" (US Bases in Romania 2013).

Despite the above mentioned controversy, the defense diplomacy between Romania and the USA continued to graduate. In October 2013, the US Defense Secretary Chuck Hagel received at the Pentagon Romania's Minister of Defense Mircea Dusa and signed with him the agreements which confirmed Romania's decision to host the Aegis Ashore missile defense systém (Baldor 2013). Hagel highly appreciated that this agreement reaffirmed and strengthened the collective defense as the basis of NATO as an Alliance (Hagel 2013). At the end of this same month, the U.S. Undersecretary of Defense for Policy James N. Miller, Romanian President Traian Basescu and NATO Deputy Secretary General Alexander Vershbow, officially inaugurated the construction of a new anti-missile base in southern Romania, signalling that the U.S. and NATO missile defense plans for Europe will press forward. U.S., Romanian and NATO officials underlined that this base will host about 200 U.S. sailors (Vandiver 2013). The "lily pad" concept (Vine 2015) paved the way to the transformation of this base into the biggest overseas military construction project within the framework of the Pentagon's European Deterrence Initiative.

The Mihail Kogălniceanu Air Base

In the past, this airport was the home of the former Romanian Air Force 57th Air Base, which operated the Mikoyan MiG-29 fighter aircraft. But after the end of the Cold War it was permanently dramatically changed. In 1999 (5 years before the adhesion of Romania to NATO), this base started to be used by the US military as one of four Romanian military facilities. During OIF 2003, it was operated by the 458th Air Expeditionary Group. The airport was transited by 1300 cargo and personnel transports to Iraq, comprising 6200 personnel and about 11,100 tons of equipment. And in 2009 (five years before Crimea) the base was transformed into one of the Permanent Forward Operating Sites (PFOS) of the USA, which are built on the territories of six continents as U.S. military bases, which are defined as "scalable, 'warm' facilit[ies] that can support sustained operations, but with only a small permanent presence of support or contractor personnel. A FOS will host occasional rotational forces, and many contain pre-positioned equipment" (United States European Command 2014).

As of October 2009, the US has spent $48 million upgrading the base. There are plans for the base to initially host 1700 US and Romanian military personnel. The new base has 78 buildings and uses the land of the former Romanian 34th Infantry Brigade base. In 2010 Romania agreed to host a part of a NATO–US missile defence system. The system became operational in 2016, with 24 SM-3 missiles based at Deveselu Airbase in southern Romania (NATO 2016). It is expected that additional NATO forces will be based in Romania to protect the system (LaGrone 2016).

With the closure of the Transit Center at Manas in Kyrgyzstan, the US military transferred to this base its processing operations for military deploying to Afghanistan and other locations. The US Army 21st Theater Sustainment Command and the Air Force 780th Expeditionary Airlift Squadron are responsible for US operations there. On 15 August 2018, four Eurofighter Typhoons of Britain's Royal Air Force that were based there were scrambled to intercept six Russian Air Force Su-24 Fencer bombers over the Black Sea under the NATO enhanced Air Policing (eAP) mission. It is also alleged to be one of the black sites involved in the CIA's network of "extraordinary renditions" (Lithuania, Romania Aided CIA Torture 2018). According to Eurocontrol data, it has been the site of four landings and two stopovers by aircraft identified as probably belonging to the CIA's fleet of rendition planes, including at least one of the widely used N379P executive jets (later registered, and more commonly cited, as N44982) (Temporary Committee 2006).

5.4 Military Consequences of the Russian Annexation of Crimea

The decisive moment came in 2014 with the Russian annexation of Crimea. The first large international reaction to this event has been formulated in June 2014 in an important document of the USA.

5.4.1 *The European Reassurance/Deterrence Initiative*

The long-term program called the *European Reassurance Initiative* (ERI) (European Deterrence Initiative 2018) was in 2017 renamed the European Deterrence Initiative (EDI). Initially, the ERI was established within the FY 2015 budget as a one-year, $1 billion emergency initiative. But it has become a long-term initiative, a long-term commitment of the USA towards the European countries (Statement by the President on the FY2017 2016) which still continues today. It is oriented mainly to the Baltic

5.4 Military Consequences of the Russian Annexation of Crimea

area) (European Deterrence Initiative 2018). The ERI confirmed that "the crisis in Ukraine has pushed the two sides over a cliff and into a new relationship, one not softened by the ambiguity that defined the last decade of the post-Cold War period, when each party viewed the other as neither friend nor foe. Russia and the West are now adversaries" (Legvold 2014). The key intention of the EDI is to "reassure allies of the U.S. commitment to their security and territorial integrity as members of the NATO Alliance." Its goal is a substantial increase of the U.S. investments in five domains (Marmei and White 2017): (1) presence; (2) training and exercises; (3) infrastructure; (4) prepositioned equipment; and (5) building partner capacity (Security Cooperation with the Baltic States 2019) (Table 5.2).

Table 5.2 The EDI and its basic characteristics

Author and guarantor	USA, the 44th President Barack Obama
Geopolitical dimension	The Baltic states and Poland The EDI reconfirms the primacy of the Baltic area
Doctrinal argumentation	The military threat represented by the RF, especially by its annexation of Crimea, and by the cross–border operation in Eastern Ukraine
Main dimensions	Presence Exercises and training Prepositioned equipment Infrastructure Building partner capacity
Military aims and measures	The strengthening of the US readiness and deterrence The increase of the US Army's war fighting capabilities and of the prepositioned equipment in Western Europe, which is far from Russia's reach Reducing Moscow's "time and space" advantage (Cancian 2016) Rebuilding the capabilities to contend with the Russian A2/AD systems
Official argumentation	The EDI is not provocative in a military sense. It is defensive in nature and demonstrates the U.S. preparedness to respond, not invade
Historical dimension	Some measures taken within the framework of the EDI/ERI had been preplanned and the annexation of Crimea only led to their enhancement (European Reassurance Initiative 2014) The other measures are new All the measures of the EDI are aimed to increase the US military presence in Europe and the readiness of the US military in Europe
Financial dimension	The EDI is included in the framework of the Overseas Contingency Operations (OCO) fund, which is not restricted by budget caps

Source Compiled by the author

5.4.1.1 The Main Dimensions of the EDI/ERI

The first dimension, called *"presence"*, is conceived as a continuing and expanding program of long-term deployments of US military units in Europe and their participation in the related military exercises since the year 2015. It is represented by the addition of another armored brigade combat team (BCT)[5] to the rotation, which means that it will be an armoured brigade that will be on the ground continuously. This BCT will coordinate its efforts with two other armoured brigades. As a result, there will thus be a total of three U.S. BCTs in Europe at all times, and four during times of handover. The Russian A2/AD systems are presented as a direct and imminent threat for the military of the USA, namely for the US military C–130 and C–17 transport planes, which are presented as "extremely vulnerable" (Joint Publications 3–17 2019). In this context, the installations of the THAAD systems, SM–6 missiles, and AN/TPY–2 radars are conceived as the US response to this threat.

Exercises and training, as the second dimension, are conceived as an increase of the number and size of the US military activities and partnership engagements in Europe. After 2014, much attention has been paid to making the exercises with the Baltic States' militaries larger and more varied, and to lowering their numbers. Within this framework, the concept of NFIUs has become an important military priority. Common exercises of the US "contributing forces" represented by the American ABCTs and BCTs, and the units of the six "hosting nations" (the Baltic States, Poland, Bulgaria and Romania) play an important role in this.

The third dimension, *"prepositioned equipment"*, is conceived as the maintenance and expansion of prepositioned sets of war-fighting equipment which are generally known as Army Prepositioned Stocks (APSs). According to the Army Doctrine Publication 4-0, the APS play an essential role in the process of timely support of national military and defense strategies in areas of national interest and treaty obligations, while significantly reducing strategic lift requirements and bypassing congested nodes (Defender-Europe 2020). The build-up of the APSs is a long-term program of the US Army aimed to preposition war-fighting stockpiles in strategic locations which enable rapid deployments of the US forces without the necessity to transport their systems over long distances. The APSs are densely consolidated storages (2015 Deploymens 2014) while the USA has a long tradition of storing of its equipment in warehouses in Europe, which has its roots in the first years of the Cold War.

APSs allow rapid reinforcement of the forces already deployed in a theatre. In an emergency, the United States needs only to transfer its military personnel from wherever they are to Europe and arm them with the prepositioned equipment (Freedberg 2020). To reduce the necessary timeline, the United States will add to the existing APSs in Western Europe a lot of additional equipment sets, including tanks, heavy artillery, weapons, ammunition, and other gear, as well as maintaining the training set already spread across the Baltic States and elsewhere in the territory of the new member states. Lastly, these new APS need a reliable backing, which

---

[5] A BCT is the Army's basic deployable maneuver unit consisting of 4000 to 5000 troops.

5.4 Military Consequences of the Russian Annexation of Crimea 111

could be assumed by an ABCT deployed out of the reach of the Russian A2/AD systems (400 km max.). In this context, Germany and Western Poland are very often mentioned (Hicks and Conley 2016, p. 73).

Infrastructure, the fourth dimension, is identified with the modernisation of air fields and bases in Eastern Europe. The EDI is oriented to making improvements, such as improvements to training ranges, which will make the bases more useful for the training of the U.S. and allied forces. The long-term aim of these improvements is to make the existing airfields more adequate not only for the training, but also for the receiving of reinforcements during an emergency (Clem 2016, pp. 74–85). And "*building partner capacity*", similarly to the last dimension, is defined as a necessity of long-term allocations leading to an important increase of the resilience of new allies and partners with the aim to counter Russian aggressiveness.

5.4.1.2 Military Measures of the EDI/ERI

The US has taken two groups of measures. The first of them is the Preplanned but Enhanced U.S. Measures, especially by the NATO Air Policing with the deployment of additional six F-15Cs to augment the four F-15Cs already in Lithuania fulfilling a NATO peacetime requirement to have quick reaction interceptor aircraft "ramp-ready" for a four-month period to ensure the integrity of the airspace above Estonia, Latvia, and Lithuania (European Reassurance Initiative and Other 2014). The second is the Land Force Deployments. As an example of such deployments, just in April 2014, approximately 600 paratroopers from the 173rd Airborne Brigade were deployed for training rotations in Estonia, Latvia, Lithuania, and Poland with the aim to enhance ongoing military-to-military relationships and demonstrate the assurance of America's commitment to its new allies.

5.4.1.3 Official Argumentation

On the negative level, the advocates of the EDI argue that the USA is moving forward deep strike weapons that could be used in attacks against the territory of the RF. They concretely mention that the U.S. fighters retained in Europe are F-15Es, which also have air-to-ground capability. And on the positive level, they argue that the F-15Cs have only counter-air capabilities. And they add that new U.S. troops are being permanently stationed in Western Europe, but not on the territory of the new member states. The new member states are in the role of the soliciting actors who urge an upgrade and reinforcement of the military presence of the active actor and the intensification of commonly organised military exercises (Judson 2019).

Furthermore, they are in the role of the referential object of the USA. As new partners, they are looking for the reinforcement of the security guaranties of the USA. As soon as they become "host nations," a new argument comes on the scene: these countries are impossible to defend (Kasekamp 2010). As a result, it is necessary to augment the military presence of the US Armed Forces as well as the number of the

Alliance military exercises. All these measures are necessary because they would play a crucial role in the multinational force in a high-end fight (Supreme Headquarters Allied Powers Europe 2014).

In this new situation, the USA as a hegemon of NATO and as the most influential active actor of NATO's expansion, is, from the military point of view, in the role of a "contributing force." After 2014, it upgrades and reinforces its role as an active actor of the expansion. The USA reacts with the reinforcement of the APS as a necessary instrument of the credibility of the deterrent of the active actor towards the passive actor. This trend is manifested by the emphasis on the reinforcement of the so-called eastern flank of the US Army force posture. This trend has been visible in four important directions.

First, there is a growing "expansion of troop presence in the Baltic states" (Hicks and Conley 2016, p. 51). Second, the annexation of Crimea has accelerated the build-up of the NFIU, which melts together the host nations with the contributing forces (units of the US Army). Third, the USA puts the main emphasis on the move from the rotational forces to the permanent forces which are perceived as a force multiplier (Bredlove 2015). Lastly, the Big 5 arms systems of the US Army are now modernised (Hawkings 2012). This is the case with the M1 Abrams tank, the M2 Bradley infantry fighting vehicle, the AH–64 Apache Attack helicopter, the UH–60 Black Hawk utility helicopter, and the Patriot air and missile defense systém (Feickert 2016). All these systems have a strategic importance (Farley 2020).

5.4.1.4 FMS, FMI and IMET

The ERI/EDI accelerated the security and military cooperation between the USA and the three Baltic countries, the new members of NATO. This security assistance has been accomplished within three important frameworks. The first of them is Foreign Military Sales (FMS). It is a U.S. Government program for transferring defense articles, services, and training to its international partners and international organizations. After 2015, the USA transferred to the Baltic States more than $450 million for the purchase of defense articles made in the USA (U.S. Department of State 2019).

The second is the fact that the Foreign Military Financing gives the eligible partner nations the possibility to purchase U.S. defense articles, services, and training through either FMS or through the foreign military financing of the direct commercial contracts (FMF/DCC) program (ibid.). Within its framework, since 2015 the Baltic countries received more than $150 million. Lastly, the third framework is that International Military Education and Training (IMET) has been activated as an instrument of the U.S. security assistance in the area of training and education (U.S. Security Cooperation With the Baltic States 2020). Its aim is to improve defense capabilities, facilitate the development of important professional and personal relationships, and provide U.S. access and influence in a critical sector of society that often plays a pivotal role. Within this framework, the Baltic countries obtained approximately $1.2 million (U.S. Department of State 2019).

The intensification of the EDI continued under the 45th President of the USA. It increased substantially during the first years of the Trump Administration, from approximately $3.4 billion in FY2017 to approximately $4.8 billion in FY2018 and approximately $6.5 billion in FY2019 (Towell and Kazlauskas 2018). For the FY2020, the Administration requested $5.9 billion in funding for the EDI; defense officials explained that the reduced request was due to the completion of construction and infrastructure projects annually per country (Mehta 2019).

5.4.1.5 Strategic Road Maps of the Bilateral Defense Cooperation

November 2018 saw the start of a new program called bilateral defense cooperation strategic road maps, which is focused on specific areas of security cooperation for the period 2019–2024. Its first aim is to strengthen cooperation in training, exercises, and multilateral operations. Second, it is oriented to new measures related to the maritime domain awareness in the Baltic Sea, and its third aim is to enhance the level of regional intelligence-sharing, surveillance, and early warning capabilities, and also of the cybersecurity capabilities (U.S. Department of Defense 2019a). This process has been crowned in May 2019, when the United States signed road map agreements with Latvia and Estonia outlining similar priorities for their long–term security cooperation (Moon Cronk 2019; U.S. Department of Defense 2019b).

5.4.2 Reactions of NATO

At the 2016 Summit in Warsaw (Warsaw Summit Communiqué 2016), NATO approved the Enhanced Forward Presence (EFP),[6] whose aim is to deploy multi-national battalion-sized (approximately 1100–1500 troops) battle groups in Poland and the three Baltic states (Stoicescu and Järvenpää 2018). Their mission is to deter Russian aggression and emphasize NATO's commitment to collective defense by acting as a tripwire (Graef 2019) that ensures a response from the whole of the alliance in the event of a Russian attack (White 2018). At the same time, the Tailored Forward Presence (TFP) is oriented to the Southern part of Eastern Europe, specifically to Bulgaria and Romania (NATO 2018a).

The perception of Russia as a highly hostile state is based on the argument that it has, since the beginning of the twenty-first Century, accelerated the build-up of its forces in this area, which was accompanied by a lot of large-scale military exercises in the Western part of its territory, and incursions by its military aircraft into the Baltic States' airspace (Insinna 2019; Schultz 2017). Here particular attention is paid to the area of Kaliningrad, which is perceived as Russia's strategic territory in

---

[6]NATO's member states approved the decision to deploy four multinational battalion battle groups on the territory of those NATO member states which were perceived as most at risk of a possible Russian attack or invasion.

the Baltic Kaliningrad (Estonia et al. 2020, p. 9). It is a 5800-square-mile Russian exclave located between Poland and Lithuania, from which the military power against NATO's northern flank can be projected. This territory hosts a lot of heavy Russian military units, including the Baltic Fleet and two airbases (Domańska 2019).

5.4.3 Reactions of the New Member States of NATO

Estonia adopted the National Security Concept 2017, which underlined the country's preference for a whole-of-society approach based on six pillars: military defense, civilian support for military defense, international action, domestic and internal security, maintenance of the state and society, and psychological defense (Republic of Estonia 2017). All the related efforts are tested in annual, whole-of-government and whole-of-society exercises (Project team 2016; Republic of Estonia Government Office 2018). The military expenditures rose from 2% of GDP in 2012 to 2.14% of GDP in 2018, with a defense budget of $636 million Republic of Estonia Ministry of Defence 2018). Last but not least, Estonia has conducted a number of exercises to test the comprehensive defense concept.

As for *Latvia*, in 2016, the Latvian National Defence Concept underlined the importance of the principles of the comprehensive/total defense, particularly cooperation among state, regional, and local authorities, as well as "the readiness and actions undertaken by individuals and legal entities during times of peace, threats and war" to support national defense (Republic of Latvia Ministry of Defence 2016). This concept underlined a long-term preparation of the population and civilian organizations for war, which is conceived as part of an integrated whole-of-society approach. The Latvian Land Forces represent the most important military force of the country. They are organized into one infantry brigade comprised of a mechanized infantry battalion and a light infantry battalion. Latvia has special operations forces trained for a variety of missions, and plans to triple the size of the forces (Kristovkis 2016).

As for *Lithuania*, the 2016 Military Strategy underlined that the Lithuanian Armed Forces (LAF) must be able to respond rapidly to conventional attacks and border violations and to act in concert with national and municipal civilian institutions. The LAF established two battalion-sized rapid-reaction battle groups to respond to hybrid threats within 2–24 hous, and have conducted large-scale exercises using an unconventional scenario with civilian institutions (Lithuanian Armed Forces 2018). And the 2017 Lithuanian National Security Strategy underlined the importance of the "will of the population to defend the State and their total preparedness to resist by providing the possibilities to acquire and enhance military training and skills to carry out nonviolent civil resistance" (Republic of Lithuania 2017).

As for *Bulgaria*, in September 2014, a few days before a NATO summit in Wales, the Bulgarian Government published a "non-paper" on defence (Bulgarian Council of Ministers 2014a). At the same time, Bulgaria, along with Estonia, Latvia, Lithuania, Poland, and Romania, became one of the countries that host NATO Force Integration Units (NFIUs), which were created within the framework of the Readiness Action

5.4 Military Consequences of the Russian Annexation of Crimea

Plan adopted at that summit. NATO decided to form six on its eastern flank—in and around Bulgaria—to support collective defence planning (Wezeman and Kuimova 2014). And in September 2015 another official document (Bulgarian Council of Ministers 2014b, 2015) spoke about the deterioration of the security environment in Bulgaria's neighbourhood. Nevertheless, it repeated the thesis that Bulgaria was not exposed to any looming and imminent direct conventional threat (Wezeman and Kuimova 2014, p. 5). Nevertheless, Bulgaria continues its cooperation with NATO, particularly with its new member states.

In 2016, a Bulgarian-Romanian multinational brigade was created and in the following year, Bulgarian President Rumen Raved spoke about the necessity to build up "strong navy forces" to "uphold [Bulgaria's] military sovereignty" and guard its "economic and energy interests" (Novinite 2017a). Bulgaria intensified its activities within the framework of the allied exercises. It co-hosted, together with Hungary and Romania, the US-led Saber Guardian army exercise in July 2017. With the participation of 14,000 US troops and 11,000 troops from 21 other NATO members and NATO partner countries, it was the biggest activity of this kind. It was also the first major activity with the participation of the Bulgarian-Romanian brigade set up in 2016, on this occasion under Bulgarian command (US Army Europe 2017; Novinite 2017b; King 2017). In May 2017, Bulgaria organised, together with Romania and Greece, one of the largest recent NATO exercises; it was called Noble Jump 2017 (Markus 2017). During this exercise, the Bulgarian armed forces tested, for the first time, their capabilities to provide logistic support to other NATO forces on a large scale, which would be an important element of any potential fast deployment of NATO forces to Bulgaria in times of crisis (Lenkin 2017).

In 2018 Bulgarian aircraft, including the Bulgarian MiG-29 aircraft, and also the US F-15C/D aircraft played an important role during the annual Thracian Star air exercise organised in cooperation with Greece, Romania and the USA (BTA 2018). The Bulgarian Navy has also participated in several international exercises and in 2018 it hosted the annual large Bris (breeze) exercise, which involved 2340 personnel and 25 combat and auxiliary ships and cutters from 11 countries, including Bulgaria, Romania, Turkey and the USA (Zdravkova 2018). Nevertheless, from the financial point of view, the Bulgarian armed forces' acquisitions of new equipment, training, salaries and operations have often been delayed and Bulgaria has limited means to modernize its largely outdated arms systems, or even to maintain troop levels (Wezeman and Kuimova 2018, p. 14).

In *Romania*, Russia's annexation of Crimea was perceived as an increased security threat. The political elites sent a request for an additional stationing of NATO forces on Romania's territory (as "rotational forces"). At the same time, Romania called for supplies of new modern heavy weapons (Chakarova and Muzyka 2015, p. 28). NATO answered with the decision to establish in 2015 a multinational division headquarters in Bucharest with 280 personnel. This was the Headquarters Multinational Division Southeast (HQ MND-SE), which was assembled from the headquarters of Romania's First Infantry Division under Romanian command, but it includes staff from 14 other NATO states (NATO 2015a). The HQ MND-SE does not have a fixed number of units under its control, and its main mission is to coordinate and command several brigades or smaller-sized units. In times of crisis, its forces will be composed of Romanian units, as well as units of other NATO states (Wezeman and Kuimova 2018, pp. 2, 8). The NFIU in Bucharest (consisting of 40 personnel, of which 20 are from Romania and the rest from 11 other NATO states) is to coordinate the support of the collective defence planning, particularly by organizing the logistics for the deployment of NATO forces to Romania in times of crisis (NATO; NATO 2018b; Butu 2016).

Romania plays an important role within the framework of the Tailored Forward Presence (TFP), whose key mission is to strengthen the security of Romania, Bulgaria and the Black Sea (Romania's Permanent Delegation to NATO 2017). The TFP is based on the MN BDE-SE and the Combined Joint Enhanced Training Initiative (CJET). The MN BDE-SE has about 5000 soldiers, is based on a Romanian brigade, and is stationed at Craiova, Romania. It is composed mainly of Romanian troops, which are supplemented by Bulgarian and Polish troops and headquarters staff from various other NATO states.

Reactions to the Russian Measures

Moreover, The RF has repeatedly deployed Iskander short-range nuclear-capable missiles in the region (Reuters 2018a), which represents a serious security threat (Davis et al. 2019). According to some strategists and experts, this area could be used to seize the Suwałki Gap (Hodges et al. 2018), the 100-kilometer border between Poland and Lithuania which separates Kaliningrad from Russia's ally Belarus (Reuters 2018a, 2018b). Some experts deduce that in the light of the Crimea experience, a comparable Russian strike could result in a quick seizure of the three Baltic States within 36–60 h (Shlapak and Johnson 2016).

On the military level, the NATO Air Policing mission in the Baltic area saw an increase of the deployments to 8 to 12 aircraft at a time. The Baltic States contribute to the mission costs, including the costs of the ground services for the aircraft and supplying aviation fuel (Estonia et al. 2020, p. 15). On the diplomatic level, in 2017 the United States signed a separate bilateral DCA with each of the Baltic States. These DCAs enhanced the defense cooperation based on the NATO Status of Forces Agreement by providing a more specific legal framework for the in-country presence and activities of U.S. military personnel (U.S. Embassy in Estonia 2017; U.S. Embassy in Lithuania 2017; Status of Forces 2017).

The cumulative consequences of the annexation of Crimea are clearly visible on three important levels. All the Baltic States are appreciated because they are reliable and, especially, grateful allies who provided the invitation for the NATO strategic engagement in this area. They offered NATO access to a new strategically important area. On the other hand, the USA confirmed its determination to play the role of a reliable security guarantor. It deployed its military units on their territory and built its (rotational) military bases there with the necessary military material and ammunitions for the organisation of common military exercises (NATO 2019a).

From the neorealist point of view, this part of Europe witnessed a rise of the numbers of the armed forces at the new Eastern border of NATO accompanied by a shortening of the distances between the armed forces of the RF and NATO member states, and a dangerous rise of the frequency of the manifestations of the military force and of their readiness to wage war in Europe. These important changes accelerated a long series of dangerous security dilemmas in the space surrounding the new frontier of the expanded NATO. All these disturbing tendencies have been crowned by a rising international tension that is political as well as military.

In November 2018, the USA and the three Baltic States agreed to develop bilateral defense cooperation strategic road maps focusing on specific areas of security cooperation for the period 2019–2024. In April 2019, the USA and Lithuania signed a road map in which they agreed to strengthen their cooperation in training, exercises, and multilateral operations with the aim to improve maritime domain awareness in the Baltic Sea; improve regional intelligence-sharing, surveillance, and early warning capabilities; and build cybersecurity capabilities (U.S. Department of Defense 2019a). And In May 2019, the United States signed road map agreements with Latvia and Estonia outlining similar priorities for the security cooperation (Moon Cronk 2019; U.S. Department of Defense 2019b).

5.4.4 Military Exercises After 2014

This part of the chapter very briefly analyses the most important military exercises which have been organised on the territory of the new member states after the second wave of NATO expansion. The text will mention the key aims of these exercises, their scenarios and participating countries and their impacts on the ISR on the Eastern frontier of the expanded NATO (Table 5.3).

5.4.4.1 The Most Important Exercises in the Baltic Area

Spring Storm
This exercise has been repeatedly organized since 2014. It is a simulated battle between two brigades with the aim to develop interoperability of the reserve forces in a variety of combat conditions. The initial stages of these exercises cover offensive and delaying actions, while the second stage simulates direct battles between brigades. These operations involve a lot of NATO countries; besides the Baltic republics, the Netherlands, the USA, the UK and Germany also participate. In 2016, Polish pilots were engaged in the exercises with their Su-22 planes and they cooperated with the British participants with Eurofighter jets, CH-47 Chinook helicopters and V-22 Osprey VTOL aircraft. These vehicles are all expected to operate within the Estonian airspace (Spring Storm in Estonia).

Saber Strike
This annual international exercise has been held since 2010 by the United States Army Europe (USAREUR). It is focused on the Baltic States and involves approximately 2000 troops from 14 countries. It trains participants in command and control as well

Table 5.3 The most important exercises in the Baltic area

Codename	Key aims	Participants
Spring Storm	A reaction of the SOF to the annexation of Crimea	Estonian, Latvian, Lithuanian, US, British, Polish, Belgian and Danish troops
Saber Strike	Training of participants in command and control as well as interoperability	USAREUR plus their European allies
Anaconda	A deterrence operation waged against the Red Alliance	Poland
Steadfast Javelin	Synchronisation of the operations of allied air and ground forces	Poland, Italy, Canada, Lithuania, Estonia, Bulgaria, Germany, Latvia, the UK and the US
BALTOPS	The largest exercise series in the Baltic Sea under the command of Naval Striking and Support Forces NATO	Canada, Denmark, Estonia, Finland, France, Germany, Greece, Italy, Latvia, Lithuania, the Netherlands, Norway, Poland, Portugal, Spain, Sweden, Turkey, the UK, and the United States

Source Compiled by the author

as interoperability with regional partners (Saber Strike). It involves a brigade-level command post exercise and a computer assisted exercise including a simulation of the US close air support (CAS) with partner nations' ground forces and a demonstration of the United States Expeditionary Medical Support (EMEDS) capability. The 2018 exercise saw a very large manifestation of this kind (The Defense Post 2018).

The Polish Anaconda Exercise
Since 2006 these exercises are organised every two years under the direction of the operational command of the Polish Armed Forces. After 2014 they were conceived as a test of the NATO countries' capabilities to protect the eastern flank of the alliance. Their scenario has the form of a deterrence operation waged against the Red Alliance, which is trying to take over a part of the Baltic Sea region, including the Baltic republics and a part of the territory of Poland, with the participation of its land forces, special forces and cyber-units (Palowski 2016). Its framework has been described as "a little bit of national regulation, a little bit of crisis, a little bit of high intensity, cyber, conventional, national, bilateral, NATO, everything [which reflects the fact that] we're living in a complex security environment" (McLeary 2019).

The Anaconda 2018 maneuvers were prepared as an activity of a spectacular dimension with the participation of about 100,000 troops, including 20,000 from Poland, with 5000 vehicles, 150 aircraft and helicopters, and 45 warships. They have been perceived as a preparation for a direct confrontation (Radziunas 2017). This confirmed the pivotal role of Poland in the Baltic area as well as the fact that the U.S. and Poland continue to share a strong defense relationship and cooperate on a wide range of programs (Milley 2020).

Steadfast Javelin

This Allied Land Command-led drill is aimed to increasing interoperability and the synchronising of complex operations between allied air and ground forces through airborne and air assault missions. It sends out a clear message that NATO is committed and ready to protect its member nations' territories at any time, especially that it is able and willing to defend the countries of Estonia, Latvia, Lithuania and Poland should the need arise (Nato-Led Exercise Steadfast Javelin II Concludes 2014). During this exercise hundreds of US Air Force (USAF) paratroopers are dropped into Latvia from C-130 aircraft with the aim to take control of and clear the airfield of the enemy's air defence and forces (ibid.).

BALTOPS

Since 2014 this exercise has been prepared as the largest exercise series in the Baltic Sea. It is under the command of Naval Striking and Support Forces NATO (BALTOPS 15 2016). Every year, it engages troops from Canada, Denmark, Estonia, Finland, France, Germany, Greece, Italy, Latvia, Lithuania, the Netherlands, Norway, Poland, Portugal, Spain, Sweden, Turkey, the UK, and the United States (NATO 2020). The latest exercise in this series went down in history because in it, a B-52 strategic bomber[7] conducted integration and interoperability training with British Royal Air Force Typhoons and French Mirage 2000s assigned to NATO's Baltic Air Policing mission. The bomber also overflew Tallinn, Estonia, Riga, Latvia, and Vaindloo Island in the Baltic Sea (The Royal Air Force 2020).

This long-range strategic bomber missions transfer to the Baltic region was presented as a visible demonstration of the US's capability to extend its deterrence globally and strengthen its relationships with NATO allies and partners while operating in the air and sea domains (B-52s Participate in BTF 2020). At the same time, this exercise included a focus on high-end war-fighting training across the entire spectrum of maritime operations, including Anti-Submarine Warfare, Air Defence, Naval Gunfire Support, Mine Warfare, Maritime Interdiction Operations, and, most significantly, Amphibious/Expeditionary Warfare.

Lastly, Crimea accelerated the intensity of the military exercises. From May to August 2019, Hungary assumed the role of the leading nation of this air-policing mission, with Hungarian Gripens joined at Šiauliai by F-18 s from Spain and British Eurofighters augmenting the mission from Ämari (NATO 2019b). Hungary was replaced in September 2019 by Belgium, with four Belgian and four Danish F-16 s operating from Šiauliai Air Base in Lithuania, which were augmented by four Czech Gripen fighters based at the Ämari Air Base in Estonia (Republic of Lithuania 2019) (Table 5.4).

---

[7] The Boeing B-52 Stratofortress is an American long-range, subsonic, jet-powered strategic bomber. The B-52 was designed and built by Boeing, which has continued to provide support and upgrades for it. It has been operated by the United States Air Force (USAF) since the 1950s. The bomber is capable of carrying up to 70,000 lb (32,000 kg) of weapons, and has a typical combat range of more than 8800 miles (14,080 km) without aerial refueling. Source: *"B-52 Stratofortress"*. *U.S. Air Force*.

Table 5.4 The most important exercises in the Black Sea area

Codename	Area	Key aims	Participants
Blue Bridge			
Thracian Summer	Black Sea area	The landing of cargo and parachutists	A Bulgaria-led exercise
Saber Guardian	Romania, Bulgaria, and Hungary	Defense against any type of aggression, rapid mobilization and concentration of forces in a short time	Albania, Bosnia and Herzegovina, Bulgaria, Germany, Great Britain, the Republic of Moldova, the Netherlands, Poland, Portugal, Romania, Spain, Turkey, Ukraine and the United States

Source Compiled by the author

5.4.4.2 The Most Important Exercises in the Black Sea Area

The *Thracian Summer* exercise has been held annually in Bulgaria since 2007. Its last version, Thracian Summer 2020, was conceived as one of the largest international training exercises conducted under the leadership of the Bulgarian Air Force. Its scenario involved landing of cargo and parachutists from US C-130 and Bulgarian Spartan military aircraft, and actions taken by Cougar and Mi-17 helicopter crews with the aim to retrieve casualties and perform an air medical evacuation, among other forms of military activities (Bulgarian and US Military 2020).

The Blue Bridge is a Bulgarian Air Force-led exercise organized in cooperation with the Romanian Air Force since 2012 and also with Canadian pilots (Canadian Enhanced Air Policing 2019). Bulgaria's Graf Ignatievo Air Force Base and Romania's Mihail Kogălniceanu Airport are largely used for all maneuvers in the training, during which the fighter aircraft are to successfully complete a set of missions, including an Air Policing one which involves the interception and the forced landing of an airplane flying without authorization through the airspace of both countries. In 2018, the Bulgarian MiG-29 and Romania's MiG-21 supersonic jet fighter fulfilled the flying task goals in the role of "airplane-intruders." At the same time, the coordination and the interoperability were tested (Bulgarian Servicemen 2018).

Saber Guardian is an exercise co-led by Romanian Land Forces and U.S. Army Europe with the aim to improve the integration of multinational combat forces that takes place at various locations in Bulgaria, Hungary and Romania. In this exercise the main attention is paid to vehicle road marches, medical exercises, multiple river crossings and an air assault (2019 Summer Exercises). This exercise aims for cohesion, unity and solidarity of the partner and allied states with a view of them defending themselves against any type of aggression, especially by a rapid mobilization and concentration of forces in a short time, anywhere in Europe. It includes staff tactical exercises and firing exercises, forced river crossing, and specific medical activities (Romanian-Insider.com 2019).

After 2014, we are witnessing a growing of the numbers of participating countries in these exercises as well as a growing emphasis on the combat against the efforts of the so-called Red Alliance to seize the territory of the new member states and also against new forms of its hybrid warfare. These exercises, together with the Russian exercises called Zapad (Woody 2020), result, of course, in a growing militarisation of this area and growing numbers of military incidents on the new Eastern frontier of NATO.

5.4.4.3 Common Features of the NATO Exercises After 2014

At the quantitative level, all the above mentioned exercises are characterised by a rising frequency as well as by rising numbers of participating soldiers and their military equipment. This tendency was typical particularly for the Alliance's military exercise Trident Juncture, which opened at the Trapani Air Force Base in Italy on 19 October 2015 for three weeks full of intensive training across Italy, Spain and Portugal with the participation of 36,000 troops from more than 30 NATO nations (NATO 2015b). At the opening ceremony, General Breedlove (the SACEUR) rightly underlined that this exercise was organised as the largest NATO exercise in over a decade with the aim to increase the readiness and the ability of the Allied states to work together and to demonstrate that NATO is capable of responding to threats from any direction (ibid.).

At the qualitative level, these exercises accelerated the doctrinal development of NATO and all the participating countries. Their scenarios were based on the protection of the Eastern frontier of NATO and repelling of the aggressions of the Red Armed Forces waging their attacks from the East with the aim to annex the territories of the new member states.

From the neorealist point of view, all these exercises resulted in the growth of the military strength of NATO's armed forces at its Eastern frontier, and a new shortening of the distances between the armed forces of NATO and Russia. They accelerated the process of the new imbalance of the security threats as well as the changes in their perceptions. As a result, they dangerously reinforced the military tension in this part of the Old Continent.

5.4.5 The Russian Exercise Zapad 2017

This exercise formally began on 14 September 2017 and ended on 20 September 2017; it was conducted in Belarus as well as in Russia's Kaliningrad Oblast and Russia's other north-western areas. It was the fourth exercise of this kind, after the preceding Zapad 1999, Zapad 2009, and Zapad 2013, but it was the first exercise of this category which was organised after the annexation of Crimea and it served as an answer to the preceding exercises that NATO organised in this area between 2014 and 2017.

This exercise generated several big controversies. The first of them resulted from the declared numbers of soldiers and their equipment. The Russians officially declared that only 13,000 personnel were to take part in the military manoeuvres, a number that was not supposed to require a mandatory formal notification and an invitation of observers under the OSCE's Vienna Document. But on the other hand, the German Minister of Defence Ursula von der Leyen declared, during the EU defence ministers' meeting in Tallinn, Estonia, that more than one hundred thousand Russian and Belorussian soldiers would participate in this exercise (Emmott 2017). At the same time, the RF was frontally criticised because of the problems with the invitation of Western military observers to the exercise.

The second controversy resulted from the scenario of this giant exercise. A wide range of the Western experts shared the conviction that this exercise was organised as "a show of force" with the aim to manifest the RF's capability to quickly absorb all the Baltic States (Worley 2017) or even Ukraine, if necessary (Shalal 2017). During this exercise, units of the 1st Tank Army stationed in the Moscow region and of the 6th Air Army were engaged. The key role was played by the ground troops, who were supported by reconnaissance units, special operations forces, air and airborne forces, air defence, and naval elements.

The third strong controversy was mirrored in the reactions of NATO and precisely articulated in a statement of the NATO Secretary General Jens Stoltenberg, who underlined, during his speech in Lithuania on 20 June 2017, the necessity to organise these kinds of exercises in full accordance with the Vienna Document, namely in accordance with the principles of transparency, predictability, and openness. The most symptomatic was his emphasis on geography: he manifested the indignation of the Alliance provoked by the Russian "military presence along our borders in this region" (Stoltenberg and Grybauskaitė 2017). And this cardinal point of the argumentation was immediately shared by a long range of military as well as political leaders of NATO (Cockburn 2017).

Lastly, the exercise Zapad 2017 had a lot of large and long-term consequences for the ISR in this area, which were manifested on two levels. On the military level, the consequence was an increase of the presence of the US military units in this area: the 2nd Armoured Brigade Combat Team (the U.S. 1st Infantry Division) stayed in Poland while the tanks (eighty-seven M1A1 Abrams tanks) and armoured vehicles of the 3rd Armoured Brigade Combat Team (the 4th Infantry Division) stayed in the region, despite the fact that the latter would have had to leave to comply with the 1997 NATO-Russia Founding Act on Mutual Relations, Cooperation and Security.

Maybe the most important of all the long-term consequences of Zapad 2017 are the political consequences, especially the meeting of the Russian president Vladimir Putin with the leadership of the MoD, the defence industry complex, and heads of ministries and regions (Putin 2017) held on 22 November 2017 in Sochi. During this high level meeting, the importance of a "quick increase of the volumes of defence products and services in a time of need" was underlined (ibid.). And these words uttered by Putin were interpreted by the Russian mainstream media as his order to industry "to prepare for war" (ibid.).

Like in the case of the preceding military exercises of the NATO countries, Zapad 2017 led to a growing militarisation of this area and new security dilemmas. It was perceived as a new step in the escalation of the military tension in this area. This dynamic of the military exercises has a bitter logic of a vicious circle. According to one US military expert, these exercises have a counterproductive messaging. On one hand, the military exercises deter, but on the other hand they destabilise. The principle is very simple: Russia views NATO's Eastern front as a buffer zone and perceives its use for military exercises as a provocation. And its responses are perceived as a direct security threat to NATO. And from the military point of view, NATO's communicated commitment to defend the post-Soviet space is a bad idea because the Alliance has not enough military power in the Baltic region to defend it in case of a sudden crisis, if not a direct Russian military attack (Clem 2018). Last but not least, this exercise was interpreted as an important military message for Belarus, a country in the sphere of vital interest of its giant Eastern neighbour (Ferris 2017).

5.4.6 Military Incidents Between the RF and Western Countries

The above-analysed military exercises organised after the Russian annexation of Crimea have been accompanied by an enormously dangerous phenomenon: the growing number of military incidents between the armed forces of the RF and NATO. The Russian seizure of Crimea, presented as a counter-measure after the second wave of the NATO expansion, was followed by the long-term Operation Atlantic Resolve, whose aim was to increase the military presence of NATO at the Southern front. It was almost immediately followed by a rise of the activities of the Russian big military units from the Western Military District, the Southern Military District and the Baltic Fleet. These Russian measures were evaluated by NATO as a large test of the military preparedness and cohesion of the Allied forces, and of the Russian determination to use force with the aim to deter any other wave of expansion (Frear et al. 2014). As a result, this part of Europe witnessed a classical vicious circle: a measure followed by a counter-measure which was followed by a counter-counter-measure, a circle which has been so typical for the Cold War.

A high number of incidents, particularly between military planes, was typical for the exercise Trident Juncture (October 2015), in which the US carrier Vicksburg operated in the Black Sea in cooperation with pilots from Canada, Bulgaria, Romania, Turkey, Germany, and Italy during training in combat manoeuvres (Giuliani 2015). And during the exercise Noble Partner 2015, parachutists from Georgia and soldiers from the 173rd Airborne Brigade of the USA, based in Vicenza in Italy, trained the coordination of their activities over a two-week period. They used the Vaziani Military Base, near Tbilisi, a base that originally belonged to the former Soviet

Army[8] but was later used by the US Army for combat preparation (LaVey 2015). From the neorealist point of view, it was an important contribution of Georgia to the external balancing of the USA, which was enormously appreciated by the US operational realists (Kucera 2015).

The above mentioned incidents started an intense discussion between Western experts. At the political level, Henry Kissinger argued that Ukraine should not immediately adhere to NATO, but nevertheless he added that this country should have the right to choose its future, including in the security field (Kissinger 2014). But Stephen Walt almost immediately answered that the USA should not adopt a deterrent model towards Russia because this country is not a rising but a declining power (Walt 2015).

And at the military level, the year 2014 opened the way for doctrinal debates and deliberations about the scenarios for the eventuality of another Russian annexation in Ukraine's neighbourhood. For example Richard Hooker[9] recommended a build-up of military bases on the territory of the new member states of NATO. He argued in favour of the transfer of a substantial part of the so-called NATO Stabilisation Force (NSF) to Poland, namely the 82nd Airborne Division of the USA and the 173rd Airborne Brigade from Vicenza. And he continued by proposing a coordination of these combat units with the 11th Airborne Brigade (11e brigade parachutiste) of France,[10] which was intended for reactions to crisis situations, and the 16 Air Assault Brigade of Great Britain.

According to this author, these two strong brigades could continue to develop their coordination for the eventuality of combat at the Eastern flank of NATO (British Army 2016). And, in extremis, the author doesn't rule out the enlargement of the cooperation between the airborne regiments of the Légion etrangere, Poland, the Netherlands, Belgium, Turkey, and Germany. Until today, this situation has generated and even accelerated a dangerous vicious circle: the growing military tension at Russia's Western frontiers is an external factor which plays into the hands of Russian authoritarian rulers. And as we know, an incomplete democratic transition creates states that have an increased risk of being engaged in international conflicts.

5.5 And What's Next

Since its beginning, the process of the NATO expansion has been accompanied by a dynamic doctrinal development. This three decades long period (including the first discussions at the beginning of the 1990's, discussions which were top secret) saw some important metamorphoses in the definition of the security threats, the

---

[8]During the Soviet period, this base was used by the 1st Guard Mechanised Corps of the Soviet armed forces.

[9]He is the director of the Institute for National Strategic Studies at the National Defense University in Washington, DC, and a former Dean of the NATO Defense College in Rome, and he was the Commander of the Airborne Brigade in Baghdad between 2005 and 2006.

[10]This brigade is located in Toulouse (the South East of France); it has 8 airborne regiments, and a total of 7500 professional soldiers.

formulation of new guidelines for the modernisation of the armed forces of the old as well new member states of NATO and, especially, the publication of new doctrinal documents which defined the use of the armed forces in the case of a direct military confrontation with the potential "challengers" or enemies.

On the following pages, three important clusters of the doctrinal thinking will be analysed. The first of them are the doctrinal ideas articulated in the speeches of Jens Stoltenberg, the 13th secretary general of NATO who assumes this post since the 1 October 2014. The second cluster is the NATO's new strategy called "stability generation." This document merits our attention because it defines the ambitions and the long-term aims of the expanded Alliance and advocates the necessity of a permanent or continuously persistent stationing of the armed forces in the NATO's Eastern countries. Lastly, a necessary attention will be payed to the document of the RAND from 2019, which very often uses the word "expansion" and explains the concepts of the total defense (TD) and of the unconventional warfare (UW) which are very typical for the Eastern area of the expanded Alliance.

5.5.1 Stoltenberg's Doctrinal Speeches

The important declarations of the doctrinal character have been articulated by Mr. Jens Stoltenberg, a man with an extraordinary long and successful political carrier. Between the years 1996–2000, he assumed the prestigious poste of the Minister of Finance and between 2000 to 2001 and from 2005 to 2013, he was Prime Minister of Norway. He is highly respected as a very experienced politician and statesman, not only in Norway, but also at the international scene, including the United Nations.[11]

During six years at the post of the GS of NATO, he presented a long serial of speeches in which he clearly defined four pivotal themes. The first of them is the necessity of the rise of the military spending of all the European member states of the NATO. Since the beginning until today, it is a real mantra of all his speeches. In the first year in his office, he invented the thesis that the security challenges of the NATO are increasing, but its defence spending is decreasing. And in the following speeches he repeated the argument that the GDP of the United States and the GDP of the Europe is almost exactly the same. Yet the United States spends more than twice as much on defence than all the other Allies combined and that the USA are providing over two thirds of total defence spending by NATO Allies.

Second Stoltenberg very often repeats his full support to the continuing NATO expansion in the post-Soviet space and underlines the responsibility of NATO in the protection and defence of all Allies against any security threat. Within this framework, Stoltenberg continues to declare the determination of the NATO to protect all its new members. He often repeats that every nation has the right to decide its own path

---

[11] In 2011, he received the Foundation's Champion of Global Change Award, as the appreciation of his extraordinary effort toward meeting the Millennium Development Goals and of his fresh ideas to global problems.

and adds that NATO fully respects it when new countries want to obtain its security guaranties and to join its structures. His argumentation on this field culminates by the declarations that if the neighbors of NATO are more stable, all the Alliance is more secure. And it is, according to Stoltenberg, the reason why NATO will continue to do so.

The third Stoltenberg's pivotal theme is the presentation of the Russia as the key security threat for the expanded NATO and, namely for its new member states in the post-Soviet space. By this way, he presents all new member states as a referential subject of the expanded alliance. And lastly, Jens Stoltenberg constantly pays a particular attention to the justification of the NATO's military measures and to the explication of their importance for the security of all the North Atlantic area.

In the light of the above mentioned four pivotal themes, three important speeches will be analysed on the following pages. All these speeches have been presented after the Russian seizure of the Crimea in 2014 and in all of them, Stoltenberg articulated attitudes which brilliantly reflected the substance of the philosophy of the NATO expansion.

Keynote address 24 November 2014[12]

In this speech, Stoltenberg spoked about new geopolitical framework after the Russian annexation of the Crimea and he continued by a moderate approach—he presented this country as the NATO's biggest neighbour. Such a presentation have any controversial potential. Nevertheless, the annexation of the Crimea and the outbreak of the civil war in the Eastern Ukraine resulted into a new definition of the RF. This country has been presented as the main security threat because of the deployment of its military units (namely the Western military district) Eastward of the new NATO borders.

In his argumentation, Stoltenberg recalled the increased military air activity of the Russia along the new NATO borders after the second wave of its expansion. He underlined that NATO had intercepted Russian planes when they are approaching NATO air space. And he added that NATO forces were following the Russian ships which were moving towards to the borders of the new member states.

And in the second part of his speech, Stoltenberg underlined the importance of three measures of the strategic importance. First, it was the decision of the NATO to increase its naval presence, to deploy more ships in the Black Sea and the Baltic Sea. Second, Stoltenberg advocated the deployment of new NATO's troops on rotational basis in the new Eastern Allied countries which are in an important role of its new referential objects. Third, Stoltenberg argued in favour of the increase of the NATO air policing and in favour of an important increase of NATO jets and AWACS planes in the Eastern part of the region. He concretely said that NATO has five times as much planes in the air than it had at the beginning of the 2014. Lastly, Stoltenberg defended the necessity of the Readiness Action Plan and of the Spearhead Force.

---

[12] Keynote address by NATO Secretary General Jens Stoltenberg at the 60th Plenary Session of the NATO Parliamentary Assembly in The Hague (including Q&A session), 24 November 2014.

Munich Security Conference, 06 February 2015[13]

Only three months later, Stoltenberg graduated his critical approach to the RF while he attributed to this country the responsibility for a dangerous shift of the international situation. He concretely underlined that nobody forced Russia to annex Crimea and nobody forced Russia to destabilize Ukraine and that Russia did it in a flagrant contradiction with the international law. When explaining the NATO's counter measures, he defended the decision to engage up to 30,000 troops within the framework of the NATO Response Force, namely the deployment of a land brigade of around 5000 troops, supported by air, sea and special forces, ready to move within as little as 48 hours.

Munich Security Conference, 13 February 2016[14]

And a year later, Stoltenberg presented three new approaches. First and maybe most important, he upgraded the construction of the threat symbolized by the passive actor. He identified the RF with the danger of the aggression or intimidation aimed against the former satellite states or even post-Soviet states who were looking for the security guaranties of the NATO. Second, during the presentation of the NATO's counter-measures, he openly declared that NATO was undertaking the biggest strengthening of its collective defence in decades. Lastly, he confirmed the determination to continue in the process of the Eastward expansion. He declared that every nation has the right to decide its own path and that NATO respected it when countries want to join NATO and also respect them if they don't want to join NATO.

In all the above analysed speeches, Jens Stoltenberg fully confirmed his ability to generate an important added value to the long-term marketing efforts of the process of the NATO expansion. He was excellent namely in the presentation of the passive actor of the expansion as an imminent and serious threat for the security of the new referential object of the active actor of this process. From the military point of view, he strongly condemned the military reactions of the passive actor to the second wave of the NATO expansion and the activities of his Navy, Air forces, and Army in the area at the new eastern border of the expanded NATO. And in the light of the neorealist approach, he brilliantly articulated critical attitudes at the address of the military activities of the passive actor of the process of the expansion and presented him as a growing threat for the active actor of this process of historical importance.

5.5.2 NATO's New Strategy of "Stability Generation"

Just a few months after the Crimea crisis, three largely respected members of the Atlantic academic community[15] published a text with a doctrinal ambition. Their

---

[13] Speech by NATO Secretary General Jens Stoltenberg at the Munich Security Conference, 06 February 2015. Available at: http://www.nato.int/cps/en/natohq/opinions_117320.

[14] Speech. By NATO Secretary General Jens Stoltenberg at the Munich Security Conference, 13 February 2016. Available at: http://www.nato.int/cps/en/natohq/opinions_128047.

[15] Franklin D. Kramer is a Distinguished Fellow and Board Member at the Atlantic Council and a former Assistant Secretary of Defense. Hans Binnendijk is a former National Security Council

document "NATO'S New Strategy: Stability Generation" (NATO 2015c) fixed a new global ambition of NATO. Its paragraphs confirm the principle of the mirror effect in the relations between NATO and the RF. The latter is seen as blameworthy simply because of the fact that it views the strategy of the NATO expansion "through a hostile lens" (p. 4).

First, this document underlined the necessity to "expand the framework nation approach in the East" (p. 9) and pre-position the US military equipment on the territory of six Eastern NATO nations and Germany (Mehta 2015). Second, a permanent or continuously persistent stationing of forces in NATO's Eastern countries would play an important role (NATO 2015d), particularly via an enlarged military cooperation of all of NATO's Baltic littoral states (Norway, Denmark, Germany, Poland, Lithuania, Latvia, and Estonia) plus Finland and Sweden as partners. Third, the Secretary General and the SACEUR should obtain the authorization to move forces under designated circumstances with the aim to avoid, in case of a crisis, the obligation to wait for a full consultation with the NAC. Lastly, the resilience is raised as a new critical requirement of hybrid war (Kramer et al. 2015).

5.5.3 Rand 2019

The growing militarisation of the Baltic area is described in an important analysis of the RAND Corporation from 2019 titled RAND 2019 (RAND 2019). This document postulates that Russia could overrun the Baltic States as quickly as in 60 h and that Russian forces could reach the outskirts of the Estonian and/or Latvian capitals within a short period of 60 h and that such a rapid defeat would leave NATO with a limited number of options without the possibility to successfully defend its most exposed members (Osborn 2019). This perception is based on seven possible scenarios.

The first is a Russia-sponsored instigating of ethnic unrest against the democratically elected governments of these countries. The second is another swift military action of little green men targeted on the critical infrastructure of the Baltic countries. In other words, the strategist are influenced by the past wars. The third is a short-warning attack with the aim being a seizure of the territory of the Baltic States led by a force of about 20 BCT reinforced by units of the SOF. The fourth is a permanent annexation of the territory occupied by Russia, which could happen within a relatively short period and push NATO into a fait accompli. In the fifth scenario, even after an initial military success of the RF, the fight would be far from over. In the sixth scenario, different segments of the society of the Baltic countries could help NATO after the beginning of its counterattack. And the last scenario specifies the active participation of these "exposed countries" in the renewal of the control.

Senior Director for Defense Policy and is currently a Senior Fellow at the School of Advanced International Studies (SAIS) Center for Transatlantic Relations. Dan S. Hamilton directs the SAIS Center for Transatlantic Relations and served as Deputy Assistant Secretary of State.

5.5 And What's Next   129

The document RAND 2019 underlines the importance of total defense (TD) and of unconventional warfare (UW) and very often uses the word "expansion." It starts with the expansion of the planning and training for crisis management, civil defense, and countering hybrid and "gray zone" attacks. It continues with the expansion of national and regional intelligence fusion centres and the expansion of the UW training of Baltic SOF and National Guard units. This approach then moves to the expansion of portable anti-armor, anti-aircraft, and mining systems. At the same time, the word "provision" is very often used. It covers the provision of enhanced sensors and associated training, critical UW equipment, decentralized stockpiles, caches, and increased strategic communications efforts. The aim is to counter Russian information warfare activities and to increase psychological resilience.

5.6 Conclusion of the Chapter

During last three decades, Europe has been witnessing a premeditated cascade of argumentation. After the dissolution of the POW, the territory of all its former member states was presented as a security vacuum with a disturbing potential of instability. The new political and military elites of these countries solicited NATO for its security guarantees. By this solicitation, they played a key role in the second wave of the NATO expansion. Thank to them, NATO obtained the control of two important areas. Their military bases could play a decisive role in case of a crisis or war, which is much more important than their economic and financial insufficiencies.

After their entry into NATO, Russia became a new direct neighbour of this expanded alliance. It provoked strong security fears on the part of the Russian elites, which resulted in a Russian intensive military build-up of new big military units, purchases of new modern arms systems, the organization of big military exercises, and the annexation of Crimea. And the story further evolved with the ERI/EDI: thanks to a new invitation, the active actor of the expansion has reached an unprecedented portfolio of external balancing, and expanded to the western frontier of the passive actor. At this moment, it speaks about the rise of a new imbalance, about a new challenge and about a new security dilemma. This new imbalance is interpreted as a result of the fact that the new eastern border of the active actor of the expansion is in the range of the A2/AD systems of the passive actor, which are perceived as an imminent threat (Farley 2014) because they could, according to two influential American generals, destroy the forward arming and refuelling points (FARP) of the active actor (Brown et al. 2015). At the same time, the US military transport planes are presented as "extremely vulnerable."

The passive actor, whose possibilities are reduced to internal balancing, is presented as an actor who has obtained the so-called "time and space" advantage, which provoked a "new geopolitical angst" on the part of the active actor's new allies (Clem 2016, p. 81). This argumentation culminates in the statement that this advantage of the passive actor must be balanced by a reinforcing of the military presence and activities of the active actor, namely by a strengthening of the US readiness and deterrence, and an increase of the US Army's war fighting capabilities. Furthermore, emphasis is put on the protection of new APSs via the build-up of a new ABCT out of the reach of Russian A2/AD systems. As a result, this part of Europe is witnessing a new vicious circle.

At the same time, the passive actor of the expansion is criticised because it places NATO at the top of the asserted security concerns in its recent national military doctrine (Trenin 2014) (2014) (The Military Doctrine of the Russian Federation 2015). The negative perception of the frontier of the active actor moving nearer and nearer to the western frontier of the passive actor is interpreted as a manifestation of the passive actor's hostility, which poses an imminent threat for the security of new member states, and therefore for the alliance as a whole.

Since 2014, the new NATO allies are presented as "the most exposed members," (Osborn 2019) as vulnerable actors who need a growing military assistance. The active actor manifests its full understanding for the so-called geopolitical anxiety of its new allies, while the passive actor has become a bona fide and growing threat to their survival (Simón 2014). The USA prepositions its arms systems and intensifies the numbers of its military exercises. It installed its troops in this area, including tanks and fighting vehicles, accelerated the modernisation of its military bases there and installed its military units with their ammunition and arms systems there. As a result, this area is witnessing a new vicious circle of measures and counter-measures, a new circle of security dilemmas.

Some scenarios of an eventual direct confrontation were prepared, and these underline the necessity of facing a strong and dangerous enemy. Military exercises have become an important counter-measure of the expanded actor. They are organised on the territory of the new member states thanks to the solicitations of their ruling elites. The soldiers of the USA and other "old" member states can use all the military facilities of this area near the Western frontier of the passive actor, which is in the role of the target. They prepare and verify their strategy in case of a direct confrontation and they represent the military dimension of the external balancing.

All the recommendations of RAND 2019 confirm the growing militarisation of this area and an intensive move from positive peace to negative peace which generates new circles of security dilemmas on the new frontier between the expanded NATO and Russia as its new neighbour. The more the active actor expands, the more it strengthens and militarises its new eastern border. This militarisation has three main pillars: the stationing of new military units, the prepositioning of the ammunitions, and the organisation of military exercises. The document of the RAND Corporation added a new dimension to this process: the preparation for the TD and UW. As the passive actor responds with the same measures, the vicious circle continues.

Sources

2015 Deployments. (2014, December 27). Back to Europe, Iraq, Other Hot Spots. *Army Times*.

2019 Summer Exercises. U.S. Army Europe. Available at: https://www.eur.army.mil/SummerExercises/.
Active Engagement. (2010, November 19). *Active Engagement. Modern Defence.* Strategic Concept for the Defence and Security of the Members of the North Atlantic Treaty Organisation adopted by Heads of State and Government in Lisbon. Available at: https://www.nato.int/cps/en/natohq/official_texts_68580.htm.
Airmen Augment Romanian Security for NATO Summit. (2008, March 7). Available at: https://www.usafe.af.mil/News/Article-Display/Article/255590/airmen-augment-romanian-security-for-nato-summit.
B-52s Participate in BTF. (2020). *BALTOPS 2020 Exercise.* Available at: https://www.afgsc.af.mil/News/Press-Releases/Article/2220464/b-52s-participate-in-btf-baltops-2020-exercise/, 15 June 2020.
Baldor, L. C. (2013, October 18). *US, Romania Agree on Air Base Rights.* apnews.com.
Ballistic Missile Defense Systém in Romania. (2016, April 17). *Agreement Between the United States of America and Romania on the Deployment of the United States Ballistic Missile Defense System in Romania.*
BALTOPS 15. (2016). STRIKFORNATO. Available at: https://sfn.nato.int/activities/past/exercises/2015/baltops-15.
Bredlove. (2015, February 25). *Statement of General Philip Breedlove, Commander U.S. Forces Europe.* docs.house.gov.
British Army. (2016, April 21). *16 Air Assault Brigade and 11e Brigade Parachutiste.* www.army.mod.uk.
Brown, C., & Spacy, B. D., & Glover, Ch. G. III. (2015, May–June). Untethered Operations: Rapid Mobility and Forward Basing Are Keys to Airpower's Success in the Antiaccess /Area-Denial Environment. *Air and Space Power Journal, 29*(3), 17–28. Available at: http://www.airpower.maxwell.af.mil/digital/pdf/articles/2015-May-Jun/SLP-Brown_Spacy_Glover.pdf.
BTA. (2018, July 16). *Joint Flights of Bulgarian, Greek, US and UK Air Forces During Thracian Star 2018 Exercise.*
Bulgaria: Bezmer and Adjacent Regions. Bulgaria: Bezmer and Adjacent Regions—Guide for American Military, p. 19.
Bulgarian and US Military. (2020, August 9). *Bulgarian and US Military in Joint Exercise Thracian Summer 2020.* Available at: https://sofiaglobe.com/2020/08/19/bulgarian-and-us-military-in-joint-exercise-thracian-summer-2020/.
Bulgarian Council of Ministers. (2014a, September 2). *Bulgaria in NATO and in European Defence 2020.* Non-paper.
Bulgarian Council of Ministers. (2014b, October 3). *National Programme: Bulgaria in NATO and in European Defence 2020.*
Bulgarian Council of Ministers. (2015, September 30). *Programme for the Development of the Defence Capabilities of the Bulgarian Armed Forces 2020.*
Bulgarian Ministry of Defence. (2010). White Paper on Defence and the Armed Forces of the Republic of Bulgaria (MOD: Sofia, 2010); and National Security Strategy of the Republic of Bulgaria, adopted by the National Assembly, 25 February 2011.
Bulgarian Servicemen. (2018, September 19). *Bulgarian Servicemen in Blue Bridge and Saber Junction 2018 Exercises.* Available at: https://bulgarianmilitary.com/2018/09/19/bulgarian-servicemen-in-blue-bridge-and-saber-junction-2018-exercises/.
Butu, A. G. (2016, July 1). NATO Units in Bucharest, Operational. *Romania Journal.*
Canadian Enhanced Air Policing. (2019, December 12). *Canadian Enhanced Air Policing Detachment About to Conclude Its Mission.* Available at: https://ac.nato.int/archive/2019/canadian-enhanced-air-policing-detachment-about-to-conclude-its-mission.
Cancian, M. F. (2016). *The European Reassurance Initiative.* Center for Strategic and International Studies (CSIS) in Washington, DC.
Chakarova, L., & Muzyka, K. (2015, November). Naval Gazing. *IHS Jane's Intelligence Review, 27*(11), 28.

Chandler, D. C. (2005, March/April). 'Lily-Pad' Basing Concept Put to the Test. *Army Logistician, 37*(2), 11–13.

Clem, R. S. (2016, Spring). Geopolitics and Planning for a High-End Fight. NATO and the Baltic Region. *Air & Space Power Journal, 30*, 81.

Clem, R. S. (2018, November). Military Exercises as Geopolitical Messaging in the NATO-Russia Dynamic: Reassurance, Deterrence, and (In)stability. *The Strategist, 29*(1), 133–136. Available at: http://dx.doi.org/10.26153/tsw/865.

Cockburn, H. (2017, 15 September). Zapad 2017: Russia Kicks Off Huge Military Exercises on Europe's Border. *The Independent*.

Coondonator, L. B. (2009). *Apoteoza lui Ceaușescu – 21 August 1968*. Iasi: Polirom.

Davis, P. K., et al. (2019). *Exploring the Role Nuclear Weapons Could Play in Deterring Russian Threats to the Baltic States*, RAND Corporation.

Defender-Europe 2020. (2020, July 22). *Army Prepositioned Stock-2*. www.army.defender.

Deletant, D. *New Evidence on Romania and the Warsaw Pact, 1955–1989*. Wilson Center. Available at: https://www.wilsoncenter.org/publication/new-evidence-romania-and-the-warsaw-pact-1955-1989.

Dikov, I. (2012, January 6). *The Bulgaria 2011 Review: Defense*. Novinite.

Domańska, M., et al. (2019, October). *Fortress Kaliningrad: Ever Closer to Moscow*. Warsaw: Centre for Eastern Studies.

Embassy of the United States, Sofia. (2008, September 9). *FAQ About U.S.-Bulgarian Shared Military Facilities*. Embassy of the United States, Sofia Bulgaria.

Emmott, R. (2017, September 7). *Germany Disputes Size of Russian Wargames, Predicts 100,000 Troops*. Reuters.

Estonia, Latvia, and Lithuania. (2020). *Estonia, Latvia, and Lithuania: Background and U.S.-Baltic Relations*, updated 2 January 2020.

European Deterrence Initiative. (2009). *European Deterrence Initiative: The Transatlantic Security Guarantee*, 9 July 2018.

European Reassurance Initiative and Other. (2014, June 3). Fact Sheet: European Reassurance Initiative and Other U.S. Efforts in Support of NATO Allies and Partners. The White House Office of the Press Secretary *obamawhitehouse.archives.gov*.

Farley, R. (2014, July 6). Five Russian Weapons of War NATO Should Fear. *The National Interest*. Available at: http://nationalinterest.org/feature/five-russian-weapons-war-nato-should-fear-10816.

Farley, R. (2020, July 24). What If the U.S. Army's 'Big Five' Weapons Programs Had Failed? *The National Interest*.

Feickert, A. (2016, April 5). *The Army's M-1 Abrams, M-2/M-3 Bradley, and M-1126 Stryker: Background and Issues for Congress*.

Ferris, E. (2017, October 4). *The True Purpose of Russia's Zapad Military Exercises: Why Moscow Wanted to Send a Message to Minsk*.

Frear, T., & Kulesa, L., & Kearns, I. (2014, November). Dangerous Brinkmanship: Close Military Encounters Between Russia and the West in 2014. *European Leadership Network*.

Freedberg, S. J., Jr. (2020, February 4). *Army Adding New Arms Stockpile in Europe: Gen. Perna*. breakingdefense.com.

Giuliani, E. (2015, March 11). NATO and Russia Simultaneously Stepping Up Military Presence in the Black Sea Region. *Politics*.

Graef A. (2019, July 25). *Graef Alexander Getting Deterrence Right on NATO's Eastern Flank*. Available at: https://berlinpolicyjournal.com/getting-deterrence-right-on-natos-eastern-flank/.

Hagel. (2013, October 18). *U.S. Defense Secretary Chuck Hagel Talks with Romania's Defense Minister Mircea Dusa, Foreground, at the Pentagon*. www.defense.gov.

Hawkings, K. (2012, September 6). *AMC-Developed Weapons Remain Vital to Army*. Available at: https://www.army.mil/article/86839/amc_developed_weapons_remain_vital_to_army.

Hicks, K., & Conley, H. A. (2016, June 29). *Evaluating Future U.S. Army Force Posture in Europe: Phase II Report*.

Hodges, B., & Bugajski, J., & Doran, P. (2018, July). *LTG (Ret.): Securing the Suwałki Corridor*. Center for European Policy Analysis.

Insinna, V. (2019, July 18). British Air Force Charts a Rise in Russian Activity Around Baltic States. *Defense News*.
Ivanov, L. (Ed.). (2007). *Bulgaria: Bezmer and Adjacent Regions—Guide for American Military*. Sofia: Multiprint Ltd.
Joint Publications 3–17. (2019, February 5). *Air Mobility Operations*. Available at: https://www.jcs.mil/Portals/36/Documents/Doctrine/pubs/jp3_17.pdf.
Judson, J. (2019). *A Modern NATO. Do the Baltics Need More US Military Support to Deter Russia?* Available at: https://www.defensenews.com/land/2019/07/15/do-the-baltics-need-more-us-military-support-to-deter-russia/, 15 July 2018.
Kasekamp, A. (2010). *A History of the Baltic States* (p. 192). New York: Palgrave Macmillan.
King, W. B. (2017, July 12). *Army Signal Soldiers Support Bulgarian-Led Multinational Brigade at Saber Guardian 17*. US Army.
Kissinger, H. (2014, March 5). To Settle the Ukraine Crisis, Start at the End. *Washington Post*.
Kramer, F., & Binnendijk, H., & Hamilton, D. (2015, June 9). Defend the Arteries of Society. *US News & World Report*. Available at: http://www.usnews.com/opinion/blogs/world-report/2015/06/09/russia-ukraine-and-the-rise-of-hybrid-warfare.
Kristovskis, G. (2016, October 5). *SOF Commander: Latvia to Triple Elite Military Units*. Defence Matters.
Kucera, J. (2015, March 13). *NATO Picks Site for Military Training Center in Georgia*. EurasiaNet. Available at: www.eurasianet.org/node/72526.
LaGrone, S. (2016, May 12). Aegis Ashore Site in Romania Declared Operational. *USNI News*.
LaVey, A. M. (2015, May 14). *US, Georgian Soldiers Train Together on Close Quarters Techniques*. Available at: www.army.mil/.../U_S___Georgian_Soldiers_train_together_on_close_quarters_techniques/.
Legvold, R. (2014, July/August). Managing the New Cold War: What Moscow and Washington Can Learn from the Last One. *Foreign Affairs*, 93(4), 74–77.
Lenkin, I. (2017, May 31). *Bulgaria Will Take Part in NATO Exercise Noble Jump*. TASS (in Russian).
Lithuania, Romania Aided CIA Torture. (2018, May 31). *Lithuania, Romania Aided CIA Torture by Hosting Secret Detention Sites, Court Rules*. www.dw.com.
Lithuanian Armed Forces. (2018). *National Defence Volunteer Forces*, webpage.
Markus, I. (2017, May 31). NATO Operation Noble Jump: Thousands of Troops Assemble in South-Eastern Europe. *Sofia Globe*.
Marmei, E., & White, G. (2017, December). *European Deterrence Initiative: Bolstering the Defense of the Baltic States*. International Centre for Defence and Security, Estonia.
McLeary, P. (2019, December 16). *From the Baltic to Black Seas, Defender Exercise Goes Big, Witch Hefty Price Tag*. breakingdefense.com.
Mehta, A. (2015, June 24). Pentagon Placing Gear in Eastern Europe. *Defense News*. Available at: http://www.defensenews.com/story/breaking-news/2015/06/23/pentagon-placing-gear-in-eastern-europe/29163461/.
Mehta, A. (2019, March 12). European Defense Fund Takes a 10 Percent Cut in New Budget. *Defense News*.
Militarybase.com. Available at: https://militarybases.com/?s=Bulgaria.
Milley M. A. (2020, January 13). Readout of Chairman of the Joint Chiefs of Staff Gen. Mark A. Milley's Meeting with Chief of the General Staff of the Polish Armed Forces Gen. Rajmund Andrzejczak. www.jcs.mil.
Ministry of National Defence, Republic of Lithuania. (2018). *Human Resources Policy: Facts and Figures*, webpage.
Moldovan, D., & Pantev, P., & Rhodes, M. (2009, September). *Joint Task Force East and Shared Military Basing in Romania and Bulgaria*. The George C. Marshall European Center for Security Studies.
Moon Cronk, T. (2019, May 22). *U.S., Estonia Sign 5-Year Road Map of Defense Cooperation*. U.S. Department of Defense.

National Guard State Partnership Program. (2019, January 18). *State Partnership Program Map.*
NATO. Headquarters Multinational Division Southeast, "About" [n.d.].
NATO. (2015a, December 3). Headquarters Multinational Division Southeast website; and NATO, "NATO Activates New Multinational Division Southeast Headquarters in Bucharest".
NATO. (2015b, October 20). *News: Alliance Kicks Off Live Military Exercise Trident.* www.nato.int.
NATO. (2015c, September 4). *NATO's New Strategy: Stability Generation—Atlantic Council.* www.atlanticcouncil.org.
NATO. (2015d, June 24). *Defense Ministers Decide to Bolster the NATO Response Force, Reinforce Collective Defence.* Available at: http://www.nato.int/cps/en/natohq/news_120993.htm.
NATO. (2016, July). NATO Ballistic Missile Defence. Fact Sheet.
NATO. (2018a, 1 February). *Boosting NATO's Presence in the East and Southeast.*
NATO. (2018b, January 31). Headquarters Multinational Division Southeast, "Closer to Final Capability Achievement".
NATO. (2019a, June 8). *News: NATO Navies Test Readiness in Baltic Sea.*
NATO. (2019b, April 17). *Hungary to Lead NATO's Baltic Air Policing, Joined by UK and Spain.*
NATO. (2020, June 9). *NATO Navies and Air Forces Exercise in the Baltic Sea.* www.nato.int.
Nato-Led Exercise Steadfast Javelin II Concludes. (2014, September 9). www.army-technology.com.
Novinite. (2017a, August 22). *Bulgarian President: 'Project for Purchase of New Fighter Should Not Be Dropped'.*
Novinite. (2017b, July 20). *Novo Selo Training Polygon Hosted the Biggest Multinational Exercise Saber Guardian 2017.*
Osborn, K. (2019, October 16). Russia vs. NATO: Who Would Win the Ultimate Showdown? Is NATO ready for War? *The National Interest.*
Palowski, J. (2016, May 11). *Heavy Equipment Headed East—Anakonda Exercise as a Test of NATO Mobility.* www.defence24.com.
Project team. (2016). Projet team non-attribution discussions in Tallinn, Estonia, September 2016.
Putin, V. (2017, November 22). Путин приказал предприятиям готовиться к войне. *Nezavisimaya gazeta.*
Radziunas J. (2017, December 13). *Anaconda 2018 Exercise in Poland Is a Preparation for War.* moderndiplomacy.eu.
RAND. (2019). Flanagan, S. J., & Osburg, J., & Binnendijk, A., & Kepe, M., & Radin, A. *Deterring Russian Aggression in the Baltic States Through Resilience and Resistance.* Available at: https://www.rand.org/content/dam/rand/pubs/research_reports/RR2700/RR2779/RAND_RR2779.pdf, p. 7.
Republic of Estonia. (2017). *Ministry of Defence, National Security Concept,* p. 3.
Republic of Estonia Government Office. (2018). *The Coordination of Security and National Defence Documents Management,* webpage.
Republic of Estonia Ministry of Defence. (2018). *Defence Budget.* webpage.
Republic of Latvia Ministry of Defence. (2016). *The National Defence Concept.*
Republic of Lithuania. (2017). Ministry of National Defence, National Security Strategy, Resolution No. XIII-202, January 17, 2017, pp. 12–14, paragraphs 18.9, 18.10, and 18.14.1.
Republic of Lithuania. (2019, September 3). Ministry of National Defence, Vice-Minister of National Defence V. Umbrasas: NATO's Air Policing Mission Will Continue to Be as Important to Lithuania, Latvia and Estonia as Eve.
Reuters. (2018a, February 5). *Russia Deploys Iskander Nuclear-Capable Missiles to Kaliningrad.*
Reuters. (2018b, 4 July). *Council.*
Rey, V., & Groza, O. (2008)."Bulgarie et Roumanie, un «entre-deux» géopolitique dans l'Union européenne. *L'Espace géographique*, 2008/4 (Tome 37), pp. 365–378.
Romania's Permanent Delegation to NATO. (2017, April). *Collective Defense.*
Romanian-Insider.com. (2019, June 3). *Over 13,500 Romanian and Foreign Military Take Part in Saber Guardian 2019 Exercise.*
Saber Strike. *Saber Strike | U.S. Army in Europe.*

Schultz, T. (2017, June 27). NATO Says More Russian Buzzing of Baltic Airspace a Risk for Deadly Mistakes. *Deutsche Welle*.

Security Cooperation with the Baltic States. (2019, July 17). US Investments in Baltic States Since 2015. U.S. Department of State, Bureau of Political Military Affairs, U.S. Security Cooperation with the Baltic States.

Shalal, A. (2017, July 20). *U.S. General Says Allies Worry Russian War Game May Be 'Trojan Horse'*. Reuters.

Shift That Esper Says Will Strengthen NATO Against Russia. (2020, July 29). *U.S. to Move Troops from Germany*. Available at: https://www.rferl.org/a/u-s-to-move-troops-from-germany-in-shift-that-esper-says-will-strengthen-nato-against-russia/30755461.html.

Shlapak, D. A., & Johnson, M. W. (2016, September 30). *Reinforcing Deterrence on NATO's Eastern Flank: Wargaming the Defense of the Baltics*. RAND Corporation.

Simón, L. (2014, Autumn). Assessing NATO's Eastern European 'Flank'. *Parameters*, 44(3), 67–79.

Spring Storm in Estonia. (2016). *6 Thousand Soldiers from 10 Countries Involed in An Exercise*. Available at: https://www.defence24.com/spring-storm-in-estonia-6-thousand-soldiers-from-10-countries-involved-in-an-exercise.

Statement by the President on the FY2017. (2016, February 2). *Statement by the President on the FY2017 European Reassurance Initiative Budget Request*. obamawhitehouse.archives.gov.

Status of Forces. (2017, January 13). *'Status of Forces' Deal Signed*. Latvian Public Broadcasting.

Stoicescu, K. & Järvenpää, P. (2018, January 28). *Contemporary Deterrence—Insights and Lessons from Enhanced Forward Presence*. International Centre for Defence and Security, Estonia.

Stoltenberg, J., & Grybauskaitė, D. (2017, June 20). *Joint Press Point with NATO Secretary General Jens Stoltenberg and Lithuanian President Dalia Grybauskaitė*. NATO.

Supreme Headquarters Allied Powers Europe. (2014, April 2). *A Key Air Training Event for NATO in the Baltics*. Available at: http://www.aco.nato.int/a-key-air-training-event-for-nato-in-the-baltics-wraps-up.aspx.

Temporary Committee. (2006, November 16). *Temporary Committee on the Alleged Use of European Countries by the CIA for the Transport and Illegal Detention of Prisoners* (Working Document No. 8) (PDF).

The Agreement. The Agrement between the Government of the United States of America and the Government of the Republic of Bulgaria in Defense Cooperation (note 11).

The Defense Post. (2018, June 3). *18000 Troops Begin US Army-Led Saber Strike in Eastern Europe*. Available at: https://www.thedefensepost.com/2018/06/03/poland-us-saber-strike-eastern-europe/.

The Military Doctrine of the Russian Federation. (2015, June 29). *London: The Embassy of the Russian Federation to the United Kingdom of Great Britain and Northern Ireland*. Available at: https://rusemb.org.uk/press/2029.

The Royal Air Force. (2020, September 3). *The Royal Air Force Complete This Years NATO Air Policing Mission*. Available at: https://usdefensestory.com/the-royal-air-force-complete-this-years-nato-air-policing-mission/usdefensestory.com.

The Way Ahead. (2017, July 7). *United States-Bulgaria Cooperation: The Way Ahead*. Available at: https://bg.usembassy.gov/united-states-bulgaria-cooperation-way-ahead/.

Towell, P., & Kazlauskas, A. D. (2018, August 8). A. D. *The European Deterrence Initiative: A Budgetary Overview*. CRS In Focus IF10946.

Trenin, D. (2014, December 29). 2014. *Russia's New Military Doctrine Tells It All*. Carnegie Moscow Center. Available at: http://carnegie.ru/eurasiaoutlook/?fa=57607.

Tudoroiu, T. (2008). From Spheres of Influence to Energy Wars: Russian Influence in Post-Communist Romania. *Journal of Communist Studies and Transition Politics*, 24(3), 386–414.

United States European Command. (2014). Strategic Theater Transformation. *2005-01-14. Archived from* the original *on 2007-02-04*. Retrieved 2007-02-07.

US Bases in Romania. (2013, October 22). GlobalSecurity.org.

US Military Chief to Land in Novo Selo. (2008, October 13). *Standard News*, Issue 786.

US Plans. (2018, August 16). *US Plans to Upgrade Military Bases in Romania, Bulgaria*. Novinite.com. Sofia News Agency.
US Army Europe. (2017, July 10). *Saber Guardian 2017*. Media information kit.
U.S. Department of Defense. (2019a, April 2). United *States, Lithuania Sign Defense Cooperation Plan*, press release.
U.S. Department of Defense. (2019b, May 10). *U.S., Latvia Reaffirm Relationship in Bilateral Meeting*.
U.S. Department of State. (2019, July 17). Bureau of Political Military Affairs, U.S. Security Cooperation with the Baltic States.
U.S. Embassy in Estonia. (2017, January 17). *Signing of Defense Cooperation Agreement—Remarks by Ambassador James D. Melville*.
U.S. Embassy in Lithuania. (2017, January 17). *United States and Lithuania Signed Defense Cooperation Agreement*.
U.S. Security Cooperation With the Baltic States. (2020, June 11). Security Assistance Programs Like Foreign Military Financing (FMF) and International Military Education and Training.
Vandiver, J. (2013, October 28). *US, NATO Move Ahead with Romanian Anti-missile Base*. Stars and Stripes Published.
Vine, D. (2015, August 25). *American Military Extends Its Reach Worldwide—Lily Pads*. Available at: https://seenthis.net/sites/779105.
Vladimirov, K. (2018). General Nicolae Rădescu: New Sources, New Perspectives, 1940s–1950s. *History, 103*(357), 610–627.
Walt, S. M. (2015, February 9). Why Arming Kiev Is a Really, Really Bad Idea. *Foreign Policy*.
Warsaw Summit Communiqué. (2016, July 8–9). Issued by the Heads of State and Government participating in the meeting of the North Atlantic Council in Warsaw.
Wezeman, S. T., & Kuimova, A. (2014). *Bulgaria and Black Sea Security*. SIPRI Publisher. http://www.sipri.org/publications.
Wezeman, S. T., & Kuimova, A. (2018, December). *Bulgaria and Black Sea Security*. SIPRI Backround Paper.
White, H. (2018, June 26). *Deterring Russia*. Available at: https://www.aspistrategist.org.au/deterring-russia.
Widome D. (2006, May 13). The List: The Six Most Important U.S. Military Bases. *Foreign Policy*.
Woody, C. (2020, August 12). *The US and NATO Are Boosting Their Presence in a Hotspot for Military Activity Near Russia*. Available at: https://www.wearethemighty.com/mighty-trending/nato-presence-russian-military-hotspot.
Worley, W. (2017, 21 August). Russia Causes Alarm with 'Largest Ever' Military Drills in Belarus. *The Independent*.
Zdravkova, G. (2018, July 16). The Bulgarian Naval Exercise BREEZE 2018 is Ongoing. *Bulgarian Military News*. Available at: http://www.aco.nato.int/-nato-warships-participate-in-exercise-breeze-2014.aspx.

Chapter 6
American Military Doctrines of the New Generation

This chapter will analyse the so-called American doctrines of the new generation which have been approved between 2012 and 2015 (Gross 2016). These documents are very important because they articulate the concretisation of the grand strategy of the US Armed Forces for their missions, and for their build-up and necessary modernisation. As all of this book examines the process of the NATO expansion after the end of the Cold War and its consequences, its last chapter is reserved for the examination of these documents. The first of them is one doctrinal document of the highest level from May 2010, which is in the category of grand strategy and which is signed by the 44th President of the USA. After this basic text, four other doctrines were published and signed by the Chairman of the Joint Chiefs of Staff of the USA, and they will be analysed on the following pages.

6.1 Key Concepts

As its mission is to explain all the important circumstances, the chapter is divided into two sections. The first one is short; it explains the basic theoretical concepts: namely grand strategy and doctrine, with their specification for the USA and its strategic culture. After this brief presentation, the section continues with a basic analysis of the key features of the international and military context of the ISR during the second decade of the present century.

And the second section represents the key part of the entire chapter and is consecrated to a detailed analysis of the US doctrinal documents. It explains the international and military context of all the important doctrinal documents as well as their key missions and aims.

© The Author(s), under exclusive license to Springer Nature Switzerland AG 2021
J. Eichler, *NATO's Expansion After the Cold War*, Global Power Shift,
https://doi.org/10.1007/978-3-030-66641-5_6

6.1.1 The Basic Concepts of This Book

The key attention of this part of the section is to explaining four basic concepts: grand strategy, security culture, strategic culture, and doctrine. Generally speaking, *grand strategy* is a very important concept. A major classic author of strategic studies, Basil Liddell Hart, defined grand strategy as a concept which is inseparable from war. Indeed it is "practically synonymous with the policy which guides the conduct of war" (Liddell Hart 1991). According to Colin Grey, grand strategy or high strategy comprises the "purposeful employment of all instruments of power available to a security community" (Gray 2007). This approach is shared by another important author, John Gaddis, who underlines that "the fighting of wars and the management of states have demanded the calculation of relationships between means and ends for a longer stretch of time than any other documented area of collective human activity" (Gaddis 2009). Lastly, Stephen Walt, one of the key neorealist authors, concludes that the first purpose of every grand strategy is to define the approach of states or alliances to the security threats which they face.[1]

Security culture represents a set of values, norms and measures. Its international dimension is defined in the light of the instrumental preferences of states. All states can opt for unilateralism or multilateralism, coercive or convictive strategy, military or non-military instruments, or prevention or pre-emption (Kirchner and Sperling 2007). And Gariup (2009) emphasises another pillar of the security culture: it is the approach to the security threats, which can be anywhere between their underestimation[2] on one hand to their exaggeration on the other.[3]

The concept *strategic culture* covers a complex of ideas, reactions and paradigms which are typical for national as well as for international communities, and which are acquired via long term education or the imitation of successful nations and their armed forces (Snyder 1977). If the security culture is primarily the job of the political leaders, the strategic culture is the job of the military leaders.

Lastly, the term *"doctrine"*[4] will be used as a common denominator for a set of central beliefs or principles for how to face existing security threats and challenges (Posen 1984). At the same time, doctrines give an answer to the question how to wage war in order to achieve the desired military ends, if it is necessary (Attrill 2015). According to the philosophy of NATO, "doctrine is defined as the fundamental principles by which the military forces guide their actions in support of objectives. It is authoritative but requires judgment in the application (AAP-6). It provides the philosophical basis for the particular action taken by military forces

---

[1] Stephen M. Walt stresses the value of understanding state action as a response to perceived threats rather than potential enemies in *The Origins of Alliances*.

[2] This behaviour was typical for J. V. Stalin and his approach to Hitler's Germany between 1939 and 1941.

[3] This behaviour was typical for G. W. Bush in his approach towards the regime of Saddam Hussein in Iraq.

[4] Generally speaking, a doctrine is defined as a set of particular principles, positions, and thoughts which define a government's orientation in the field of national and international security.

and the reasons behind that action". Every doctrine has its direct implications for the force structure, training, and equipment of the related armed forces (Gray 1999); it creates a framework for their engagement in a concrete strategic environment (de Montbrial and Klein 2000).

6.1.2 The International and Military Context of the US Doctrinal Documents Approved Between 2012 and 2015

All the doctrinal documents from the period 2012–2015 are based on a profound and systematic analysis of the development of the ISR during the two preceding decades. They have five important common denominators which resulted from the dynamic of the international, historical, and military context after the end of the Cold War and which will be examined on the following pages.

6.1.2.1 The International and Historical Context

All these documents reflected the profound political, economic as well as military changes which happened during the two decades after the end of the Cold War on the political and military fields. They articulated American reactions to the profound changes that happened during the last three decades, namely the Eastern expansion of NATO, the enormous successes of the US military in the wars after 1990, and the long-term general weakening of Russia, which contrasted with the above mentioned successes of the USA. The Russian Federation, the successor state of the USSR, lost more than 5 million km^2 and 140 million inhabitants when the USSR was dismantled (Strategic Trends 2017). In terms of general economic force, Russia fell to the 12th place in the world, behind Canada and South Korea (IMF 2016). Its military budget dropped to under the level of 10% of the budget of the USA (The Balance 2016; Russia & India Report 2016). This Russian general decline clearly contrasted with the unprecedented rise of the USA, and especially with its strengthened self—confidence.

As Chapters 3 and 4 of this book have shown, after two waves of its expansion, NATO entered into the so-called vacuum on the territory of the POW and even in the North-Western part of the post-Soviet space. During the presidency of G. W. Bush, the large Northern and Southern part of the post-Soviet space passed under the direct (namely the three Baltic states) or indirect economic and political control (namely Ukraine and Georgia) of the USA and its allies. Of course, the numbers of the US units on the territory of the post-Soviet space are modest. They are much more modest than the numbers in the case of the overlarge military units (regiments, divisions, army corps, military districts) of the USSR during the Cold War.

The US doctrines reflect the fact that the USA and it its allies are present on this strategically important territory, which could be, in case of an international crisis or war, used for projections of military force in directions leading towards St. Petersburg,

Moscow and other important Russian cities (Sprūds and Bukovskis 2014). This large space represents the military pillar of a large and rich portfolio of advantages of the external balancing of the USA as the hegemon of NATO after the first two waves of its post-Cold War expansion. All these strategic advantages determine the ambitions of the US doctrinal documents approved during the third decade after the end of the Cold War.

The doctrinal documents of the new generation covered the second decade of the new century, which means that they offered a vision and orientation for the two following decades, if not until the middle of the twenty-first century. It is no surprise that they fixed the concrete strategic and military ambitions, aims, and tasks of the US military in the post-Soviet area. Lastly, the US doctrines reacted to the fact that with the beginning of the new century, Russia started its long-term initiative aimed to reduce its military backwardness, underdevelopment, and inferiority in comparison with the USA. The key attention was paid to the build-up of A2/AD systems on its North-Western frontier (Frühling and Lasconjarias 2016). The numbers of the planes on the air bases as well as those of mechanised brigades and divisions rose to the maximum levels from the beginning of the 1990s (Jones 2012).

6.1.2.2 The Military Context of the US Doctrinal Documents in 2012–2015

From the military point of view, the A2/AD arms systems represent a common denominator of all these documents. They manifest the determination of the US operative realists to show that they will not hesitate to use the US's contemporary spectacular military supremacy against all "challengers with A2/AD arms systems." Before 2014, only China and Iran had been concretely mentioned as countries with systems of the category A2/AD. But even during this period, it was evident that huge concentrations of these arms systems were typical particularly in the post-Soviet space, and that Russia was the power with the strongest arsenal of these arms systems. Yes, this country was not directly mentioned in these doctrines, but nevertheless all these documents send an implicit, between-the-lines message that the post-Soviet space is a new important area of the American grand strategy and particularly of the following military doctrinal documents for the next decades.

The documents signed between 2012 and 2015 concretise the basic tasks for the A2/AD warfare. It is a warfare which includes hybrid and ambiguous instruments and methods in the new military environment, which has a lot of typical features (Gross 2016, p. 1). The first of them is a dramatic increase in the levels of military activity in the early phases of operations as well as increased modularity, agility, and flexibility across the functions of war. Second, the wars waged after 1990 confirmed the growing importance of the integration of intelligence and operations as well as of deception, stealth, and ambiguity in terms of complicating enemy calculations from the beginning until the end of military hostilities. Lastly, the military combat with A2/AD systems implies new concepts of combined arms and sea power; and it facilitates a philosophic return to the roots of war (Table 6.1).

6.1 Key Concepts

Table 6.1 The hierarchy of the American doctrinal documents of the new generation

Category	Name of the doctrinal document	Guarantor(s)	Month and year of publication
The highest political level (grand strategy)	NSS 2010	The President of the USA	May 2010
The highest political level (grand strategy)	Sustaining U.S. Global Leadership: Priorities for twenty-first century Defence	The President of the USA	January 2012
Military level	JOAC: Joint Operational Access Concept	The Chairman of the Joint Chiefs of Staff (CJCS)	January 2012
Military level	Air-Sea Battle (ASB)	The Chiefs of the Army, Marine Corps, Navy, and Air Force	May 2013
Military level	The Joint Concept for Entry Operations (JCEO)	The Chiefs of the Army, Marine Corps, Navy, and Air Force	April 2014
Military level	The Joint Concept for Rapid Aggregation (JCRA)	The Chiefs of the Army, Marine Corps, Navy, and Air Force	May 2015

Source Compiled by the author

Besides the above mentioned documents, some others have been published. These are the Joint Concept for Command and Control of the Aerial Layer Network (JC2ALN, or JALN), signed in March 2015 (JC2ALN 2015), the Joint Concept for Health Services (JCHS), signed in August 2015 (JCHS 2015), and the Joint Concept for Logistics (JCL), signed in September 2015 (JCL 2015).

All of them are very important, particularly in the field of the so-called globally integrated logistics, which plays an important role in modern warfare (Ross 2018). Nevertheless, they will not be analysed in the following text particularly because of the fact that they represent "only" the application of the four above mentioned pivotal documents of basic importance. Instead, attention will be paid to the document which created the basic framework for the A2/AD warfare and articulated the most important tasks for the US soldiers in the A2/AD environment.

From the military point of view, all these documents were written with the aim to specify the role of the US military and technological superiority across all domains in the era of unimpeded operational access within the framework of long distance force projection. Under the phrase "unimpeded operational access", it is necessary to understand the access to the decisive areas and targets, and quick control of them. This phrase demonstrates the determination of the U.S. to carry out as quickly as possible the positioning of its armed forces overseas with the aim to manage crises and prevent war, or defeat an enemy in a war (JOAC 2012).

6.2 From the NSS 2010 to the JCRA

This part of the chapter will analyse the most important doctrinal documents which have been approved within the relatively short period between 2012 and 2018. It will not cover all the documents from this period, but only the most important ones among them. The key attention will be paid to the documents which have a clear relevancy for the NATO expansion and its consequences in the field of ISR in post-Cold War Europe. The chapter will start with an analysis of the document in the category of grand strategy which has been signed by the 44th President of the USA Barack Obama, and it will be closed with an examination of the document JCRA, which fixes the concrete tasks of the US commanders and soldiers in the field of rapid aggregation of their military units.

6.2.1 The Grand Strategy and Security Culture of Barack Obama

6.2.1.1 From Obama as a Candidate...

All the US doctrines of the new generation have been written and published during the two mandates of Barack Obama, the 44th President of the USA. Before entering the White House, this former teacher of constitutional law at the University of Chicago Law School and former senator from Illinois (2003–2008) was known thanks to his views on health care reform and his exceptionally critical (and perspicacious) attitude towards the so-called Global War on Terror (GWOT) of the 43rd President of the USA and, especially, towards the war in Iraq. He shared the conclusion of Francis Fukuyama that global terror was not an existential threat, but a threat generated by the US foreign policy in the Middle East (Fukuyama 2006). From the point of view of the key topic of this book, is necessary to remember that the process of NATO expansion was not his big priority. But once elected as the new President, Barack Obama was in the position of a statesman who inherited this process, with all its international consequences, from his two predecessors B. Clinton (the political guarantor of the first wave) and G. W. Bush (the political guarantor of the second wave).

6.2.1.2 To Obama as the President

And during his first mandate (2009–2014), he presented his original security culture, which had two basic dimensions: the negative and positive ones. *The negative dimension* of the security culture of Barack Obama has its roots in his famous speech against the Iraq War (Obama 2002). In this speech, delivered in Chicago on October 2, 2002, the then senator did not hesitate to call this war a dumb and rash war which had been cynically pushed by Richard Perle and Paul Wolfowitz.[5] In this sense, Obama fully shared the critical attitude of Zbigniew Brzeziński, who gave G. W. Bush an F grade when assessing his foreign policy (Brzeziński 2007). He did not relativise the danger of Saddam Hussein and his dictatorial rule, but nevertheless, he openly declared that Saddam posed no imminent and direct threat to the United States or his neighbours. In this sense, he clearly refuted the basis of the dominant US security culture, which was based on the exaggeration of this threat and a clear preference of a military approach and military instruments. And this courageous attitude, this negation of the negative attitude towards Iraq that was so typical for the then US mainstream approach, led Obama to a clear formulation of his own security culture.

The positive dimension of the security culture of Barack Obama was articulated in his programme from 2007 (Obama 2007). In this document, Obama, as a presidential candidate, presented his alternative vision, in which he advocated the demilitarisation of the security strategy of the USA and underlined the necessity to fight not only military threats, but also non-military ones, such as ignorance and intolerance, corruption and greed, and poverty and despair. And his logic of the negation of the negative foreign policy of his country resulted in the appeal to force the so-called allies in the Middle East, the Saudis and the Egyptians, to stop oppressing their own people, suppressing dissent, tolerating the corruption and inequality in their countries, and mismanaging their economies. Last but not least, Obama underlined the necessity of the renewal of an active security cooperation with Russia, namely in the field of nuclear arms control.

6.2.1.3 Negation of the Negative Features of the US Foreign Policy

Obama's emphasis on the negation of the negative aspects of the foreign policy of his country gained the support of some important thinkers in the USA. Samuel P. Huntington and Steve Dunn appreciated the move from hegemonic thinking towards a cosmopolitan approach which meant that the USA should react and act as a member of a large international community (Huntington and Dunn 2004). And Obama's emphasis on the demilitarisation of the US security strategy was strongly supported by Philip Gordon, a leading US thinker[6] in this field due to his widely cited book (Gordon 2007–2008). Lastly, John Ikenberry, a leading author of liberal institutionalism, openly supported the move from the power-based international order towards international cooperation (Ikenberry 2014).

Just at the beginning of his first mandate, Obama managed to attract a global attention, especially by his famous Prague Speech in April 2009 (Obama 2009), in which he underlined that the existence of thousands of nuclear weapons is the most

---

[5] Two enormously radical and influential proponents of this war.
[6] During his career, he held a number of research and teaching positions, especially those at the Brookings Institution in Washington, D.C. and the International Institute for Strategic Studies in London.

dangerous legacy of the Cold War. At the same time, he declared his commitment to seek the ways towards a world without nuclear weapons, even if the realisation of this dream may exceed his lifetime.

6.2.2 NSS 2010

Obama's initiative in the field of security culture and grand strategy continued with the National Security Strategy 2010 (NSS 2010a). This important document was published during the second year of his first mandate. It reflects his original approach toward the stakes of peace and war and towards the role of force and diplomacy. The then new president underlined that it was a strategy of national renewal and global leadership and that the US's long term security would come not from its ability to instil fear in other peoples, but through its capacity to speak to their hopes (NSS 2010b). And he continued by being critical towards the US overuse of its military might, its actions imposed without partners, and the overstretching of the US military.

At the same time, the new President accepted that the use of force is sometimes necessary, but he argued that it should come only after the exhausting of other options and a careful reflection of the costs and risks, and under the conditions of a broad international support and with a clear mandate of the U.N. Security Council. In his preface to the Nuclear Posture Review 2010, he underlined, once again (Sanger and Shanker 2010), his determination to make nuclear weapons obsolete, and to create incentives for countries to give up any nuclear ambitions they might have (NPRR 2010).

Of course, within the USA, Barack Obama provoked a lot of criticism. For example, Charles Krauthammer reproached him for his hesitation, delays, indecision and plaintive appeals to the (fictional) "international community" (Obama 2011). According to another US author, Obama's foreign policy, particularly that in Libya in 2011, was a debacle (Kuperman 2015). And one of the most influential critics condemned Obama as the first "post-American" president, who reduced the emphasis on US hegemony in world politics and decreased the American military potential abroad, which is the most important pillar of the US exceptionalism (Bolton 2009).

From the global point of view, we can conclude that in the field of grand strategy and security culture, Barack Obama acted as a typical Wilsonianist of the twenty-first century. He put a key emphasis on the demilitarisation and denuclearisation of the security strategy of the USA, the respect for the international and the unavoidable role of the UN SC. Thanks to his courage, the world witnessed an incontestable move towards positive peace. And from the point of view of the NATO expansion, Obama paid key attention to the grand strategy and the security culture, while the doctrines, especially military doctrines, and strategic culture stayed under the authority of the US generals, namely the Chairman of the Joint Chiefs of Staff and the Chief of Staff of the United States Army. And they continued to modernise the doctrines for the space of the expanded NATO.

6.2.3 Sustaining U.S. Global Leadership: Priorities for Twenty-First Century Defense

On the following pages, the doctrinal document with the title above will be called simply the *Priorities for twenty-first century Defense*. It was approved in the period which was characterised by the military and technological superiority of the USA and the backwardness of the Russian Federation (Zapfe and Haas 2016, p. 36). Its strategic and historical importance relies on two pillars. First, the *Priorities* opened a new era in the doctrinal thinking in the USA, which can be called the era of military activities in the A2/AD environment. At the same time, they paved the way for the following doctrinal documents which fixed concrete priorities for the Army, Navy and Air Force of the USA.

The *Priorities for twenty-first century Defense* were approved after a long series of important changes which had happened during the 1990s. First, the ISR have profoundly changed since the RF removed its big military units from the territories of its former satellite states (the RDA, Czechoslovakia, Hungary, Poland, the three Baltic states, Bulgaria, and Romania) and relocated them eastward, namely to the area of Kaliningrad and, sometime later, under the commandment of the Western Military District, to St. Petersburg (Friedman 2015). This movement of historical importance confirmed that Russia definitively lost all its strategic depth (Frühling and Lasconjarias 2016). Moreover, the area of Kaliningrad witnessed a reduction of the numbers of tanks (by one half), fighters (from 155 to 28) and submarines (from 42 to 2) (Hyde-Price).

Second, the *Priorities for twenty-first century Defense* reflected the four spectacular military successes that the USA obtained in the following large military operations: ODS in 1991, OAF in 1999, OEF in 2001, and OIF in 2003. All these operations showed the American military supremacy in comparison with all other countries of the contemporary world and led to manifestations of the growing American political as well as military engagement and responsibility in the post-Cold War world. These big successes of the US military resulted in profound changes of the ISR after the Cold War.

In reaction to the above mentioned changes, the document *Priorities for twenty-first century Defense* was conceived as a general political framework for the use of the US military superiority for the projection of American military forces into areas with Anti-Access/Area Denial systems. It has two basic characteristics. In its negative sense, this doctrine very often uses the word "challengers," which represents a non-confrontational, maybe more "digestible" expression or label for possible military adversaries who could become military obstacles for the projection of American military power over great distances.

And in its positive sense, this doctrine declares the necessity to assure that the US soldiers have a free access to all areas where their challengers have their A2/AD systems. This document creates a general framework for the use of the US technological superiority in the most favourable conditions. It defines the concept of Anti-Access (A2) as a large set of actions intended to slow the deployment of friendly

Table 6.2 A2/AD systems thirty year after the end of the Cold War

Main systems	Their capabilities
surface-, air- and submarine-launched ballistic and cruise missiles	They have the capability to carry out very accurate and precise attacks against forwarding bases (in peacetime) and deployed U.S. forces (during crisis and war operations)
Ballistic missiles with conventional heads	They can destroy important US installations, particularly military airports
Kinetic and non-kinetic anti-satellite weapons	They can destroy space systems vital to U.S. force projection, namely C2 and ISTAR systems
Submarine forces and anti-ship missiles	They can interdict U.S. and friendly sea lines of communications in both sovereign and international waters between U.S. bases and the theatre of possible operations
Air–defence systems	They have the potential to complicate the realisation of the ASB strategy, particularly the entry operations
Long-range reconnaissance and surveillance systems	They provide necessary targeting information, including information related to satellites, aircraft, and land- and ship-based radars

Source Compiled by the author

forces into a theatre or force them to operate from distances farther from the locus of conflict than they would otherwise prefer. The A2 concept covers all the related activities, including the movement of military forces to a theatre. And the concept of Area-Denial (AD) is defined as a large set of actions intended to impede friendly operations within areas where an adversary cannot or will not prevent access. This means that the AD concept affects military manoeuvres within a theatre far away from the territory of the USA (Table 6.2).

The US doctrinal documents never explicitly mentioned Russia as an adversary or as a challenger, even if it was generally known that the RF was the state with the biggest quantity of A2/AD systems and that its A2/AD systems were at a very respectable level. The document only explained the key characteristics of the A2/AD systems, but all experts working with it understood the true context and message of this explosive subject and its importance for the future (Zapfe and Haas 2016, p. 36). The Russian arms systems of the A2/AD category are, since the beginning, at the disposal of the Western Military District and the forces on the Crimea peninsula. From among them, much attention is paid to the batteries of the S-300 and S-400 (Majumdar 2015) missiles which were furnished to the Russian military units with the aim to strengthen the capacities of the air defence (Freedberg 2015). Another important measure came with the introduction of the system of regular large scale military exercises whose aim is to reinforce the system of defence (*RT News* 2014) (Table 6.3).

6.2 From the NSS 2010 to the JCRA

Table 6.3 The most important Russian A2/AD systems in the light of American doctrines

The name of the system	The key mission of the system	Location
SAM = surface-to-air missile SAM-300 and SAM-400	Protection of Russian units and important centres	Kaliningrad and Crimea
K–300 P Bastion mobile systems	Littoral anti-ship capabilities = attacks against enemies landing military vessels[a]	The Baltic Fleet The Black Sea Fleet
Krasucha	Electronic warfare	The Baltic Sea and Crimea

Source Compiled by the author
[a] With the use of SS–N–26 Strobile missiles, 636. 6 Varšavjanka (Kilo) non-nuclear submarines and shallow-water mines

Out of the above mentioned systems, the Krasucha radars raise particular concerns in the USA. These systems can paralyse radar signals at a distance of 150–300 km, and they are able to jam land radars and radars of supersonic planes and drones. Moreover, they have the capacity to analyse the trajectories of their flights and the use of their arms systems; they are thus called "anti-plane radars" (Zapfe and Haas 2016, pp. 34–41).

6.2.3.1 The Challenger in the Role of the Weak Actor

The basic characteristics of the Priorities for twenty-first century Defence rely on an implicit categorisation of the key actors in a hypothetical direct military confrontation in case of a projection of the US military forces at great distances. This implicit categorisation indicates that the military units of the USA and its allies represent the strong actor, while the units of the target state of that projection are in the role of the weak actor. In all the analysed doctrines, this weak actor is called the "challenger" and this relatively impartial label will be used on the following pages of this book for the explication of the substance of the entire philosophy of A2/AD. If the strong actor carries out a projection of its armed forces, the weak actor is determined to resist, his aim being to complicate the projection, or to deny it.

Within this implicit categorisation, the "challenger," in the role of the weak actor, has no possibility to carry out a counter-offensive against the strong actor. The stronger actor projects his military units over very long distances so that they are far away from his own territory, which means that his homeland has the status of a sanctuary. On the other hand, the ambition of the weak actor, of the "challenger", is much more modest. His ambition is to reduce and weaken the military superiority of the strong actor who carries out the projection of his offensive units to the targeted territory. This basic circumstance explains the fundamental importance of the A2/AD systems—they give the "challenger" the possibility to reduce the military superiority of the strong actor and complicate his offensive operations.

According to this doctrinal approach, the so-called "challenger" relies on his A2/AD systems with two key aims. His minimal aim is to reduce the speed of the projection of the military forces of the strong actor. In this case, the tactics called attrition can happen. The maximal aim of the weak actor is to stop the projection of the strong actor and defeat him. In this case, the victory of the weak actor could discredit the strong actor and force him to forget his ambition to project his military units over a very long distance (Krepinevich 2010).

6.2.4 The Joint Operational Access Concept (JOAC) of January 2012

The JOAC (2012) is the first document to concretise the above analysed Priorities for twenty-first century Defence and apply them to the military level. It was published only two weeks after this document of the category of grand strategy. As it fixes the concrete tasks for all units and Headquarters conceived as a general conceptual framework for A2/AD warfare which fixes the tasks for the combat activities of US soldiers during their projections over long distances into areas with a high concentration of A2/AD systems.

6.2.4.1 The Cascade of Arguments

This doctrinal document is based on a sophisticated cascade of arguments which has the six following levels: the American way of life (AWL), its pillars, foreign actors (challengers) who could threaten the AWL, the instruments that they have at their disposal, the US determination to eliminate these threats, and the key instruments that it can use with the aim to face its challengers.

At the first level, the USA defines itself as a global power with global interests. Its political as well as military elites are convinced that the AWL represents the top political value of all its doctrines, including the JOAC. At the same time, the AWL represents the basis for the arguments on all five of the following levels. At the second level, the AWL rests on two mutually intertwined pillars: the USA categorically requires *a free access* to the global strategic resources (as a part of the so-called global commons) as well as to the global markets. At the same time, the JOAC underlines that the USA has not only the right, but also *the duty to send its soldiers* into areas where the USA or its allies could be exposed to imminent and serious security threats.

On the third level, the cascade of arguments continues with the presentation of *the serious and imminent threats* to which the USA and its allies are exposed. These threats are identified with the so-called challengers, which concretely means the countries which could try to limit the freedom of action of the USA and its allies during the projection of their armed forces over long distances into every place of the globe. This document identifies the future enemies as both states and nonstate

6.2 From the NSS 2010 to the JCRA

actors which would see the adoption of an anti-access/area-denial strategy against the United States as a favourable course of action for them (JOAC 2012, p. 13).

At the fourth level, the key instrument of these *"challengers"* is identified as their arsenal of A2/AD arms systems. The JOAC concretely mentions the most dangerous A2/AD systems, which could be used with the aim to deny the projection of force of the US military units. It divides these instruments into two categories. The first of them is the category A2, which includes the long-range systems designed to prevent an opposing force from entering an operational area. This category concretely includes missiles launched from land, planes or military ships whose range is more than 1000 miles, long range radars and anti-satellite systems. The second category is identified with AD systems, systems of a shorter range designed not to keep an opposing force out, but to limit its freedom of action within the operational area; these systems are engaged with the aim to oppose the military activities of projected forces which managed to enter the given territory, which is called the operational area. This category includes particularly air forces, air defence, precision guided missiles, artillery, land forces and drones (JOAC 2012, p. 17).

At the fifth level, the cascade of arguments continues with the declaration of *the determination of the USA* to eliminate these systems with projections of force, and it is crowned by an open declaration that the JOAC is a warfighting concept. On the sixth level, the instruments of the USA are charged with the projection of force and forcible entries into the territories of states that are perceived as challengers or even as threats for the USA or its allies. The JOAC states that the preparation of the units charged with these tasks is oriented in two basic directions. The first of them is that of the system of long term preparation of the operation in the A2/AD environment, which could be regularly organised on the territory of the USA or of its allies. And the second is that of the realisation of entry operations which open the way for the following quick advancement into the territory of the enemy armed with A2/AD systems.

The JOAC underlines that the most important ability of the US armed forces is force projection, which is defined as the ability to project a military instrument of national power from the United States or another theatre in response to requirements for military operations (DOD Dictionary). Also, the document explains the importance of operational access, which is defined as the ability to project military force into an operational area with sufficient freedom of action to accomplish the mission (JOAC 2012, p. 1). Lastly, this doctrine emphasises the role of assured access, which is defined as open access to the maritime, air, space and cyberspace domains (NATO's Act 2011). From a military perspective, the Alliance relies and increasingly depends on assured access to all four domains—often simultaneously (NATO's Act 2011, p. 3). The aim of the JOAC is to assure the unhindered national use of the global commons and select sovereign territories, waters, airspace and cyberspace, which is achieved by projecting all the elements of national power.

On the sixth level (instruments of the USA), the JOAC mentions not only the instruments, but also *the abilities* which are necessary for success in the field of projection of force into a so-called A2/AD environment. It starts by discussing operational access in the face of armed opposition. The following general principles, when applied to each situation through planning and execution, amplify that basic concept with an additional level of description. Among them, the Operational Access Precepts play a very important role. They are based on the requirements of the broader mission, while also designing subsequent operations to lessen access challenges.

At the same time, the JOAC underlines the importance of the preparation of the operational area in advance with the aim to facilitate access, namely to seize the initiative by deploying and operating on multiple, independent lines of operations. The Precepts include provisions for the exploitation of the advantages in one or more domains to disrupt enemy anti-access/area-denial capabilities in others, the disruption of enemy reconnaissance and surveillance efforts while protecting friendly efforts, as well as the creation of pockets or corridors of local domain superiority to penetrate the enemy's defences and maintain them as required to accomplish the mission. Lastly, the JOAC underlines the importance of direct manoeuvres against key operational objectives from a strategic distance, in-depth attacks against enemy anti-access/area-denial defences and the maximisation of surprise through deception, stealth, and ambiguity to complicate enemy targeting (JOAC 2012, p. 17).

The concept of *deception* has two basic meanings in this case. On the level of grand strategy, this behaviour includes, according to Mearsheimer (2018) three key methods. The first is lying, which is defined as knowingly making an untrue statement. The second is spinning, in other words emphasising or de-emphasising of certain facts. And the last is concealment, which is withholding information from the public that might undermine or weaken a favoured policy. As a result, deception creates distrust, weakens the rule of law, undermines policy making, and provokes a loss of faith among the public which might lead the given society to be open to an authoritarian regime.

On the military level, deception is defined as a complex of measures designed to mislead the enemy by manipulation, distortion, or falsification of evidence and to induce the enemy to react in a manner prejudicial to its interests. In the US military doctrines, military deception (MILDEC) is conceived as a complex of actions executed with the aim to deliberately mislead adversary military, paramilitary, or violent extremist organization decision makers, thereby causing the adversary to take specific actions (or inactions) that will contribute to the accomplishment of the friendly mission (MILDEC 2012). And the doctrines of the new generation define it as a large portfolio of actions which are executed with the aim to deliberately mislead adversary military decision makers in regard to friendly military capabilities, intentions, and operations, thereby causing the adversary to take specific actions (or inactions) that will contribute to the accomplishment of the friendly mission (JOAC 2012, p. 25).

6.2.5 Air-Sea Battle, May 2013

The third of the doctrinal documents of the new generation was approved in the spring of 2013 under the name Air-Sea Battle (2013). The basic philosophy of this

6.2 From the NSS 2010 to the JCRA

enormously important document was inspired by the Air-Land Battle (ALB) concept from the last decade of the Cold War, whose aim was to face the conventional quantitative superiority of the POW. The ALB doctrine put the main emphasis on the combat activities of the Allied Air Forces, namely their massive attacks against the armies in the second and even third echelons on the territory of the former Czechoslovakia, the DDR, and Poland and the Eastern parts of the USSR. This doctrine paid decisive attention to a close coordination between land forces acting as an aggressively manoeuvring defence, and air forces attacking rear-echelon forces feeding the front line enemy forces (Grant 2001).

The ALB doctrine was approved in 1982 (AirLand Battle 2018) as a warfighting concept of the US Army for the war in the European theatre and served as a doctrinal base until the end of the Cold War (Winton 1996). Its key purpose was the elimination of the large conventional superiority of the USSR and its satellite states (Starry 1981). This doctrine oriented the efforts of the US armed forces toward the destruction of the conventional forces and of all of their logistics pertaining to the territories of the satellite countries.

6.2.5.1 The International Context of ASB

The philosophy of the above mentioned ALB was so consistent that it became the basic inspiration even for the concept of Air-Sea Battle. More than 20 years after the end of the Cold War, the ASB doctrine was elaborated with the aim to develop the long tradition of the integrated battle doctrine which became official in February 2010. Thus ASB's name was changed to the Joint Concept for Access and Maneuver in the Global Commons (JAM-GC) in 2015 (Goldfein 2015). The primary target of this doctrine is not the post-Soviet space, but the "asymmetrical threats" in the Western Pacific and the Persian Gulf. This doctrine was elaborated as the US response to the military modernisation of two problematic countries in the Eastern hemisphere: China and Iran (Gady 2015). For their detailed and profound analysis, the Pentagon created a China Integration Team (CIT) composed of U.S. Navy officers. Following their military analysis and recommendations, the Obama Administration declared in 2010 that freedom of maritime navigation in the South China Sea was a U.S. national interest (Glain 2011) (Table 6.4).

Table 6.4 The basic definition of ASB

General aims	Concrete aims
Operational superiority of the armed forces of the USA	The ability to operate in the A2/AD environment
The USA will have the advantage of the escalation of military activities	The USA will decide about the conditions and circumstances of the employment of the destructive arms systems

Source Compiled by the author

Even if this new doctrine is not specifically oriented to the area of the South China Sea, its key principles could be applied even at the Eastern frontier of the expanded NATO. This is especially the case with the North Eastern area, where four new member states of NATO (Poland and the three Baltic countries) are littoral countries with strategically important coasts which could be used, if necessary, for the projection of military forces over necessary distances. In the South-Eastern frontier of the expanded NATO, Bulgaria and Romania, as new member states of NATO, don't offer the same possibilities for the projection of military forces, but in case of the inclusion of Ukraine and Georgia in NATO, the geostrategic importance of this area could enormously grow.

6.2.5.2 Military Aims of ASB

The above mentioned circumstances explain the strategic and military importance of the ASB doctrine and of its emphasis on a large portfolio of tasks for the coordination of the Air Force and Navy for cases of invasive operations in the areas of A2/AD operations (Krepinevich 2010). In this new international context, ASB presents new doctrinal priorities as well as new general and concrete aims for the military at the beginning of the new century (Lock-Pullan 2005).

The ASB doctrine underlines three military aims for the US military in the A2/AD environment. The first of them is defined as a successful fight against the A2/AD systems, a fight which must be based on the operational superiority of the US armed forces across all domains. The second aim is to have an escalation advantage within the framework of all military operations. Lastly, ASB is oriented toward the projection of military force and unlimited freedom of actions in the so-called global commons. The phrase "global commons" is not used here with the aim to identify any concrete territory. It refers to the air, waters, space, and cyber-space which are in the possession of no state, but which have vital importance for the USA, namely for the projection of its military force towards a hostile territory. The more GCs the USA has under its control, the more platforms it can use for the application of its Priorities for twenty-first century Defense and other doctrines of the new generation, namely for the projection of force.

6.2.5.3 The 3D Missions and Their Importance

Another important pillar of ASB is represented by the so-called 3D missions, which have a common denominator: intensive and concentrated attacks into the depths of the "challenger" with the aim to destroy the maximum number of their A2/AD systems (O'Hanlon and Steinberg 2012). They are conceived as integrated operations in all five domains: air, land, sea, space and cyberspace. This means that ASB covers the large space between a doctrine and a military concept (O'Hanlon 2012).

From the geopolitical point of view, ASB is not a strategy of combat against a concrete enemy or state; it is not conceived for a concrete region. It is conceived

6.2 From the NSS 2010 to the JCRA

Table 6.5 The "3D" Missions

Name of the mission	The key purpose of the mission
Disrupt	To destroy the adversary's C4IS systems
Destroy	To destroy the adversary's A2/AD systems
Defeat	To destroy the adversary's combat units

as a strategy for the entire globe. Its key attention is paid to modern arms systems, which represent the most important obstacles for entry operations of the US armed forces (O'Hanlon and Steinberg 2012). The phrase "arms systems" is used to refer to the following systems: ballistic missiles, cruise missiles, sophisticated systems of air defence, and systems of electronic combat which are able to destroy C4ISR systems.[7] Since the beginning, all these systems have been deployed eastward from the contemporary Eastern border of NATO; more specifically, they are at the disposal of the Western Military District in St. Petersburg.

And from the military point of view, this doctrine has two basic missions. The first is to augment the combat superiority of the US Armed Forces at any place of the world and across all domains. The second mission of ASB is to assure a full escalation advantage of the US military units. It puts a particular emphasis on a perfect coordination and integration of military operations in all the dimensions: land, sea, air, space and cyberspace. Within this framework, ASB underlines the importance of the following key aims. The first is the manoeuvres in the A2/AD milieu, and the second is the freedom of action in the projection of force into the so-called global commons (GC), which can be used as the bases from which it is possible to reach the hostile territory (Table 6.5).

In comparison with ALB, the ASB doctrine manifested two basic changes. The first is the rising importance of the intensity as well as the extensity of the military operations of the USA and its allies. The second is that the missions of the Air Force are now enlarged from the initial support of the land forces in the case of ALB to the support of the maritime infantry during large and intensive sea landing operations in the countries with a strong potential in terms of A2/AD arms systems in the case of ASB.

---

[7]C4ISR is an acronym used by the U.S. Department of Defense, U.S. intelligence agencies, and the defense community which stands for Command, Control, Communications, Computers, Intelligence, Surveillance, and Reconnaissance.

6.2.6 The Joint Concept for Entry Operations (JCEO) of April 2014

The fourth in the line of the doctrinal documents of the new generation was published in April 2014 and represents an important document which presents concrete missions and aims of the armed forces of the USA and its allies during their projections over long distances into environments saturated by A2/AD systems (JCEO 2014). Before its detailed examination, it is necessary to remember that the USA has a long and deeply rooted tradition of so-called long distance entry operations which covers the long period from the Korean War (namely the battles at Pusan /Utz 1994/ and the Yalu/MacArthur 1964/) to Operation Restored Hope in Somalia (Stewart 1994).

The Joint Concept for Entry Operations is a doctrinal document of the US Army and it has been authorised in spring 2014 by General Martin E. Dempsey.[8] This four-star general[9] underlined in his message that the JCEO is a vision for how joint forces will enter a foreign territory and immediately employ their capabilities to accomplish a full variety of possible assigned missions. The entry operation should be conducted in the presence of an armed opposition which would be characterised by increasingly advanced area-denial systems in places where the environment and infrastructure may be degraded or austere. Like in the other doctrinal documents, possible enemies are referred to as "opponents," or "adversaries" (Air-Sea Battle 2013, p. 7). They are characterised as forces that will limit the freedom of action of the US mission-tailored joint forces or military forces, which are operating in a difficult security environment far away from their homeland. The key aim of this doctrine is to gain and maintain accessions of foreign territory (JCEO 2014, p. vi).

The US military activities are defined as forcible entries against armed opposition with the aim to fulfil broader strategic goals. Entry operations of this kind are conceived as sea and air penetrations of the foreign territory with the aim to fulfil all the strategic aims of the USA and its allies. Forcible entries as one the most important mission types are defined as the seizing and holding of a lodgement in the face of armed opposition (Joint Chiefs of Staff 2017). The word lodgement refers to a designated area in a hostile environment which has been seized and held with the aim to assure a continuous landing of troops and materials there and to provide manoeuvre space for subsequent military operations within the framework of the projection of force over long distances (JCEO 2014, p. 1) (Table 6.6).

This doctrinal document defines not only new missions of the armed forces and the capabilities necessary for their fulfilment but also new types of armed forces that should realise these operations in case of war: entry forces, support forces, support of entry forces and follow-on forces. Last but not least, this document pays much attention to the military bases of the USA and its allies in the territories far from the

---

[8] He has in his background the functions of the commander of a regiment, the commander of armored divisions and even the commander of the Vth Corps.

[9] The 18th Chairman of the Joint Chiefs of Staff, in office from October 1, 2011 until September 25, 2015.

6.2 From the NSS 2010 to the JCRA

Table 6.6 Basic characteristics of entry operations

Key missions	Projection of force over a long distance
	Rapid manoeuvres of navy and air assaults
	Forcible entries into foreign territories
Key tasks	Defeating all resistance of adversary forces
	Rapid entries and destroying the adversary's A2/AD systems.
Key types of manoeuvres	Envelopment, infiltration and penetration

Source Compiled by the author

Table 6.7 Military bases of the USA

Types of military bases	Main tasks
Bases near the possible entry operations	Rapid manoeuvres
Rotational forward bases	Preparation of entry operations
Homeland bases	Long-term preparation for the military activities in the A2/AD environment

US homeland and as near as possible to the frontiers of "challengers" armed with A2/AD systems. These bases are enormously important, and they represent one of the pillars of the doctrinal thinking (Table 6.7).

ASB is characterised by a clear definition of three key types of military manoeuvres: envelopment, infiltration and penetration. The first type is described as a quick military action on the territory of the enemy based on technological superiority and high mobility. The aim of the second type of manoeuvre is the destruction of the cohesion of a potential enemy and, particularly, of its A2/AD systems. And penetration, as the third type, is defined as a series of rapid attacks against the defensive units of the enemy.

Finally, several key instruments are defined within the framework of ASB: multinational operations, modern intelligence and the growing firepower aimed particularly against air defence and anti-navy A2/AD systems. The same logic is characteristic for the contemporary doctrine JCEO from April 2014. This doctrine is officially presented as a warfighting concept (Department of Defence 2012) against all "adversaries" or "opponents" who could limit the freedom of action of the US military forces in the environment with A2/AD systems.

The main mission of the JCEO is to gain and maintain access to foreign territories against the so-called armed opposition of states which could use their A2/AD systems with the aim to stop the military units of the USA and its allies. This means that forcible military entries represent the key instrument of this doctrine (JCEO 2014, p. vi). The USA is determined to carry out these large and rapid entry operations at every place in the contemporary world where its vital interests could be exposed to a menace.

At the same time, the JCEO doctrine explains the main forms of war to be waged against states with A2/AD systems. It underlines the key importance of air and sea assaults and operations prepared and waged in accordance with the Air-Sea Battle concept. Within this framework, the US soldiers should be able to satisfy all the criteria of projection of military power and forcible entries in all parts of the contemporary world, and operate at global distances (Department of Defence 2012, p. 3).

According to this doctrine, the forcible entry operation will be followed by the so-called joint entry operations, which are to be realised by the specialised mission–tailored joint forces. During the first stages of these operations, the combat units of the USA and its allies have the mission to search for the weak and vulnerable elements of the adversaries and to transform them into entry points not only for the first echelons, but also for the units which will reinforce the potential of the projected attack forces.

6.2.7 *The Joint Concept for Rapid Aggregation (JCRA) of May 2015*

The month of May 2015 saw the publication of the first doctrinal document approved after the Russian annexation of the Crimea. Nevertheless, this dramatic event had no direct impact on the JCRA (2015), which is based on a continuity with the philosophy of the Priorities for twenty-first century Defense of 2012. The JCRA openly declares that it takes its inspiration particularly from current doctrines, lessons learned from recent operations, best practices, and ongoing development work, and their evaluation for the purpose of finding a solution to the problem of the future operational environment (JCRA 2015, p. iii).

From the military point of view, the JCRA represents a coherent operational platform for the combined forces which are charged with the so–called globally integrated operations—GIO. These operations are characterised by high flexibility, decentralised cooperation with all the Allied commanders, a high preparedness for combat and a capability to take part in combat in the A2/AD environment. They are conceived as the US strategic approach to a large portfolio of global security tasks (MECC 2018). In the definition of this doctrine, General Martin Dempsey, the Chairman of the Joint Chiefs of Staff, underlined the global dimension and mission of this doctrine. According to him, the USA has the ambition to create a "globally postured Joint Force" which will be able to operate "anywhere in the world with a wide array of partners." This means that "[t]here may be times when a large centralized force is needed, but more often than not, the Joint Force will operate as a decentralized network that can aggregate on demand and dial capabilities up or down depending on the mission and the operating environment."

The entirety of this doctrinal document is based on two basic words. The first of them is the substantive "aggregation", which is defined as the ability "to collect units or parts into a mass or whole" with the aim to form "a group, body, or mass composed of many distinct parts or individuals able to achieve unity of effort in the accomplishment of common objectives." And the adjective "rapid" (Merriam Webster) denotes the speed of action required to aggregate forces under the compressed timelines of crises. Ultimately, the necessary response speed is relative to the mission's tempo as it unfolds.

The key aims of this doctrine are to improve the US's ability to rapidly aggregate forces, to achieve efficiencies and synergies at a qualitatively new level, and to quickly connect with a diverse and evolving set of partners and networks with substantively improved collaborative tools and practices. Rapid aggregation aims toward a significant strategic and operational agility which would be achieved by increasingly globally integrated planning and resourcing strategies. Its final aim is to generate and aggregate the military forces necessary for successful operations. The JCRA concept orients the military training of the US armed forces towards gaining the ability to realise so-called globally integrated operations which are characterised by a high flexibility, decentralised cooperation with all the Allied commanders, a high preparedness for combat and a capability to take part in combat in the A2/AD environment.

6.3 The Conclusion of the Chapter

This entire chapter has been consecrated to the analysis of the American doctrinal documents approved during the half-decade 2010–2015. These documents symbolise a new stage in the history of the US security and strategic culture. They have been analysed on two basic levels: those of grand strategy and military doctrines.

The category of grand strategy is represented by the NSS 2010 and the Priorities for twenty-first century Defense—both of which have been signed by the 44th President of the USA and shaped by his emphasis on the demilitarisation and denuclearisation of the US security culture, and on the move from unilateralism towards multilateralism. Within this general framework, the NATO expansion and its political and military aspects did not play a central role. These aspects have been reserved for the category of military doctrines.

From the geopolitical point of view, all the military doctrines from the period 2012–2015 were written as a concentrated reaction of American operative realists to the fact that the second Russian president initiated, after the so-called lost decade symbolised by his predecessor, a large and intensive modernisation of the Russian Armed Forces which, since the beginning, had two basic characteristics. First, it had been motivated by the Russian fears of encirclement after the second wave of the NATO expansion. Second, as the fears of Russian operative realists were identified particularly with large amphibious invasive anding operations, the modern A2/AD anti-landing systems became the pillar of this intensive modernisation. Their mission is limited to attacking and destroying all systems which can be used to approach the territory of the RF with the aim to carry out an entry operation. This concretely means that they are to attack military vessels, submarines, planes and systems of navigation and reconnaissance, including modern satellites.

From the military point of view, the US military doctrines have four common denominators. First, they reflect the US's *growing military self-confidence* acquired after a lot of successful military operations and regime changes after 1990 (Zapfe and Haas 2016, p. 38). Second, they react to the so-called challengers' *obsession with offensive operations* with an emphasis on quick attacks on the arms systems in the depths of the given territory. Third, they underline *the enlargement of the Western values* as well as of the right of other countries to demand and obtain security guarantees from the USA. Lastly, they are oriented towards offensive entry operations (Zapfe and Haas 2016, p. 38) waged with the aim to destroy as much as possible of the A2/AD systems. No wonder that Michael Haas concludes that these doctrines have no "altruistic basis" (Haas 2014, p. 69).

The growing military self-confidence of the USA is manifested in three important directions. First, the US military doctrines send out an implicit general message that the post-Soviet space, particularly its Western part, is seen as an area vital for the American hegemonic system. Second, they underline the strategic importance of the American technological and military primacy. Third, they overtly manifest the determination of the US elites to use the US's military primacy not only in peace but also, if necessary, on the military field. Lastly, all the US doctrinal documents are oriented towards offensive entry operations that would go into the depths of states equipped with A2/AD systems. They reflect the determination of the American operative realists to accumulate as much destructive force as possible and locate it as close to the Eastern frontier of the enlarged NATO as possible. Nevertheless, all the doctrines could have some counterproductive consequences.

In peacetime, the risk of a regionalisation of NATO could grow. This risk results from the fact that the Eastern frontier of NATO is characterised by a high degree of military tension and of danger of a direct military confrontation. On the other hand, the Western flank of the Alliance can differ from the new member countries, and they could differ especially in their perceptions of security threats. This situation could lead to a so-called regional security dilemma and internal tension in the Alliance, as was so precisely explained by Snyder (1997) and Massala (2010). Today, the border with the RF represents the most controversial area of all of NATO, and it is characterised by an enormously high military tension. On the one hand, the Poles and the Baltic states live with major security fears regarding their Eastern neighbour. On the other hand, the threat perception of the South-Western flank of NATO is profoundly different (Zapfe and Haas 2016, p. 35).

And *in case of war*, there is a risk of a counterproductive and unintended military escalation and of big losses on the part of the Allied forces during the first days of armed hostilities. As the Allied VJTF and NRF military units require between 2 and 5 days for their transfer, the fate of the Baltic countries would be sealed without any armed conflict in this scenario (Haas 2014). The Baltic States could be annexed by Russia without a single shot being fired (Fiott 2016).

6.3 The Conclusion of the Chapter

6.3.1 The Primordial Importance of the Bay of Finland

The years that followed the publication of the above analysed documents confirmed the primordial importance of the Bay of Finland. Russia accelerated the production and the deployment of the new A2/AD systems, while none of them can be used to attack the territory of the USA or that of the so-called old member countries of NATO. In this category of Russian arms systems, there is only one partial exception: the new missile called SS-26 Stone or "Iskander," a road-mobile short-range ballistic missile (SRBM) with a range of up to 500 km (SS-26 Iskander 2016). Using a common transporter-erector-launcher (TEL) and support vehicles, the system can also fire 9M728 (R-500, SSC-7) and 9M729 (SSC-8) cruise missiles. The installation (*The Guardian* 2016) of these systems has been interpreted as the Russian answer to the American antimissile systems in Europe (Richardson 2011). This measure provoked an enormously controversial reaction because the Iskanders can be launched against targets at a distance of 700 km, which means that they could reach the Eastern part of the FRG (Akulov 2016).

As the Baltic area and particularly the Bay of Finland represent a doorstep to the Northern part of the RF, the Russian operative realists pay key attention to the modernisation of the Baltic Fleet. This important unit of the Russian Navy obtained new corvettes of the class Steregushchiy (Russian: Стерегущий, lit. 'Vigilant') (Global Naval Forces). It is a new category of multipurpose corvettes which was designed for combat in littoral zone operations, namely for engagement against three key military threats: enemy submarines, surface ships, and gun support of landing operations (rusnavy.com 2012).

6.3.2 Military Exercises and Growing Tension

But on the other hand, the USA and its allies continue to object that these systems represent a threat for the security of the new member states. As a result, this part of our continent is witnessing a growing military tension which is manifested particularly during military exercises. Among them, a large test of the above mentioned corvettes played an important role. March and April 2020 saw six corvettes participating in large-scale drills of the Russian Navy. Since the beginning this exercise was planned and largely presented as an answer (BMPD 2020) to the largest NATO post-Cold War simulation of amphibious landing in Europe, which received the code name DEFENDER-Europe 20. It was a large U.S.-led multinational exercise that included NATO's participation. During this deployment of U.S.-based forces to Europe, the largest in more than 25 years, more than 20,000 soldiers were deployed directly from the U.S. to Europe. This exercise was planned with the aim to demonstrate the U.S. commitment to NATO and its resolve to stand by its European allies and partners (Defender Europe 20).

Today, we know that this regularly repeated military exercise carried out all over Europe, as well as the exercises Dynamic Front, Saber Strike, and Swift Response, was cancelled due to the ongoing COVID-19 pandemic (Milevski 2020). Nevertheless, the plans and the preparations of this large scale, multi-national drill provoked a Russian response in the form of an exercise of the Baltic Fleet. This escalation confirmed the dangerous logic of the mirror security behaviour between NATO and the RF. The annexation of the Crimea was followed by the exercises of NATO and they were followed by the exercise of a big Russian unit. As a result, the military tension between the RF and NATO continues to rise to a very dangerous and explosive level.

Sources

AirLand Battle. (2018, August 1). The Army's Cold War Plan to Crush Russia. Available at: …nationalinterest.org › blog › buzz.
Air-Sea Battle. (2013, May). *United States Department of Defense [PDF]*. Available at: https://arc hive.defense.gov/pubs/ASB-ConceptImplementation-Summary-May-2013.pdf, p. 7.
Akulov, A. (2016, October). *Iskander Missiles Deployed in Kaliningrad: Whom Do They Threaten?* Available at: https://www.strategic-culture.org/…/iskander-missiles-deployed-ka…,13.
Attrill, M. (2015). NATO Doctrine. *The Three Swords Magazine*, p. 14.
BMPD. (2020). Крепкая Балтика. *bmpd*, April 4.
Bolton, J. (2009, October). President Obama's Foreign Policy: An Assessment. *Imprimis, 38*(10).
Brzeziński, Z. (2007). *Second Chance: Three Presidents and the Crisis of American Superpower*. New York: Basic Books.
Defender Europe 20. Available at: https://shape.nato.int/defender-europe.
de Montbrial, T., & Klein, J. (Eds.). (2000). *Dictionnaire de stratégie* (p. 193). Paris: Presses universitaires de France.
Department of Defence. (2012). P. 3.
DOD Dictionary. *DOD Dictionary of Military Terms*. Available at: http://www.dtic.mil/doctrine/dod_dictionary/.
Fiott, D. (2016, April–May). Modernising NATO's Defence Infrastructure with EU Funds. *Survival: Global Politics and Strategy, 58*(2), 77–94.
Freedberg, S. J. Jr. (2015, September 11). Russians 'Closed the Gap' For A2/AD: Air Force Gen. Gorenc.
Friedman, G. (2015). *Flashpoints: The Emerging Crisis in Europe*. New York: Doudleday.
Frühling, S., & Lasconjarias G. (2016). NATO, A2/AD and the Kaliningrad Challenge. *Survival, 58*(2), 103.
Fukuyama, F. (2006). *America at the Crossroads. Democracy, Power and the Neoconservative Legacy*. New Haven: Yale University Press.
Gaddis, J. L. (2009). *What Is Grand Strategy?* Presented at a meeting of the FPRI-Temple University Consortium on Grand Strategy, Philadelphia, Pennsylvania, September 10, 2009.
Gady, F.-S. (2015, September 9). China or Iran: Who Is the Bigger Threat to U.S. Airpower?
Gariup, M. (2009). *European Security Culture: Language, Theory, Policy*. Burlington, VT: Ashgate.
Glain, S. (2011). The Pentagon's New China War Plan. *Salon*, August 13.
Global Naval Forces. (2008, December 29). News and Defence Headlines. IHS Jane's 360.
Goldfein, D. (2015, January 8). *Document: Air Sea Battle Name Change Memo*. Available at: www.news.usni.org. Pentagon.
Gordon, P. H. (2007–2008). Winning the Right War. *Survival, 49*(4, Winter 2007–2008), 17–46.

Grant, R. (2001). Deep Strife. *Air Force Magazine*, June 1. Available at: https://www.airforcemag.com/article/0601airland/.
Gray, C. (1999). *Modern Strategy*. Oxford: Oxford University Press.
Gray, C. (2007). *War, Peace and International Relations: An Introduction to Strategic History* (p. 283). Abingdon and New York City: Routledge.
Gross, G. M. (2016). The New Generation of Operational Concepts. *Small Wars Journal*, January 8.
Haas, M. (2014). *Foreign Policy Begins at Home: The Case for Putting America's House in Order*. New York: Basic Books.
Huntington, S. P., & Dunn, S. (2004). *Who are We? The Challenges to America's National Identity*. New York: Simon & Schuster.
Hyde-Price, A. NATO and the Baltic Sea Region: Towards Regional Security Governance? NATO Research Fellowship Scheme 1998–2000 Final Report.
Ikenberry, J. (2014). *Power, Order, and Change in World Politics*. Cambridge: Cambridge University.
IMF. (2016, October 4). *World Economic Outlook Database*.
JC2ALN. (2015, March 20). *Joint Concept for Command and Control of the Joint Aerial*. Available at: www.hsdl.org › abstract.
JCEO. (2014). *Joint Concept for Entry Operations, Joint Chiefs of Staff, 7 April 2014. Paperback—26 June 2014*. Available at: https://www.jcs.mil/Portals/36/Documents/Doctrine/concepts/jceo.pdf?ver=2017-12-28-162000-837.
JCHS. (2015, August 31). *Joint Concept for Health Services. Joint Chiefs of Staff*. Available at: www.jcs.mil › Doctrine › concepts.
JCL. (2015, September 25). *Joint Concept for Logistics—Center for Joint and Strategic*. Available at: cjsl.ndu.edu › Portals › Documents.
JCRA. (2015, May 22). *Joint Concept for Rapid Aggregation (JCRA)*.
JOAC. (2012, January 17). *Joint Operational Access Concept—United States*. Available at: archive.defense.gov › pubs › pdfs.
Joint Chiefs of Staff. (2017, September 16). *JP 3-18, Joint Forcible Entry Operations CH 1*. Available at: www.jcs.mil › Doctrine › pubs.
Jones, B. (2012). Russia Rejuvenates Kaliningrad Naval Base. *Janee's Navy International, 117*(3).
Kirchner, E. J., & Sperling, J. (Eds.). (2007). *Global Security Governance: Competing Perceptions of Security in the 21st Century*. London: Routledge.
Krepinevich, A. F. (2010). *CSBA: Why AirSea Battle?* (PDF). Center for Strategic and Budgetary Assessments (CSBA).
Kuperman, A. J. (2015). Obama's Libya Debacle: How a Well-Meaning Intervention Ended in Failure. *Foreign Affairs, 94*(2), 66–70, 71–77.
Liddell Hart, B. H. (1991). *Strategy* (2d rev. ed., pp. 321–222). Toronto: Meridian.
Lock-Pullan, R. (2005). How to Rethink War: Conceptual Innovation and AirLand Battle Doctrine. *Journal of Strategic Studies* [online], *28*(4), 679–702. Available at: http://www.tandfonline.com/doi/pdf/10.1080/01402390500301087.
MacArthur, D. (1964). *Reminiscences*. New York: Ishi Press.
Majumdar, D. (2015). American F-22s and B-2 Bombers vs. Russia's S-300 in Syria: Who Wins? *National Interest*, September 22.
Massala, C. (2010). Alliances. In M. D. Cavelty & V. Mauer (Eds.), *Routledge Handbook of Security Studies* (p. 387). London: Routledge.
Mearsheimer, J. J. (2018). Liberalism as a Source of Trouble. In *The Great Delusion: The Liberal Dreams and International Realities* (pp. 154–187). New Haven and London: Yale University Press.
MECC. (2018, October). *Globally Integrated Operations, 30 October 2018*. Available at: https://www.jcs.mil/Doctrine/Joint-Education/MECC2018/.
Merriam Webster. Available at: http://www.merriam-webster.com/dictionary/rapid.

MILDEC. (2012, January 26). *Military Deception (MILDEC)—Joint Forces Staff College*. Available at: jfsc.ndu.edu Additional_Reading.
Milevski, L. (2020, March 30). *Military Exercise Defender Europe-20 Is Cancelled: What Does It Mean for the Baltic States?* Available at: www.fpri.org.
NATO's Act. (2011, February 25). *Assured Access to the Global Commons*. Available at: https://www.act.nato.int/images/stories/events/2010/gc/aagc_recommendations.pdf.
NPRR. (2010, April 6). *Nuclear Posture Review Report*. Available at: www.hsdl.org › abstract.
NSS. (2010a, May 1). *National Security Strategy—Obama White House*. Available at: obamawhitehouse.archives.gov › files.
NSS. (2010b). *National Security Strategy 2010 (PDF)*. United States Government. Retrieved 21 April 2011.
Obama, B. (2002). *Transcript: Obama's Speech Against The Iraq War: NPR*. Available at: www.npr.org › story › story. Barack Obama delivered this speech in Chicago on 2 October 2002.
Obama, B. (2007). Renewing American Leadership. *Foreign Affairs*, July–August.
Obama, B. (2009). *Remarks by President Barack Obama in Prague as Delivered*. The White.
Obama, B. (2011, April 5). The Obama Doctrine: Leading from Behind. *Washington Post*, April 28. Available at: www.washingtonpost.com › opinions. House, Office of the Press Secretary.
O'Hanlon, M. (2012). The Case for a Politically Correct Pentagon. *Foreign Policy*, September 18.
O'Hanlon, M., & Steinberg J. (2012). Going Beyond 'Air-Sea Battle'. *The Washington Post*, August 3.
Posen, B. (1984). *The Sources of Military Doctrine: France, Britain, and Germany Between the World Wars* (p. 13). Ithaca and New York: Cornell University Press.
Richardson, D. (2011). Russia Plans More Iskander-M Systems. *Jane's Missiles & Rockets*, 15(9).
Ross, T. W. (2018, January 9). The Power of Partnership Security Cooperation and Globally Integrated Logistics. *Joint Force Quarterly, 88*.
RT News. (2014). Russian Military Completes Rapid Deployment Drills in Kaliningrad. *RT News*, December 16. Available at: https://www.rt.com/news/214667-russiadrills-kaliningrad-region/.
rusnavy.com. (2012). Russian Navy to Receive Corvette Boiky by Year End. *rusnavy.com*, November 16. Available at: http://rusnavy.com/news/navy/index.php?ELEMENT_ID=16470&sphrase_id=2327045.
Russia & India Report. (2016). Russian Military Spending Cut Significantly. *Russia & India Report*, November 2.
Sanger, D. E., & Shanker, T. (2010). White House Is Rethinking Nuclear Policy. *New York Times*, February 28.
Snyder, J. L. (1977). *The Soviet Strategic Culture: Implications for Limited Nuclear Operations*. Santa Monica: RAND Corporation.
Snyder, J. (1997). *Alliance Politics*. Ithaca and New York: Cornell University Press.
Sprūds, A., & Bukovskis, K. (2014). *Security of the Broader Baltic Sea Region: Afterthoughts from the Riga Seminar*. Riga: Latvian Institute of International Affairs.
SS-26 Iskander. (2016, September 22). *Missile Threat*. Available at: https://missilethreat.csis.org/missile/ss-26-2/.
Starry, D. A. (1981). Extending the Battlefield. *Military Review*, March, pp. 31–50.
Stewart, R. W. (1994). *The United States Army in Somalia 1992–1994*. Washington, DC: United States Army Center of Military History.
Strategic Trends. (2017). *Key Developments in Global Affairs*, CSS Zurich 2017, p. 17.
The Balance. (2016, October 26). U.S. Military Budget: Components, Challenges, Growth. *The Balance*. However, the GDP share of defence in Russia (3.3 percent in the 2017 budget) is comparable with the situation in the US.
The Guardian. (2016). Russia Transfers Nuclear-Capable Missiles to Kaliningrad. *The Guardian*, October 8, World News. Available at: https://www.theguardian.com › World › Nuclear Weapons.
Utz, C. (1994). *Assault from the Sea: The Amphibious Landing at Inchon*. Washington, DC: Naval Historical Center.

Winton, H. R. (1996). Partnership and Tension: The Army and Air Force Between Vietnam and Desert Shield. *Parameters*, (Spring 1996), 100–119.

Zapfe, M., & Haas, M. C. (2016, June–July). Access for Allies? NATO, Russia and the Baltics. *The RUSI Journal, 161*(3).

Chapter 7
Conclusion: Waiting for a New Gorbachev and for a New Reagan

All of this book has been consecrated to an analysis of the two-decades-long process of the post-Cold War expansion of NATO and its consequences in the field of international security relations. This process profoundly changed the frontiers in the so-called Old Continent as well as the whole political climate there. The first chapter of this book articulated four research questions. This part of the book will start by answering these questions.

RQ 1: Why did the relations between the USA and the RF move from a security cooperation (which was so typical for the first half of the 1990's) towards confrontation? Why are they moving from positive peace towards negative peace?

The basic cause of the move from the security cooperation to the confrontation resulted from the asymmetric end of the Cold War and the following disharmony of the security interests between the winner and the loser of this four-decades-long indirect confrontation. The process of NATO expansion reinforced this asymmetry because the Russian operative realists perceived it, since the beginning, as a typical zero-sum game played to the detriment of their country. They were particularly frustrated by the fact that all the former satellites of the USSR joined NATO, which gave this alliance the advantage of a new strategic depth covering about 1 million km^2.

As a result, Russian political and military elites became obsessed with their deeply rooted security fears and their typical sentiments of Russia being an encircled country with hardly defendable frontiers. They reacted with the formation of new military units and the installations of new arms systems at the Western frontiers of their country. Even if the aim of these measures is to resist possible invasive navy and air operations, they provoked strong security fears in the new member states of NATO. As these states became a new referential object of the Alliance, the political as well as military counter-measures of NATO followed. As a result, we are witnessing the rise of new security dilemmas and a growing military tension.

RQ 2: What kinds of approaches were prevailing in, and which decisions were the milestones of the process of NATO expansion?

The first milestone is identified with the secret decision of the administration of the 41st President of the USA George H. W. Bush concerning the future of European security. He made the decision to preserve NATO as a basic pillar of the international system even after the end of the Cold War. His strategy TLDA (to leave the door ajar) had two fundamental consequences. First, NATO gained the time which had been necessary for its survival in a new environment after the vaporisation of its raison d'etre. Second, this strategy prepared the way for the future rising of the importance and influence of NATO within the framework of the new security architecture of Europe. Lastly, it opened the perspective for the future eastward enlargement.

The second milestone came with NATO's air war against Serbia in 1999. This war confirmed the high value and relevancy of Huntington's concept of the so-called kin-country syndrome. Russian elites perceived and interpreted this war as an aggression against their Orthodox little brother and an arrogant form of unilateralism and a profound and humiliating disdain for their country. And unilateralism has been typical even for the third milestone, which came with the policy of G. W. Bush, namely the US withdrawal from the ABM Treaty and his active support of the by-passes of pipelines from the Caspian area. These two decisions were seen and largely interpreted by Russian operative realists as an arrogant disrespect for the interests of their country and also as openly hostile acts against their country.

The fourth milestone is the second wave of NATO expansion and its two consequences of historical importance. First, as the frontiers of NATO moved 1,000 km eastward, all of the former buffer zone of the USSR changed into the buffer zone of NATO. Second, this move enormously strengthened the security fears of the Russian elites because NATO entered into two areas with a strategic importance: the Baltic Sea and the Black Sea. These areas are perceived, particularly by the Russian strategists, as two large territories which can be used, in case of a military confrontation, for invasive navy and air operations directed against the Russian territory and also against the Russian armed forces, namely against their A2/AD systems.

The fifth milestone is symbolised by the installations of Russian A2/AD systems on Russia's northwestern frontier, in the Moscow area, and in the Crimea. These systems have been, since the beginning, perceived as a grave and imminent threat for the security of the new member states of NATO, which are in the role of new referential objects of the security strategy of NATO. These Russian A2/AD systems have a profound impact on the strategic thinking in the USA and it is no surprise that they opened the way for work on the doctrinal documents of the new generation.

The sixth decisive moment came with the so-called five-day war between Georgia and the Russian Federation in 2008. Putin and the Russian generals used Saakashvili's risky raids against two separatist regions as a pretext for a massive attack against Georgia, which is relatively small, but enormously important from a geopolitical point of view. Even if this short war exposed the obsolescence of the Russian armed forces and their backwardness in comparison with those of the USA and other Western countries, it manifested the willingness of the Russian operative realists to use military force against another post-Soviet state which could aspire to NATO membership. From the politico-military point of view, the use of force had an open and clear dissuasive message addressed to potential candidates for the MAP.

The most dramatic milestone came with the annexation of the Crimean Peninsula in 2014. This action resulted from the security fears and irritations of Russian operative realists. In comparison with the war against Georgia in 2008, this military operation showed the progress in the Russian use of force. From the military point of view, it was a move from the robust bombing with a lot of victims in 2008 to a surgical but bloodless use of the force. Also, the long-term concentration of military troops in 2008 was replaced by a surprising secret action in the latter case.

But from the political point of view, the annexation was an illegal and illegitimate operation which provoked a large condemnation from other countries, especially in the Western world. It was condemned even by the United Nations General Assembly Resolution 68/262 as well as by the Wales Summit Declaration of NATO from 5 September 2014, which condemned it in the strongest terms as Russia's escalating and illegal military intervention in Ukraine and demanded that Russia stop and withdraw its forces inside Ukraine and along the Ukrainian border. As a result, the annexation of the Crimea provoked the most serious international crisis since the end of the Cold War and an unprecedented growth of military tension between NATO and the RF.

RQ 3: Why is the structure of the international security relations (ISR) at the Eastern border of NATO so confrontational?

The key cause of the growing controversy is the gradual rise of numbers of military units on the two sides of the new frontier between NATO and the RF. At its Eastern part, the Western Military District (WMD) with its armies, divisions and brigades of the Russian Army, Navy and Air Force provokes the security fears of new member states of NATO. As these countries become a new referential object of the USA and other so-called old member states, these fears are shared by all of the Atlantic alliance and we are thus witnessing a growing military tension.

On the other hand, the Russian operative realists don't contest that the WMD is a big and strong unit, but they object that this big unit is located in the Russian territory. And they repeat that this case is very different from that of the units of the USA and other NATO countries that are deployed abroad, and very close to the Western frontiers of Russia. At the doctrinal level, the Russian security fears are reinforced by the US doctrines and concepts of invasive and entry operations. Finally, military exercises, especially those organised by the RF, also represent an important source of the growing military tension.

RQ 4: What are the consequences of this trend?

Unfortunately, the third decade after the end of the Cold War has been decisively marked by the growing military rivalry between NATO and the RF, two actors which have been preparing for a possible mutual direct confrontation. As a result, we are witnessing a growing number as well as a growing seriousness of military incidents between the military units of NATO and the RF. These incidents have become the most typical and the most dangerous consequences of the military tension on the border between them as the new dividing line in Europe. Each of these incidents has a big potential to escape from the political control over it and result in an open and direct confrontation.

The RF is the weakest actor of the contemporary rivalry—in the economic, financial, geopolitical, and demographic and especially the military domains. Today this Russian inferiority across all domains is typical even for the Russian conventional forces (which represents a big difference from the Cold War) and has very disturbing consequences. It leads a growing number of Russian strategists to enormously dangerous reflections and debates about the possibility of nuclear weapons use with the aim to avoid a quick conventional defeat in case of an unfavourable development of a possible conventional conflict. In their heads, the use of nuclear weapons came back to the domain of the thinkable.

7.1 NATO Expansion in the Light of the Key Pillars of Realism

The process of the NATO expansion confirmed the academic value of all three pillars of realism. First, groupism is typical for this process. The entry of new countries into NATO resulted in an unprecedented enlargement of the group of countries with security guarantees of the USA. But at the same time, Russia, as an outsider of this group, continues to present itself as a loser, as a country whose security interests have not been taken into consideration and continue to be ignored.

Second, egoism has been typical for the new member states as well as for the USA. The new member states were satisfied by the security guarantees of the strongest state of the contemporary world, regardless of the international consequences. And the USA obtained new allies, and, especially, a new strategic depth in case of a military confrontation. On the other hand, Russia presented its egoism by its uses of force in 2008 and especially in 2014. As a result, we are witnessing a clash of two forms of security egoism, which results in a dangerous move from positive peace (which was so typical for the first half of the 1990's) towards negative peace.

Finally, power-centrism has been manifested by the maximisation of power of the USA to the detriment of the power of the RF. This trend was typical not only for the hard power (namely the enlargement of the territories and the building of new military bases and garrisons as strong instruments of the external balancing) but also, if not especially, for the soft power (the attractiveness of the Western way of life, and the force of the West's example and conviction) of these two competitors.

7.2 NATO Expansion in the Light of the Key Pillars of Neorealism

First, the process of NATO expansion has been concentrated in four very important areas of the Old Continent: Central Europe, the Baltic Sea, the Black Sea and the Western Balkans (which are, from the neorealist point of view, much less disturbing in this respect than the three other areas). As a result, it completely changed the European environment in terms of the theory of balancing, as so precisely formulated by

7.2 NATO Expansion in the Light of the Key Pillars of Neorealism

Kenneth Waltz. On the one hand, the USA, as a central and dominant state of NATO, gained an unprecedented portfolio for its external balancing, which is reinforced by the enormous gratitude of the political and military elites of the new member countries. On the other hand, the RF lost all the advantages of the former USSR from the period of the Cold War. Today, its possibilities of balancing are reduced only to the internal balancing.

Second, the NATO expansion profoundly changed the distances between the two key actors of this process: the USA as an active actor, and the RF as a passive one. At the same time, it changed the offensive capabilities of their armies, the perception of security threats and the balance of threats. Lastly, this process confirmed the role of ideology as a secondary factor of the balance of threats. This gives us the right to conclude that it fully confirmed the value of the theory of Stephen Walt.

Third, the run of the elites of the former states of the Warsaw Pact for the security guarantees of the USA and especially the American readiness to satisfy their solicitations confirmed the academic value of Mearsheimer's theory of offensive realism. During the two decades between 1999 and 2019 the process of NATO expansion has enormously strengthened and reinforced the US hegemony in Europe. This hegemony covers both of the key dimensions—hard power (namely the geographic expansion) and soft power (the attractiveness of the American way of life and the run for the US security guarantees). As a result, we are witnessing a hegemony by invitation, not a hegemony by coercion like that which was so typical for the security behaviour of the USSR in the Warsaw Pact during the Cold War.

The confrontational structure of the ISR on the border between NATO and the RF was very precisely reflected in the original doctrinal speech of Jens Stoltenberg presented in Vilnius in June 2017. Speaking in the name of the active actor of an unprecedented expansion and an actor which benefited from the enormously large advantages of the external balancing, the General Secretary dramatically manifested a profound indignation at the shortening of the distance between the armed forces of NATO and the RF. From the neorealist point of view, according to the sophisticated logic of Jens Stoltenberg, the active actor expands towards the passive actor. He enlarges his territory and particularly his strategic depth by the adhesion of new member states, which are in the role of his referential object and which participate very actively and with a high willingness in the dynamic process of external balancing. And this remarkable logic culminates in Stoltenberg's statement that the passive actor of the expansion become a threat to the security of the new allies of the active actor of this process, and therefore also to all members of the expanding alliance.

7.3 Likudisation as an Inspiration for the NATO Expansion?

The comparison of Likudisation and the NATO expansion may be surprising and controversial; nevertheless, it can help us to better understand and explain an omitted aspect of the international security relations after the end of the Cold War. The term Likudisation or the Likud doctrine was introduced by Naomi Klein to describe and explain the strong and long-term influence of the strategic culture of the State of Israel on the security and strategic culture of western countries, especially that of the USA.

Naomi Klein used this concept at the beginning of the twenty-first Century with the aim to explain the role of the Israeli military in providing the security for the new settlements built during the Israeli expansion on the occupied Palestinian territory after the Six-Day War in 1967 (Klein 2004a). The process is as follows. The new villages being built, the leaders of the settlers once again ask the Israeli Defence Forces (IDF) to send new military units with a mission to assure their security against the threat of Palestinian protests or attacks. After the arrival of the units of the IDF the process of the build-up of new settlements continues and, as a result, new military units are regularly sent to the occupied territories with the aim to assure their security. This behaviour continues as a typical vicious circle. As a result, it is criticised not only by Klein, but also by some critical Israeli authors (B'Tselem 2002) who warn about the possible counterproductive consequences of a continued and gradually increasing expansion (Talmon 1980).

The conclusions of Naomi Klein have an incontestable potential to explain the global importance of the process of Likudisation (Klein 2004b). And where is the parallel between the two compared cases, between the Likudisation and the process of NATO expansion? In the first case, the settlers on the occupied territories solicit new security guarantees; this means that they can be called "soliciting actors." And the State of Israel is in the role of the "solicited actor." It reacts positively and provides security for the required guaranties, which means that it assumes the role of the active actor of the process of expansion. On the other hand, Palestinians are reduced to the role of passive actors.

And in the second case, that of the NATO expansion, the role of the soliciting actors is assumed by the former member states of the POW, and the USA as the hegemon of NATO, is in the role of the solicited actor. And the Russian Federation is in a role largely comparable to that of the Palestinians. Both are in the role of a passive actor which faces the active actor of the expansion, which increasingly approaches nearer to it.

In both of the compared cases, the active actors of the expansion have an incontestable superiority and they prefer a confrontation of choice. They bet on preemption, which opens for them a way to the enlargement of their strategic depth. After every new stage of expansion, they require a new referential object that will need and ask for their security guarantees in the foreseeable future. This means that until they face a strong resistance of the passive actor, the expansion and its rationalisation have the character of a vicious circle.

At the same time, constructivism plays an important role in the argumentation of the active actors of the expansion. The active actors of the expansion underline that they cannot leave behind the referential objects of their expansion: the settlers on the occupied territories or the new member states in the post-Soviet area. The passive actors of the expansion are presented as security threats for the new referential objects. And more importantly, in the two compared cases, we are witnessing continuing profound changes in the distance between the active and passive actors, and between their armed forces, which leads to changes in the balance of threats. In other words, in both of the compared cases, constructivist arguments are largely used to justify a typical neorealist policy of expansion.

As a result, we are witnessing, three decades after the end of the Cold War, a declining trend in the security environment in the Old Continent. It is symbolised by a decline from the very promising security cooperation between the former rivals, which was so typical particularly for the first decade after the end of the bipolar confrontation, towards a growing tension caused dominantly by the process of NATO expansion, particularly by its second wave and the plans which anticipated the entry of the new post-Soviet states into NATO. The culmination of this negative trend came with the annexation of Crimea, an extreme manifestation of the Russian security fears caused by the approaching of NATO toward the frontiers of the RF.

7.4 A Clash of Two Contradictory Narratives

The frontier between the new member states of NATO and western Russia has become an area with a growing military tension. This shared neighbourhood is characterised by a clash of two irreconcilable narratives.

On the one hand, the Western narrative is very critical towards Russia, namely its president: it reproaches them for the annexation of Crimea, their support of the Russian separatists in Eastern Ukraine and their provocative military activities near the Eastern frontier of NATO. This narrative has been materialised by the decision to strengthen the defensive potential of NATO in this area. And on the other hand, the Russian narrative reproaches the West for its zero-sum game, its strategy of the encirclement of Russia and, more and more often, for its determination to impose a regime change in Russia. No wonder that this situation is seen as a dialogue of deaf actors and that it tends to lead to a growing number of military incidents.

And the logic of the dialogue of the deaf is typical even for the doctrinal domain. New doctrines of the USA confirm that the post-Soviet space is a long zone (from the Finland Bay in the North to the Black Sea in the South) of a merciless competition between two rivals. The doctrines of the USA as the active actor of the expansion after the end of the Cold War, reflect its upgraded military self-confidence, which it gained especially thanks to its four remarkable victories in the big wars it waged after 1990. They put the main emphasis on the access to all areas which play a vital role for its own security as well as for the security of its allies. As the concrete instruments are concerned, these doctrines prefer offensive before defensive actions. They are oriented to quick invasive entry operations waged with the aim to destroy the A2/AD arms systems on the territory of their "challengers."

And the doctrines of Russian Federation, as the passive actor of the contemporary competition, are oriented to the build-up of the A2/AD arms systems which are positioned on the western frontier of the RF and which are conceived as necessary instruments against the threat of invasive operations which could threaten the strategically important major cities in the western part of the country. From the geopolitical point of view, the decisive attention is paid to the Finland Bay (an ideal space for an invasive operation in the direction to St. Petersburg), and from the military point of view, the Baltic Fleet is in the role of the preferred military unit within the process of modernisation.

Moreover, the military doctrines of the two rivals are mutually intertwined with the military exercises which are organised on their common frontier. On one hand, these doctrines fix the tasks for the combat activities, and on the other hand, the exercises verify the feasibility of the new military doctrines. The intertwined development of the military doctrines and exercises led to a growing militarisation of the entire space of the shared frontier between NATO and the RF. As the military exercises are accompanied by growing numbers of military incidents with an enormously explosive potential, the new military doctrines and military exercises of the two competing actors lead to a growing military tension on the large and explosive zone between the expanded NATO on one hand and the increasingly paranoid RF on the other. This tension represents a serious threat for the stability and security in all of Europe.

Twenty years after the beginning of the process of the NATO expansion, the tension between the West and the RF is at its highest level since the end of the Cold War. These competing actors face a common challenge: they have to do the maximum to avoid a hot conflict and a direct military confrontation. And just after this aim is fulfilled, they must move from the confrontation towards a new détente of the international tension. Once they find the necessary political courage, they can follow the heritage of Olaf Palme with his emphasis on the common security. And at the political level, they can take an example from the extraordinary security cooperation between R. Reagan and M. Gorbachev in the second half of the 1980's, which was crowned by the signature in Washington in 1987 of the Intermediate-Range Nuclear Forces Treaty (INF), the first disarmament treaty in the nuclear age, which opened the way to a long series of treaties pertaining to arms control, which was symbolised mainly by the Treaty on Conventional Forces in Europe (CFE) signed in Vienna in November 1991.

Sources

B'Tselem (2002). *Land Grab: Israel's Settlement Policy in the West Bank*. Available at: https://www.btselem.org/publications/.../200205_land_grab, May 2002.

Klein, N. (2004a). The Likud Doctrine. *The Guardian*. Available at: https://www.theguardian.com/world/2004/sep/10/russia.comment1, 10 September 2004.

Klein, N. (2004b). The Likudization of the World: The True Legacy of September 11. *Common Dreams*. Available at: https://www.commondreams.org/views/2004/09/10/likudization-world.

Talmon, J. (1980). *"The Homeland Is in Danger." An Open Letter to Menahem Begin*. Available at: https://www.dissentmagazine.org/.../the-homeland-is-in-danger-an.

Printed in the United States
by Baker & Taylor Publisher Services